# James Purdy
## *A Bibliography*

Compiled and Annotated by
### Jay L. Ladd

Arranged and Edited by
### Nels P. Highberg

The Ohio State University Libraries
*1999*

# Contents

# In Tribute to Jay L. Ladd

## March 26, 1932 - June 6, 1997

A resident of Columbus for 37 years, Jay L. Ladd was born in St. Louis, Missouri. After receiving his Bachelor and Master of Library Science degrees from Florida State University in 1953 and 1954, he served in the U. S. Army for two years, then began his career as a librarian at the University of New Mexico in 1956. Joining The Ohio State University Libraries in 1960, he worked in a number of increasingly responsible positions. In 1968 Jay became head of department libraries, and in 1984 he was promoted to the position of Assistant Director for Department and Undergraduate Libraries. Responsible for the administration of 13 department and undergraduate libraries, he also spearheaded the planning and construction of a number of new library facilities on the Columbus campus. He was very active professionally, belonging to several local and national professional library organizations. He was instrumental in the founding of the Academic Library Association of Ohio and served for three years as editor of the Ohio Library Bulletin.

Jay was also an avid collector of pattern glass and contemporary art glass, and he had a great love of books, movies, bridge, gardening, cooking and entertaining. His special love of cats was a well-known fact to his many friends and family. A longtime patron of the arts, he supported both the theater and the fine arts in Ohio. His prized collection of works by and about American author James Purdy has now become part of the Special Collections at The Ohio State University Libraries.

Those who knew Jay will always remember his positive, outgoing personality, his firm commitment to libraries and library service, and his generosity and genuine concern for the needs of others. According to Jay's wishes, his body was cremated and his ashes were scattered beneath the Chinese Elm dedicated in his honor southeast of the main entrance to The Ohio State University Main Library.

# Foreword

This bibliography of works by and about James Purdy is the product of twenty-five years of scholarship by Jay L. Ladd, which was inspired by and derived from his exhaustive collecting and study of Purdy materials. Jay almost achieved the goal of seeing his labors into print; but he succumbed to cancer in June 1997, just short of being able to complete the final editing, cross-checking and arrangement necessary for publication. Fortunately, Nels P. Highberg [1], a graduate student at The Ohio State University (OSU), was available and willing to take on the critical task of organizing the bibliography into a standard arrangement, under the able guidance of Dr. James Bracken (the specialist Librarian for English, Theatre, and Communication at OSU). Jay Ladd's good friend and colleague, Steve Rogers (Reference/Map Librarian at OSU), then spent many hours on verification and additional editing, as well as creating the index.

A copy of this bibliography is being sent to each member of the Association of Research Libraries so as to insure ample availability throughout North America.

**William J. Studer**
*Director of Libraries*
*The Ohio State University*
August 1998

---

[1] Nels P. Highberg earned M.A.'s in Women's Studies and Comparative Studies at The Ohio State University, where his research focused primarily on cultural representations of AIDS. He entered the Ph.D. program in Language, Literacy, and Rhetoric in the Department of English at the University of Illinois at Chicago in 1998.

# Introduction

I first learned of James Purdy a decade ago while reading the 1988 collection *Men on Men 2: Best New Gay Fiction* where his story "In This Corner" appears. The story is marked by intensity in characterization and plot. The protagonist, Hayes, feels extreme passion for a young man he meets one night, a passion that exerts a hold upon every aspect of his life. He ventures to his Wall Street job unshaven and unable to work and often wanders around New York City in a quest for the man who has ignited such feelings. *James Purdy: A Bibliography* collects varied writings by numerous reviewers and critics that continually refer to similar intensities running throughout Purdy's fiction, poetry, and plays. Those who read his work will often find characters on a journey for answers to the questions that plague them, for relief from the pain that they suffer. Sometimes with a touch of camp and sometimes with a focus on drama, Purdy centers his attention on a search for meaning that has grown with the passing of recent decades.

James Purdy was born in Ohio in 1923, and he moved to Chicago while in his teens. Later, he attended the University of Chicago. His first short story, "A Good Woman," appeared in 1939 and he has continued to publish well into the 1990s. Although a prolific writer, Purdy has never achieved celebrity status or national fame. He remains somewhat on the margins of the literary establishment largely because he wrote openly about obsessive love, homosexuality, fratricide, alienation, and dysfunctional families long before audiences sought to read such stories. Still, his texts have influenced younger writers and his work continues to generate a steady amount of critical interest.

This bibliography attempts to bring together both Purdy's entire body of work and the scholarship and criticism that it has generated. Jay Ladd spent a great amount of time compiling an alphabetized, annotated list of the hundreds of sources that appear in this bibliography. I arranged the entries into standard categories. For example, I separated primary and secondary sources and divided reviews for other critical commentary; reviews of adaptations appear in II.E. All citations and their accompanying annotations, however, are in Ladd's own writing. Ladd provided numerous details about each entry and noted, for example, whether reviews were positive or negative. I have not verified the information in either the citations or the annotations. I know that some gaps do exist, but I wanted Ladd's words to prevail as much as possible. Shifts in citation style are also Ladd's work. I often let these shifts remain as long as the information provided still enables readers to find the source at hand. Earlier bibliographies that scholars can use to verify information in older entries can be found in II.F.1. My goal has been to create a working document that can lead others to a wide range of sources, and this bibliography will hopefully increase understanding and appreciation of Purdy, a writer of ability who has much to teach readers today.

**Nels P. Highberg**
July 1998

# Works by James Purdy

## A. Books and Separate Publications

1      *The Brooklyn Branding Parlors*. New York: Contact II Publications, 1986.

> Limited edition of 1000 copies with 26 signed by author and artist. Numbered. Contains seven poems by Purdy and each poem is accompanied with art work by Vassilis Voglis whose work was inspired by the poems. Poems included are "Don't Let the Snow Fall," "I Have Told You Your Hands Are Salt," "Merman," "He Watched Me," "The Brooklyn Branding Parlors," and "A Wild Bitter Boy." Also contains portrait of Purdy on the back cover by Adam Berger.

2      *Cabot Wright Begins*. New York: Farrar, Straus & Giroux, 1964.

> First American edition of the novel.

3      *Cabot Wright Begins*. London: Secker & Warburg, 1964.

> First English edition of the novel.

4      *Cabot Wright Begins*. New York: Avon Books, 1965.

> Cover illustration by Barron Storey.

5      *Cabot Wright Begins*. London: Penguin Books, 1967.

> Cover design by Michael Peters.

6      *Cabot Wright Begins*. New York: Bantam Books, 1972.

7    *Cabot Wright Begins*. New York: Carroll & Graf, 1985.
Cover Painting: Edwin by Alex Katz.

8    *The Candles of Your Eyes*. New York: Nadja Editions, 1985.

Limited edition of 226. Original illustration by Ed Colker.

9    *The Candles of Your Eyes and Thirteen Other Stories*. New York: Weidenfeld & Nicolson, 1987.

Contains: "Some of These Days," "Scrap of Paper," "Summer Tidings," "Mr. Evening," "Lily's Party," "On the Rebound," "Ruthanna Elder," "Sleep Tight," "Short Papa," "Mud Toe the Cannibal," "How I Became a Shadow," "Dawn," "The Candles of Your Eyes," "Rapture."

10    *The Candles of Your Eyes and Thirteen Other Stories*. San Francisco: City Lights Books, 1991.

Contains: "Some of These Days," "Scrap of Paper," "Summer Tidings," "Mr. Evening," "Lily's Party," "On the Rebound," "Ruthanna Elder," "Sleep Tight," "Short Papa," "Mud Toe the Cannibal," "How I Became a Shadow," "Dawn," "The Candles of Your Eyes," "Rapture."

11    *The Candles of Your Eyes and Thirteen Other Stories*. London: Peter Owen, 1988.

12    *Children is All*. New York: New Directions, 1961.

Contains: "Daddy Wolf," "Home by Dark," "About Jessie Mae," "The Lesson," "Encore," "Night and Day," "Mrs. Benson," "Sermon," "Everything Under the Sun," "Goodnight, Sweetheart" and *Children Is All* and *Cracks*.

13    *Children is All*. London: Secker & Warburg, 1963.

Contains: "Daddy Wolf," "Home by Dark," "About Jessie Mae," "The Lesson," "Encore," "Night and Day," "Mrs. Benson," "Sermon," "Everything Under the Sun," "Goodnight, Sweetheart" and *Children Is All* and *Cracks.*

14 *Children is All.* New York: New Directions, 1971.

  Contains: "Daddy Wolf," "Home by Dark," "About Jessie Mae," "The Lesson," "Encore," "Night and Day," "Mrs. Benson," "Sermon," "Everything Under the Sun," "Goodnight, Sweetheart" and *Children Is All* and *Cracks.*

15 *Children is All.* London: Panther Books, 1972.

  Contains: "Daddy Wolf," "Home by Dark," "About Jessie Mae," "The Lesson," "Encore," "Night and Day," "Mrs. Benson," "Sermon," "Everything Under the Sun," "Goodnight, Sweetheart" and *Children Is All* and *Cracks.*

16 *Collected Poems.* Amsterdam, Netherlands: Athenaeum-Polak & Van Gennep, 1990.

  Published in both a hardback and paperback edition.

17 *Color of Darkness.* New York: New Directions, 1957.

  Anthology contains: "Color of Darkness," "You May Safely Gaze," "Don't Call Me by My Right Name," "Eventide," "Why Can't They Tell You Why?," "Man and Wife," "You Reach for Your Hat," "A Good Woman," "Plan Now to Attend," "Sound of Talking," "Cutting Edge," *63: Dream Palace.*
  Jacket adapted by Owen Scott from Philip Featheringill's painting.

18 *Color of Darkness.* New York: J. B. Lippincott Company, 1961.

  Introduction by Dame Edith Sitwell. Eleven stories and a novella.

19 *Color of Darkness & Children Is All.* New York: Avon Books, 1965.

  Cover design by Nick Fasciano.

3

20  *Color of Darkness: Eleven Stories and a Novella.* New York: Bantam Books, 1970.

> Contains: "Color of Darkness," "You May Safely Gaze," "Don't Call Me by My Right Name," "Eventide," "Why Can't They Tell You Why?," "Man and Wife," "You Reach for Your Hat," "A Good Woman," "Plan Now to Attend," "Sound of Talking," "Cutting Edge," and *63: Dream Palace*.

21  *Color of Darkness & Malcolm.* New York: Doubleday, 1974.

> Contains: "Color of Darkness," "You May Safely Gaze," "Don't Call Me by My Right Name," "Eventide," "Why Can't They Tell You Why," "Man and Wife," "You Reach for Your Hat," "A Good Woman," "Plan Now to Attend," "Sound of Talking," "Cutting Edge," and *63: Dream Palace* along with *Malcolm*. This edition has an introduction by Tony Tanner.

22  *Colour of Darkness.* London: Secker & Warburg, 1961.

> Contains: "Colour of Darkness," "You May Safely Gaze," "Don't Call Me by My Right Name," "Eventide," "Why Can't They Tell You Why?," "Man and Wife," "You Reach for Your Hat," "A Good Woman," "Plan Now to Attend," "Sound of Talking," "Cutting Edge," and *63: Dream Palace*. This edition has a preface by Dame Edith Sitwell. Jacket design by Peter Edwards.

23  *Colour of Darkness: Eleven Stories and a Novella.* London: Four Square Books, 1963.

> Contains: "Colour of Darkness," "You May Safely Gaze," "Don't Call Me by My Right Name," "Eventide," "Why Can't They Tell You Why?," "Man and Wife," "You Reach for Your Hat," "A Good Woman," "Plan Now to Attend," "Sound of Talking," "Cutting Edge," and *63: Dream Palace*. This edition has a preface by Dame Edith Sitwell.

24     *A Day After the Fair: A Collection of Plays and Short Stories*. New York: Note of Hand Publishers, 1977.

> Contains: *A Day After the Fair, Scrap of Paper,* "Mr. Evening," "On the Rebound," *Wedding Finger*, "Lily's Party," "Summer Tidings," "Some of These Days," "Short Papa," and *True*.

25     *Did I Say Yes, Did I Say No*. Binghamton, New York: Bellevue Press, 1978.

> Prose poem. Broadsides number 20. Printed by Stuart McCarty.

26     *Don't Call Me by My Right Name and Other Stories*. New York: William-Frederick Press, 1956.

> Purdy's second published book. With illustrations by the author. Anthology contains: "Don't Call Me by My Right Name," "Eventide," "Why Can't They Tell You Why?," "Man and Wife," "You Reach for Your Hat," "A Good Woman," "Plan Now to Attend," "Sound of Talking," "Cutting Edge."

27     *Don't Let the Snow Fall: a poem ; Dawn: a story*. Edited by Andre Bernard. Utrecht: Sub Signo Libelli, 1984.

> This is a limited edition of the poem "Don't Let the Snow Fall" and the short story "Dawn" contained in one paperback volume.

28     *Dream Palaces*. New York: Viking Press, 1980.

> Foreword by Edward Albee. Includes three Purdy novels: *Malcolm, The Nephew*, and *63: Dream Palace*.

29     *Eustace Chisholm and the Works*. New York: Farrar, Straus & Giroux, 1967.

> First American edition.

30     *Eustace Chisholm and the Works*. New York: Bantam Books, 1968.

31     *Eustace Chisholm and the Works*. London: Jonathan Cape, 1968.

First English edition. Introduction by Paul Binding.

32    *Eustace Chisholm and the Works*. London: Panther Books, 1970.

33    *Eustace Chisholm and the Works*. London: GMP, 1984.
      Introduction by Paul Binding.

34    *Garments the Living Wear*. San Francisco: City Lights Books, 1989.

35    *The House of the Solitary Maggot*. New York: Doubleday, 1974.
      Sequel to *Jeremy's Version*; part two of the *Sleepers in Moon-Crowned Valleys* trilogy.

36    *The House of the Solitary Maggot*. London: Peter Owen, 1986.
      Sequel to Jeremy's Version, part two of the Sleepers in Moon-Crowned Valleys trilogy.

37    *I Am Elijah Thrush*. New York: Doubleday & Company, 1972.

38    *I Am Elijah Thrush*. London: Jonathan Cape, 1972.
      Jacket design by Bill Batten.

39    *I Am Elijah Thrush*. New York: Bantam Books, 1973.

40    *I Am Elijah Thrush*. London: Guernsey Press, 1986.
      Introduction by Paul Binding. Cover art: Morning Prayer by Glyn Phipot. Series: Gay Modern Classics.

41    *In a Shallow Grave*. New York: Arbor House, 1975.

42    *In a Shallow Grave*. New York: Arbor House, 1976.
      Introduction by Jerome Charyn.

43    *In a Shallow Grave*. London: W. H. Allen, 1978.

44    *In a Shallow Grave*. London: GMP, 1988.

45    *In a Shallow Grave*. San Francisco, California: City Lights Books, 1988.

46    *In the Hollow of His Hand*. New York: Weidenfeld & Nicolson, 1986.

47    *In the Night of Time and Four Other Plays*. Amsterdam: Athenaeum-Polak & Van Gennep, 1992.

> Contains: "Ruthanna Elder," "Enduring Zeal," "The Rivalry of Dolls," "The Paradise Circus," and "In the Night of Time."

48    *I Will Arrest the Bird That Has No Light*. Northridge, California: Santa Susana Press, 1977.

> Limited edition of the poem. Printed by Pall Bohne on the Shniedewend Washington hand-press. This poem was printed for the Bibliographical Society to commemorate the inauguration of Herb Yellin as its President. The editor of the project was Norman Tanis. The artist was Irving Block. This is an edition of one hundred copies, numbered and signed.

49    *Kitty Blue*. Brooklyn, New York: James Purdy, 1992.

50    *Jeremy's Version*. New York: Doubleday & Company, 1970.

> Subtitled "Part One of *Sleepers in Moon-Crowned Valleys*."

51    *Jeremy's Version*. New York: Bantam Books, 1971.

> Part one of *Sleepers in Moon-Crowned Valleys*.

52    *Jeremy's Version*. London: Jonathan Cape, 1971.

> Subtitled "Part One of *Sleepers in Moon-Crowned Valleys*."

53    *Lessons & Complaints*. New York: Nadja Editions, 1976.

A limited edition of the poem of 174 numbered copies of which twenty-six are lettered and reserved.

54  *Malcolm.* New York: Farrar, Straus & Giroux, 1959.

55  *Malcolm.* London: Secker & Warburg, 1960.
    Jacket design by A. B. Saunders.

56  *Malcolm.* London: Four Square Books, 1963.

57  *Malcolm.* London: Penguin Books, 1966.
    Cover photography by Christopher Ridley.

58  *Malcolm.* New York: Avon Books, 1967.
    Cover illustration by Saul Lambert.

59  *Malcolm.* New York: Noonday Press, 1967.
    With an introduction by David Daiches.

60  *Malcolm.* New York: Bantam Books, 1971.

61  *Malcolm.* London: Penguin Books, 1980.
    Foreword by Edward Albee.

62  *Malcolm.* New York: Weidenfeld & Nicolson, 1987.
    Cover illustration: "Arnold Comes of Age" by Grant Wood. Cover design by Cindy LaBreacht.

63  *Malcolm.* London, England: Serpent's Tail, 1994.

64  *Mourners Below.* New York: Viking Press, 1981.
    [Part three of the *Sleepers in Moon-Crowned Valleys* trilogy.]

65  *Mourners Below.* Middlesex, England: Penguin Books, 1981.

66  *Mourners Below.* New York: Viking Press, 1981.
    An unrevised and unpublished proof not for the public.

67    *Mourners Below*. New York: Penguin Books, 1982.
      The Penguin Contemporary American Fiction Series.

68    *Mourners Below*. London: St. Edmundsbury Press, 1984.

69    *Mourners Below*. London: Arrow Books Limited, 1986.
      An Arena Book.

70    *Mr. Evening: A Story & Nine Poems*. Los Angeles: Black
      Sparrow Press, 1968.
      Limited edition to 300 numbered copies sewn in
      wrappers and seventy-five numbered copies hand-
      bound in boards each with an original drawing by James
      Purdy.  Designed and printed by Saul and Lillian Marks
      at the Planten Press, Los Angeles.  Nine poems are:
      "Come Ready and See Me," "It Came to This and It
      Came to That," "Come Down from the Moon,"
      "Canaries Whose Voices Blend," "Pink Was What
      Was Said," "Except through Bees," And "Pigeons &
      Gulls and Sparrows & Jays."

71    *Narrow Rooms*. New York: Arbor House, 1978.

72    *Narrow Rooms*. Surrey, England: Black Sheep Books,
      1980.

73    *Narrow Rooms*. London: Guernsey Press, 1985.
      Introduction by Paul Binding.  Cover art: Ben Shahn
      Brothers.  Series: Gay modern classics.

74    *The Nephew*. New York: Farrar, Straus & Cudahy, 1960.

75    *The Nephew*. London: Secker & Warburg, 1961.

76    *The Nephew*. New York: Avon Books, 1962.

77    *The Nephew*. London: Four Square Books, 1963.

78    *The Nephew*. New York: Avon Books, 1966.
      Cover illustration by Saul Lambert.

| 79 | *The Nephew*. New York: Noonday Press, 1967. Foreword by R. W. B. Lewis. |
|----|----|
| 80 | *The Nephew*. New York: Farrar, Straus & Giroux, 1967. Foreword by R. W. B. Lewis. |
| 81 | *The Nephew*. London: Panther Books, 1973. |
| 82 | *The Nephew*. New York: Bantam Books, 1973. |
| 83 | *The Nephew*. New York: Penguin Books, 1980. Foreword by Edward Albee. Cover design by Neil Stuart. Cover illustration by Spencer Kelly. |
| 84 | *The Nephew*. New York: Weidenfeld & Nicolson, 1987. |
| 85 | *On Glory's Course*. New York: Viking Press, 1984. |
| 86 | *On Glory's Course*. New York: Penguin Books, 1985. |
| 87 | *On Glory's Course*. London: Peter Owen, 1985. |
| 88 | *On the Rebound: A Story & Nine Poems*. Los Angeles: Black Sparrow Press, 1970. Limited edition of 300 copies hand-bound in boards by Earle Gray all numbered and signed by the author. Printed in Santa Barbara by Noel Young. Design by Barbara Martin. Nine poems are: "Cruel Zoo," "Speckled with Stars and Flowing with Milk the Summer Night," "Small Birds with Voices of Men," "Flowers at My Feet in the Dark Whisper Sweet," "There Will Be Fancy Dress Balls and Gay Masquerades," "Big Bears Whose Snouts Are Smeared with Honey And Gray," "After Six Months They Met Again," "Lessons Learned Too Late by Boys In Old Hollows," And "Bang the Kettles." |
| 89 | *Out with the Stars*. London: Peter Owen, 1992. |
| 90 | *Out with the Stars*. San Francisco: City Lights Books, 1992. |

91     *An Oyster Is a Wealthy Beast*. San Francisco, California: Black Sparrow Press, 1967.

> Limited edition of the short story "Scrap of Paper" and eleven poems of two hundred and fifty copies; fifty copies numbered 1 - 50 bound in boards, each hand-illustrated by the author, and two hundred copies numbered 51-250 sewn in wrapper, all signed by the author. The poems are: "Pass by the Yellow Dock, with Grass, Yarrow," "Carl Van Vechten," "White Possum by the Fire," "An Oyster Is a Wealthy Beast," "Join Won't You Please," "Two Madrigals: Bartholomew Green," "Come Down from The Parapet, Haughty Girl," "Water Bird," "Fading Violets Go," "The Lovely Listless Wind Has Sighed," And "Bridget Girl-Baritone."

92     *Proud Flesh*. Northridge, California: Lord John Press, 1980.

> The four plays contained in this volume are *Strong, Clearing in the Forest, Now* and *What Is It, Zach?*

93     *Reaching Rose*. Brooklyn, New York: Avalon Press, 1994.

> Single short story in limited numbered edition, hardcover with frontispiece by Purdy. Printed simultaneously with a Dutch translation. Contains a letter to Jan Erik Bouman by the Dutch poet and novelist Kees Ouwens and translated into English by Jonathan Bragdon.

94     *The Running Sun*. New York: James Purdy, 1971.

> A limited edition of sixteen poems of 300 copies, each of which is signed and numbered by the author. Purdy wrote "there are really only about 200 copies in existence, as the remaining copies of the original 300 were spoiled."

95     *Scrap of Paper and The Berry-Picker*. Los Angeles: Sylvester & Orphanos, 1981.

> Limited edition.

96    *She Came Out of the Mists of Morning.* Binghamton, New York: Bellevue Press, 1975.

Poem published as a postcard.

97    *63: Dream Palace: A Novella.* New York: William-Frederick Press, 1956.

First edition, privately published. Covers designed by James Purdy.

98    *63: Dream Palace.* London: Victor Gollancz, 1957.

Anthology contains: *63: Dream Palace*, "Eventide," "Why Can't They Tell You Why?," "Man and Wife," "You Reach for Your Hat," "Don't Call Me by My Right Name," "A Good Woman," "Plan Now to Attend," "Sound of Talking," and "Cutting Edge." First commercially published edition.

99    *63: Dream Palace: Eleven Stories and a Novella.* London: Panther Books, 1961.

Preface by Dame Edith Sitwell. Contains: "Colour of Darkness," "You May Safely Gaze," "Don't Call Me by My Right Name," "Eventide," "Why Can't They Tell You Why?," "Man and Wife," "You Reach for Your Hat," "A Good Woman," "Plan Now to Attend," "Sound of Talking," "Cutting Edge," and *63: Dream Palace.*

100   *63: Dream Palace and Other Stories.* New York: Penguin Books, 1981.

Contains: "Color of  Darkness," "Your May Safely Gaze," "Don't Call Me by My Right Name," "Eventide," "Why Can't They Tell You Why?," "Man and Wife," "You Reach for Your Hat," "A Good Woman," "Plan Now to Attend," "Sound of Talking," "Cutting Edge," and *63: Dream Palace.* Foreword by Edward Albee. Cover design by Neil Stuart. Cover illustration by Spencer Kelly.

101   *63: Dream Palace: Selected Stories 1956-1987.* Santa Rosa, California: Black Sparrow Press, 1991.

Anthology contains: "Color of Darkness," "You May Safely Gaze," "Don't Call Me by My Right Name," "Eventide," "Why Can't They Tell You Why?," "Man and Wife," "You Reach for Your Hat," "A Good Woman," "Plan Now to Attend," "Sound of Talking," "Cutting Edge," *63: Dream Palace*, "Daddy Wolf," "Home by Dark," "About Jessie Mae," "The Lesson," "Encore," "Night and Day," "Mrs. Benson," "Sermon," "Everything under the Sun," "Goodnight, Sweetheart," "Some Party," "On the Rebound," "In This Corner ..." Design by Barbara Martin. Edition is published in paper wrappers. There are 300 hardcover trade copies. 150 copies have been numbered and signed by the author and numbered copies have been hand-bound in boards by Earle Gray each with an original drawing by James Purdy.

102     *Sleep Tight*. New York: Nadja Editions, 1979.

Limited edition of the short story of one hundred numbered copies of which twenty-six are lettered and reserved.

103     *Sunshine Is an Only Child: Poems*. New York: Aloe Editions, 1973.

Limited edition consisting of one hundred and fifty signed copies, of which twenty-six are lettered and reserved. Edition, designed and printed by Ronald Gordon at The Oliphant Press in New York. The nine poems are: "Sunshine Is an Only Child," "Let All Footed Beasts Then Parade," "He Has Gone on Wings to the Lake," "I Will Arrest the Bird That Has No Light," "I Have Warned Small Chickens Not to Approach the King of Beasts," "Over Green Leaves That Stretch to the Sea," "A Great Cry to the Core of the Earth," "Richard Is Not One He Is Three and in Water Makes Love to the Sea," And "Over the Night and over the Waves."

104     *Two Plays*. Dallas, Texas: New London Press, 1979.

The two plays contained in this volume are *A Day after the Fair* and *True*.

# B. Works in Anthologies, Periodicals and Edited Collections

## 1. Short Fiction

105    "About Jesse Mae." *New Yorker* 33 (25 May 1957): 87-88, 90, 92.

106    "Anonymous Anomalous Letters I-IV." *Conjunctions* 1 (winter 1981/1982): 176-185.

   Reprint of the "Letters" which first appeared in New Directions annuals. This inaugural double-issue of *Conjunctions* is a festschrift in honor of James Laughlin, publisher of *New Directions*.

107    "The Anonymous/Anomalous Letters of Passion: The Saga of S. Vireo." In *An International Anthology of Poetry and Prose*. Edited by James Laughlin. New York: A New Directions Book, 1979.

   Short story on pages 23-35.

108    "The Anonymous/Anomalous Letters of Passion: The Saga of S. Vireo." *Christopher Street* 12 (January 1990): 10-15.

   Includes a full-page photograph of Purdy which first appeared in the September 1989 issue.

109    "The Anonymous/Anomalous Letters of Passion." In *More Like Minds*. Edited by Ben Goldstein. London: GMP, 1991.

   A collection of fourteen gay short stories. Purdy's story is on pages 163-178

110    "Bonnie." *Village Voice Literary Supplement* 38 (9 February 1993): SS32.

111    "Brawith." *Antioch Review* 52 (spring 1994): 199-208.

112    "The Candles of Your Eyes." In *Anthology: Forty Years of Independent Publishing*. Edited with and introduction by Peter Owen. London: Peter Owen, 1991.

Short story on pages 139-143.

113    "Children Is All." *Mademoiselle* 56 (November 1962): 108-9, 164-173, 184-6.

114    "Color of Darkness." In *Short Story: A Thematic Anthology*. Edited by Dorothy Parker and Frederick B. Shroyer. New York: Charles Scribner and Sons, 1965.

An anthology of thirty-eight short stories arranged under the headings of Youth, Cruelty, Love, Loneliness, Death, Humor, Fantasy and Symbol. Purdy's story is under "Loneliness" on pages 149-158.

115    "Color of Darkness." In *The Short Story*. Edited by Willoughby H. Johnson and William C. Hamlin. New York: American Book Company, 1966.

A collection of twenty-six short stories arranged in four parts: Reading for Theme; Stories of Comparison; Stories with Questions, and Stories for Analysis. The collection of short stories has been chosen to act as a textbook for teaching the art of the short story. Eighteen of the stories are by well-known American authors including Anderson, Bierce, Faulkner, Hemingway, O'Connor. Purdy's story is paired with O. Henry's "The Gift of the Magi" In part two. The two stories are followed by a section of comments. The story is on pages 145-156.

116    "Color of Darkness." In *Insight Through Fiction: Dealing Effectively with the Short Story*. Edited by John Antico and M. K. Hazelrigg. Menlo Park, California: Cummings Publishing Company, 1970.

An anthology of thirty-eight short stories to be used as a textbook. Purdy's story is on pages 132-143. The book also contains a short entry on Purdy listing his publications, recreations, and address.

117     "Crucifiction." *Penthouse: The International Magazine for Men* 9 (May 1978): 132-134, 164-166, 170-174.

         Excerpt from *Narrow Rooms*.

118     "Cutting Edge." In *Coming Together: Modern Stories by Black and White Americans*. Edited by Adam A. Casmier and Sally Souder. Encino, California: Dickenson Publishing, 1972.

         An anthology of twenty-five short stories suitable for college students in undergraduate literature courses. Includes a section "About Authors" with individual author photographs. Purdy's story is on pages 292-299.

119     "Cutting Edge." *Evergreen Review* 1 (1957): 99-109.

120     "Cutting Edge." In *Literature in America: The Modern Age*. Edited by Charles Kaplan. New York: Free Press, 1971.

         A three-volume anthology of which this is the third volume. The arrangement is thematic; Purdy' short story is included in the section entitled "Manners and Morals" on pages 138-146.

121     "Cutting Edge." In *The Process of Fiction: Contemporary Stories and Criticism*. Edited by Barbara McKenzie. New York: Harcourt, Brace & World, 1969.

         An anthology of twenty short stories by ten outstanding contemporary American writers with "critical essays that interpret the first story of each pair." Purdy's stories "Cutting Edge" and "Why Can't They Tell You Why?" are included along with questions for discussion of each story, a bibliography of primary and secondary sources and a brief biographical sketch. On pages 299-304 and 313-321.

122     "Cutting Edge." In *Fiction: The Universal Elements*. Edited by Pearl and Ralph Gasarch. New York: Van Nostrand Reinhold, 1972.

An anthology of thirty-one short stories related to the five universal life stages: Childhood—The Loss of Innocence; Youth—Self Awareness Takes Root; The Search for Love—Venturing Outward; Marriage—The Shared Life ; Later Life—New Toys, New Sorrows. The short story "Cutting Edge" is contained in the anthology on pages 97-105. Of special importance is Purdy's response to the invitation to discuss his work. Purdy writes, "My work has always been by its nature and form 'against the grain.' At the beginning of my career, Dame Edith Sitwell quoted John Cowper Powys's description of my fiction as an exploration 'under the skin' of my characters. To explore what is 'inside' will always be unpopular or taboo so far as any 'establishment' is concerned. Similarly, my style, based on the rhythm and idiom of common American speech, from my own small-town Ohio background, jarred and still jars on the ears of the spokesman-salesman for blue-skim homogenized prose a la New York City. The public, however, devourers of bestseller fiction, demand now as always candy-wrapped lies. They will applaud anything, provided they are not required to feel. Anaethesia is the boon they have always asked of the writers applauded by the New York book trade.... The advantages, in my case, however, of having no public are considerable. There is no one I need to please except myself, and since I have never been 'in,' I cannot fear being 'out.' Thus I am free to pursue my own way, while at the same time I am creating an audience of 'followers' who are willing to go imaginatively 'under the skin,' through the medium of my stories, written in 'native American diction,' and in the 'cadence and idiom' of the psyche."

123    "Cutting Edge." In *Reading for Insight: A Perceptual Approach to College English*. Edited by J. Burl Hogins and Gerald A. Bryant, Jr. 2nd edition. Beverly Hills, California: 1974.

A collection of 190 pieces including: "paintings, poems, editorials, advertisements, anecdotes, articles, cartoons, color photographs, speeches, song lyrics, short-stories, folktales, and photo-essays divided into six thematic units, each ending with questions designed to provoke thought, concerning ideas, events and personalities, as well as current movements and trends." These units are entitled People: Perceiving Individuality; Women's Libertism; Drugs and Dissent; Marriage, Mortality and the Future; Environment; Alienation. Purdy's story is the first story in the first unit, pp. 7-11.

124     "Cutting Edge." In *The Shape of Fiction*. Edited by Alan Casty. 2nd edition. Lexington, Massachusetts: D. C. Heath and Company, 1975.

A collection of short stories for teaching and study which includes study aids or questions at the end of each paired set of stories. Twenty-two stories are paired and eleven more are paired for additional study. The stories were selected because all stories after many readings will still move one; all stories have enduring literary value; have a strong dramatic and emotional impact; the surface impact is direct; and all stories demonstrate the subtle power of fiction to catch the human situation in all its complexity. Authors selected range from Hawthorne and Melville to Welty and Albert Camus. Purdy's "Cutting Edge" is paired with Walter Van Tilburg Clark's "The Rapids." Purdy's story is on pages 168-175.

125     "Daddy Wolf." In *New World Writing* 17. Edited by Stewart Richardson and Corlies M. Smith. Philadelphia: J. B. Lippincott, 1960.

Story on pages 151-160.

126     "Daddy Wolf." In *New Sounds in American Fiction*. Edited by Gordon Lish. Menlo Park, California: Cummings Publishing, 1969.

A collection of twelve short stories by living American authors. "This book is coordinated with a series of recordings brought out by Cummings Publishing Company under the same title, the recording series presents a dramatic reading of each story collected

18

herein and a conversation with each author." Each reading is performed by a different person. Purdy's reading is by Ken Lynch and the conversation with James Purdy was recorded in his Brooklyn apartment. The Purdy recording is program seven and runs for twenty-seven minutes. The volume of short stories is intended to be used as a textbook. Each story is prefaced with a page of biographical information and followed by a series of questions. Purdy's short story and added material is on pages 110-127. Also included is a manuscript page from "Daddy Wolf" showing Purdy's changes.

127    "Daddy Wolf." In *Big City Stories by Modern American Writers*. Edited by Tom and Susan Cahill. New York: Bantam Books, 1971.

A collection of thirty stories arranged in five sections: Growing Up; Loving; Working; Dying and Looking Ahead. All of the stories "tell of the city's impact on its people." Purdy's story is under Dying and on pages 327-334.

128    "Dawn." In *Growing Up Gay/Growing Up Lesbian: A Literary Anthology*. Edited by Bennett L. Singer. New York: The New Press, 1994.

An anthology of fifty-six works divided into four sections: Self-Discovery; Friendships/Relationships; Family; Facing the World. The writings span almost the entire century. Purdy's short story appears under Family and is on pages 175-178.

129    "Dawn." In *The Faber Book of Gay Short Fiction*. Edited with a foreword by Edmund White. London: Faber and Faber Limited, 1991.

An anthology of thirty-two gay literary pieces ranging from the early writers of Henry James, Ronald Firbank, E. M. Forster to contemporary authors including Alan Hollinghurst, David Leavitt, and Lev Raphael. Purdy's story is on pages 234-237.

130    "Don't Call Me by My Right Name." In *New Directions in Prose and Poetry* 16 (1957): 46-53.

131    *Don't Call Me by My Right Name.* New York: Tsurumi Shoten, 1957.

>    Four stories with Japanese notes for a Japanese release.
>    Purdy's story is contained on pages 53-66.

132    "Don't Call Me by My Right Name." In *New Directions Reader.* Edited by Hayden Carruth & James Laughlin. Norfolk, Connecticut: New Directions Books, 1964.

>    An anthology of stories, poems and excerpts from novels, plays, and books of literary criticism published in celebration of the 25th anniversary of the publishing firm of New Directions. Purdy's short story is on pages 178-186.

133    "Don't Call Me by My Right Name." In *Black Humor.* Edited by Bruce Jay Friedman. New York: Bantam Books, 1965.

>    Thirteen literary pieces which Friedman defines as examples of "black humor." Authors included in this anthology are Pynchon, Heller, Donleavy, Nabokov, Barth, and Southern. Purdy's short story is on pages 139-145.

134    "Don't Call Me by My Right Name." In *The Shape of Fiction: British and American Short Stories.* Edited by Leo Hamalian and Frederick R. Karl. New York: McGraw-Hill Book Company, 1967.

>    A collection of thirty-nine short stories from Hawthorne (1835) to Randall (1965), arranged by "basic aspect of the genre: plot, character, mood, theme, style and point of view." After each story there is an analysis and questions to help "lead the student toward valid critical conclusions." Purdy's short story is included in the section "Style and Point of View."

135    "Don't Call Me by My Right Name." In *How We Live: Contemporary Life in Contemporary Fiction.* Edited by

Penney Chapin Hills and L. Rust Hills. New York:
Macmillan Company, 1968.

> The anthology is divided into three major parts and nine
> sections. Purdy's story is in part one, "The Way We
> Live" section in "In Families." Basic theme of the
> collection is to "celebrate" contemporary fiction. The
> end of each selection contains brief biographical sketch
> and analysis of short story. Purdy's story is on pages
> 361-367.

136    "Don't Call Me by My Right Name." In *Four Modes: A
       Rhetoric of Modern Fiction*. Edited by James M. Mellard.
       New York: Macmillan Company, 1973.

> An anthology of contemporary short stories. The
> appendix includes five references to Purdy's writing.

137    "Don't Call Me by My Right Name." In *Outside, Inside*.
       Edited by Laurie Urbscheit and Jerrod Brumfield. New
       York: Holt, Rinehart and Winston, 1973.

> An anthology of 134 literary pieces designed for
> freshmen English composition classes. The selections
> were chosen "for their varying ability to move, touch,
> anger the student—in short, to produce a reaction that
> 'constructively upsets' him." The collection is divided
> into eleven sections with Purdy's story in Unit 1,
> "Identity," on pages 27-32.

138    "Don't Call Me by My Right Name." In *The Shape of
       Fiction: British and American Short Stories*. Edited by
       Leo Hamalian and Frederick R. Karl. 2nd edition. New
       York: McGraw-Hill Book Company, 1978.

> Purdy's story appears in this collection of thirty-nine
> short stories from Hawthorne (1835) to Randall
> (1965).

139    "Don't Call Me by My Right Name." In *Studies in
       Fiction*. Edited by Blaze O. Bonazza, Emil Roy and
       Sandra Roy. 3rd edition. New York: Harper & Row, 1982.

> A collection of short stories for "developing
> understanding and appreciation of the short story by

providing a guide to systematic critical reading." Each story is followed by a series of questions for discussion. Purdy's story is on pages 706-710.

140      "Encore." In *Identity: Stories for This Generation*. Edited by Katherine Hondrus. Chicago: Scott, Foresman, 1966.

A collection of "seventeen modern short stories ... all of high literary excellence [that] deal with the intellectual and emotional problems of American youth." Purdy's story is on pages 44-51.

141      "Encore: A Story." *Commentary* 28 (March 1959): 243-247.

142      "Encore." In *Prize Stories 1960: The O. Henry Awards*. Edited by Mary Stegner with an introduction by Wallace Stegner. Garden City, New York: Doubleday, 1960.

Purdy's story is on pages 228-236. First published in the magazine *Commentary*.

143      "Encore." In *Contemporary American Short Stories*. Selected and introduced by Douglas and Sylvia Angus. New York: Fawcett Premier Book, 1967.

An anthology of twenty-three short stories written during and following World War II. Purdy's story is on pages 372-379.

144      "Encore." In *Family: Stories from the Interior*. Edited by Geri Giebel Chavis. Saint Paul, Minnesota: Graywolf Press, 1987.

A collection of twenty-five short stories which focuses on dynamic family relationships. Purdy's story is found in the section "Mothers and Sons" on pages 266-274.

145      "Eventide." In *Understanding Fiction*. Edited by Cleanth Brooks and Robert Penn Warren. New York: Appleton-Century Crofts, 1959.

A collection of fifty short stories. Purdy's story is on pages 223-232. Because the book has been devised as a textbook, each story is followed by an interpretation and questions.

146    "Eventide." In *The Scope of Fiction*. Edited by Cleanth Brooks and Robert Penn Warren. New York: Appleton-Century-Crofts, 1960.

This volume is an abridged version of the editors' *Understanding Fiction*.

147    "Eventide." In *Interpretation: An Approach to the Study of Literature*. Edited by Joanna H. Maclay and Thomas O. Sloan. New York, Random House, 1972.

An anthology of eighty-one pieces of nonfictional prose, poetry and prose fiction selected for teaching literature. Each literary selection is accompanied by a series of study questions. Purdy's short story is on pages 352-358.

148    "Eventide." In *The Art of the Tale: An International Anthology of Short Stories 1945-1985*. Edited with an introduction by Daniel Halpern. New York: Viking, 1986.

An anthology of eight-two short stories that the editor hopes is "capable of surviving the vagrancies of time and fashion, the fickleness of our short memory and our impatience." Purdy's story is on pages 622-628.

149    "Everything under the Sun." *Partisan Review* 26 (summer 1959): 363-370.

150    "Everything under the Sun." In *American Short Stories Since 1945*. Edited with an introduction by John Hollander. New York: Harper & Row, 1968.

An anthology of twenty-six contemporary short stories which aims "to show the major shapes taken by shorter fiction in America since the end of World War II." Purdy's story is on pages 384-391.

151    "Garments the Living Wear." *Art: Mag* 12 (1989): 1-9.
Excerpt from novel by the same name.

152      "Garnet Montrose and the Widow Rance." *Fiction* 4 (1975): 2-6.

      An excerpt from *In a Shallow Grave*, Purdy's eighth novel.

153      "Gertrude's Hand." *Antioch Review* 51 (summer 1993): 327-341.

      Short story.

154      "A Good Woman." *Creative Writing* 1 (January-February 1939): 5-10.

      Purdy's first published short story. *Creative Writing* was published in Chicago and lasted only three volumes (vols. 1-3, no. 3, November 1, 1938-March/April, 1941. It changed its name to *New Horizons* with volume three). On page thirty-one: "James Purdy has his first published story, 'A Good Woman,' in this issue and we hope that subsequent issues will present more of his work. At twenty-two he has a Masters Degree from the University of Chicago and has written his first novel, which has not been published."

155      "A Good Woman." In *Writer's Choice*. Edited with an introduction by L. Rust Hills. New York: D. McKay, 1974.

      In addition to the short story Purdy has written a preface explaining why he chose this story and provides background information. He also takes this opportunity to lambaste "American publishers, critics, and the media, and its debrained puppet, the public." Purdy's story is on pages 339-349.

156      "Goodnight Sweetheart." *Esquire* 54 (October 1960): 106-108.

157      "Goodnight Sweetheart." In *Coming Together: Modern Stories by Black and White Americans*. Edited by Adam A. Casmier and Sally Souder. Encino, California: Dickenson Publishing Company, 1972.

An anthology of twenty-five short stories suitable for college students in undergraduate literature courses. Includes discussion questions and writing suggestions. Also includes a section "About the authors" with individual author photographs. Purdy' s "Goodnight Sweetheart" appears on pages 160-171. This volume also includes Purdy's "Cutting Edge," which is on pages 292-299.

158     "Goodnight Sweetheart." In *12 From the Sixties*. Selected and introduced by Richard Kostelanetz. New York: Dell Publishing, 1967.

An anthology of short stories by distinguished American writers. "Madness and the absurdity of society are the two themes which obsess these authors" in this collection. Purdy's story is on pages 36-47.

159     "Goodnight Sweetheart." In *Grooving the Symbol*. Edited with a preface by Richard W. Lid. New York: The Free Press, 1970.

A collection of sixty-nine contemporary American readings for college students. The collection is arranged in nine sections: Some Ancestors: Old and New; Some Descendants: Recent and Contemporary; Some Futurists; Identify: The Gap; Society: The Microcosm; Education: Here and Now; The Media and the Arts: Pop, Mod, Fad; Making It: Gut, Soul, Cortex; and Symbol and Myth. Purdy's story is on pages 284-295.

160     "Goodnight Sweetheart." In *The Naked I: Fiction for the Seventies*. Edited by Frederick R. Karl and Leo Hamalian. Greenwich, Connecticut: Fawcett World Library 1971.

An anthology of twenty-seven literary works arranged in three sections: Discontinuity With Design; An Earlier Generation; and Nonfiction. In the stories "which make up this collection, the naked 'I' perceives, creates, and then communicates to the reader its own unique and personal vision of that world." Purdy's story is on pages 311-322.

161  "Goodnight, Sweetheart." In *Killing Time: A Guide to Life in the Happy Valley*. Edited by Robert Disch and Barry Schwartz. Englewood Cliffs, New Jersey: Prentice-Hall, 1972.

A collection of poems, short stories and short plays illustrating "those areas of human experience where sociologists and psychologists tell us the society is showing dangerous stress, where individuals are suffering because of their inability to understand the forces that cause tension and anxiety in their lives." Purdy's story is on pages 11-20.

162  "Green Knowledge." *New Directions in Prose and Poetry* 32 (1976): 132-134.

163  "Home by Dark." *Harper's Bazaar* 91 (June 1958): 89, 110-111.

164  "Home by Dark." *London Magazine* 5 (June 1958): 39-45.

165  "Home by Dark." *New Directions in Prose and Poetry* 17 (1961): 192-200.

166  "Home by Dark." In *The Uncommon Reader*. Edited by Alice S. Morris. New York: Avon Books, 1965.

An anthology of thirty-five stories by contemporary authors from fourteen countries. These works were selected from one hundred and eighty-six stories that have appeared in *Harper's Bazaar* under the editorship of Alice Morris. Purdy's short story is on pages 319-326.

167  *"The House of the Solitary Maggot." TriQuarterly* 33 (spring 1975): 5-69.

An excerpt from Purdy's novel *The House of the Solitary Maggot*. Issue is entitled "Ongoing American Fiction" and is illustrated by William E. Biderbost. Contains the note, "For my grandmother, Minnie Mae."

168    "How I Became a Shadow." *New Directions in Prose and Poetry* 36 (1978): 124-126.

    "An excerpt from the novel-in-progress *Narrow Rooms*."

169    "How I Became a Shadow." *Nimrod* 22 (spring/summer 1978): 66-68.

170    "I Am Elijah Thrush." *Esquire* 76 (December 1971): 194-201, 246-264.

    An early version of his novel which was later published in book form by Doubleday in 1972. Illustrated by Barry Zaid.

171    "I Am Elijah Thrush." In *The Secret Life of Our Times: New Fiction from Esquire*. Edited by Gordon Lish. Introduction to the book by Tom Wolfe. Garden City, New York: Doubleday & Co., 1973.

    An anthology of thirty-one selections from *Esquire*. Story is on pages 81-145

172    "In the Hollow of His Hand." *Antaeus* 55 (autumn 1985): 254-275.

    Excerpt from the novel.

173    "In This Corner ..." In *Men on Men 2: Best New Gay Fiction*. Edited with an introduction by George Stambolian. New York: New American Library Books, 1988.

    A collection of eighteen gay fiction stories by contemporary American writers. "Many of the stories deal with AIDS, particularly with the intense conflicts the disease has produced between love and fear, compassion and discrimination ... others give new insights into the ageless problems of family life." Purdy's story is on pages 74-86.

174    *Jeremy's Version*. In *Works in Progress* (No. 1). Edited by William Ewald. New York: Literary Guild of America, 1970.

This is an excerpt from the novel *Jeremy's Version*. On pages 193-209.

175      "Kitty Blue." *Conjunctions* 18 (spring 1992): 24-41.

This issue has the subtitle "Fables, Yarns, Fairy Tales."

176      "The Lesson." *Texas Quarterly* 1 (winter 1958): 72-79.

177     "Lily's Party." *New Directions in Prose and Poetry* 29 (1974): 99-109.

178      "The Longer I Serve Him the Sweeter He Grows." *New Directions in Prose and Poetry* 35 (1977): 178-182.

"Excerpts from *Four Thousand Afternoons with the Forest*." A combination of prose and poetry.

179      "Mr. Evening." *Harper's Bazaar* 101 (September 1968): 168+.

On page 232 there is a brief note on Purdy including a photograph.

180      "Mr. Evening." *New Directions in Prose and Poetry* 21 (1969): 30-49.

181      "Mrs. Benson: A Story." *Commentary* 28 (October 1959): 329-333.

182      "Mud Toe the Cannibal." *Bomb* 7 (1983): 34-37.

183      "Night and Day." *Esquire* 50 (July 1958): 108-112.

184      "On Glory's Course." *Antaeus* 51 (autumn 1983): 158-177.

Excerpt from Purdy's novel *On Glory's Course*.

185      "On the Rebound." *New Directions in Prose and Poetry* 23 (1971): 14-21.

186      "Out With the Stars." *Conjunctions* 19 (1992): 19-28.

Excerpt from the Purdy novel. Issue has subtitle: "Other Worlds."

187   "Out With the Stars." *Bastard Review* 5/6 (n.d.): 11-20.
      An excerpt from his novel.

188   "Q & A." *Esquire* 79 (May 1973): 134, 232.
      A fictional piece written in questions to Prince Antelope and answered by him. Note in "Backstage with Esquire," (p. 116): "James Purdy's play *Wedding Finger* is to be produced at the Cafe La MaMa in New York this fall."

189   "Rapture." *New Directions in Prose and Poetry* 50 (1986): 237-245.
      This is the 50th Anniversary Issue.

190   "Scrap of Paper." *Evergreen* 11 (August 1967): 23-25, 81-82.

191   "Scrap of Paper." *New Directions in Prose and Poetry* 20 (1968): 34-44.

192   "A Selection from *Garments the Living Wear*." *Art: Mag* 11 (spring/summer 1989): 12-20.
      An excerpt from the novel *Garments the Living Wear*.

193   "Sermon." *New Directions in Prose and Poetry* 17 (1961): 188-191

194   "Shoot!" *New Directions in Prose and Poetry* 25 (1972): 144-145.

195   "Short Papa." *Antioch Review* 34 (summer 1976): 420-427.
      First appearance of this short story.

196   "Short Papa." *Antioch Review* 50 (winter/spring 1992): 246-253.
      The 50th Anniversary Issue.

197 "Short Papa." In *Early Sorrow: Ten Stories of Youth.* Selected by Charlotte Zolotow. New York: Harper & Row, 1986.

> A collection of short stories that deal "with loss, separation, unrequited or unspoken love, divorce or death of those we care about." Purdy's story, about loss and the death of a father, is on pages 121-134.

198 "Sleep Tight." In *Wonders: Writings and Drawings for the Child in Us All.* Edited and introduction by Jonathan Cott and Mary Gimbel. New York: Summit Books, 1980.

> A collection of 126 pieces of literature in response to a request for "a story, or a poem, or a fantasy, or a fable—whatever you [the writer] have in mind—that you might like to tell a child (of any age)." Purdy's story is on pages 481-487.

199 "Sleep Tight." *Antioch Review* 37 (winter 1979): 27-35.

200 "Some of These Days." *New Directions in Prose and Poetry* 31 (1975): 53-62.

201 "Some of These Days." *A Shout in the Street: A Journal of Literary & Visual Art* 2 (1979): 64-74.

202 "Some of These Days." In *On the Line: New Gay Fiction.* Edited with an introduction by Ian Young. Trumansburg, New York: The Crossing Press, 1981.

> A collection of eighteen stories written since the Stonewall riot of 1969 dealing primarily with gay men. Purdy's story is on pages 109-116.

203 "Some of These Days." In *Mae West Is Dead: Recent Lesbian and Gay Fiction.* Edited by Adam Mars-Jones. London: Faber and Faber, 1983.

> A collection of twenty-one stories representing the best of contemporary lesbian and gay fiction both in Great Britain and the United States. Purdy's story is on pages 92-102.

204 "Some of These Days." In *The Penguin Book of Gay Short Stories*. Edited by David Leavitt and Mark Mitchell. New York: Viking Press, 1994.

A collection of thirty-nine short stories. "For the purpose of this anthology, then, a gay story has been defined as one that illuminates the experience of love between men, explores the nature of homosexual identity, or investigates the kinds of relationships gay men have with each other, with their friends, and with their families." Purdy's story is on pages 266-274.

205 "Sound of Talking." *The Black Mountain Review* 5 (summer 1955): 153-164.

206 "Summer Tidings." *Esquire* 82 (December 1974): 186-187, 232-238.

Illustrated by Martin Lemelman.

207 "Summer Tidings." *New Directions in Prose and Poetry* 30 (1975): 103-111.

208 "Summer Tidings." In *All Our Secrets Are the Same: New Fiction from Esquire*. Edited with a foreword by Gordon Lish. New York: W. W. Norton & Company, 1976.

A second anthology of thirty-eight short stories from *Esquire*. Purdy's story is on pages 9-11.

209 "Summer Tidings." *Granta: A Magazine of Fiction and Prose* (autumn 1979): 105-110.

This issue has subtitle "New American Writing."

210 "Summer Tidings." In *In Another Part of the Forest*. Edited by Alberto Manguel and Craig Stephenson. New York: Crown Trade Paperbacks, 1994.

An international collection of forty-five short stories. Each story in the anthology includes a brief introduction to the author with quotes by the author. Purdy's story is on pages 362-370.

211     "The Vorago: A Chapter from a Novel in Progress."
*Christopher Street* 12 (September 1989): 18-21.

      Includes a full page photograph of Purdy.

212     "The Vorago." *Satchel* 1 (1989): 47-56.

      This is an excerpt from a novel in progress

213     "The White Blackbird." *Conjunctions* 20 (1993): 104-126.

      Issue has subtitle "Unfinished Business."

214     "Why Can't They Tell You Why?" In *Twenty-Nine
Stories*. 2nd edition. Edited by William Peden. Boston:
Houghton Mifflin Company, 1967.

      A collection of short stories of writers ranging from Poe
and Hawthorne to Purdy, O'Connor and Roth. Purdy's
story is on pages 329-336. At the end of the story
there is a brief biographical section and five discussion
questions.

215     "Why Can't They Tell You Why?" In *The Process of
Fiction: Contemporary Stories and Criticism*. Edited by
Barbara McKenzie. New York: Harcourt, Brace & World,
1969.

      An anthology of twenty short stories by ten
outstanding contemporary American writers with
"critical essays that interpret the first story of each
pair." Purdy's story is on pages 299-304 along with
questions for discussion and a bibliography of primary
and secondary sources and a brief biographical sketch.

216     "Why Can't They Tell You Why?" In *An Introduction to
Short Fiction and Criticism*. Edited by Emil Hurtik and
Robert Yarber. Waltham, Massachusetts: Xerox College
Publishing, 1971.

      The stories in this collection "were chosen for their
intrinsic interest as well as for their literary and critical
significance. There are several generations of writers
represented; the emphasis is on the present." Purdy's
story is on pages 322-325.

217    "Why Can't They Tell You Why?" In *American Models:
       A Collection of Modern Stories*. Edited by James E.
       Miller. Glenview, Illinois: Scott, Foresman, 1973.

       An anthology of twenty-two short stories including
       works by Anderson, Barthelme, Capote, Faulkner,
       Hemingway, McCullers, Stafford, Welty, and Purdy.
       Purdy's short story is on pages 170-175.

218    "Why Can't They Tell You Why?" In *Evening Games:
       Tales of Parents and Children*. Edited by Alberto
       Manguel. New York: Clarkson N. Potter, 1987.

       A collection of sixteen short stories exploring various
       relationships of parents and children. Each selection is
       preceded by brief biographical information and
       background notes to the short story. Purdy's story is
       on pages 139-147.

219    "Why Can't They Tell You Why?" In *Fiction's Many
       Worlds*. Edited by Charles E. May. Lexington,
       Massachusetts: D. C. Heath, 1993.

       An anthology of 142 stories. At the end of each
       selection are questions for students that will enhance
       the study and understanding of each piece.

220    "You May Safely Gaze." In *The Other Persuasion: An
       Anthology of Short Fiction about Gay Men and Women*.
       Edited by Seymour Kleinberg. New York: Vintage Books,
       1977.

       A collection of twenty-six short fiction pieces. "One
       purpose of this collection is to assist definition by
       exploring some meanings of the experience that the
       word [gay] has connoted in the past, and by noting the
       change in meaning, tentative but clear, as we approach
       the present." Purdy's story is on pages 195-202.

221    "You May Safely Gaze." In *The Signet Classic Book of
       Contemporary American Short Stories*. Edited by Burton
       Raffel. New York: New American Library, 1985.

       A collection of short stories written after 1945. Each
       story is preceded by a brief biography and a note of

criticism. Raffel states that Purdy's prose is "exemplary, idiosyncratic, and exceedingly carefully controlled. What often seems to be a kind of poetic indulgence usually turns out, on close examination, to be a deliberately calculated effect. Purdy is a superb craftsman." Purdy's story is on pages 128-138.

222    "You May Safely Gaze." In *No Need to Knock: Stories and Fragments Focusing on Men in the Office.* Selected by Arie-Jan Gelderblom. Design and illustrations by Mart Kempers. Amsterdam, Netherlands: Ahrend Group NV, 1990.

Eleven stories providing "a picture of people, springing from writers' imaginative powers." Purdy's short story is on pages 39-44.

223    "You Reach For Your Hat." *Prairie Schooner* 20 (spring 1946): 185-192.

One of Purdy's earliest commercially published short stories. Information on the contributors notes "James Purdy, of Havana, Cuba is also a new contributor." Quotes Purdy as stating "After being honorably discharged from the army, I have been living in Mexico and Cuba. I have no real home in the United States, but I think the place which influences me most there is Chicago. I went to the University there, and it was a group of Chicago writers who encouraged me to write. Robert Williams published one of my stories in his *Creative Writing* (later *New Horizons*) just about the time of the war."

224    "You Reach for Your Hat." In *A Short Wait Between Trains: An Anthology of War Short Stories by American Writers.* Edited by Robert Benard. New York: Dell Publishing, 1991.

A collection of twenty-two short stories, from the Civil War to the Vietnam War. A few of the authors included in the anthology are Stephen Crane, Ernest Hemingway, William Faulkner, Irwin Shaw, James Jones, and Wright Morris. Purdy's story is on pages 171-182.

225    "You Reach for Your Wraps." *Mademoiselle* 44 (March 1957): 104-105.

226    "You Reach for Your Wraps." In *40 Best Stories From Mademoiselle, 1935-1960*. Edited by Cyrilly Abels and Margarita G. Smith. New York: Harper & Brothers, 1960.

    A collection of short stories which first appeared in the magazine *Mademoiselle*. Purdy's story is on pages 362-370 and was his first national magazine publication.

227    "You Reach for Your Wraps." In *Best Stories From Mademoiselle*. Edited by Cyrilly Abels and Margarita G. Smith. New York: Harper & Brothers, 1961.

    Twenty-nine short stories selected from *40 Best Stories from Mademoiselle, 1935-1960*. Purdy's story is on pages 261-270.

## 2. Plays

228    *Adeline: A Short Play. Second Coming* 10 (1-2) (1981): 6-20.

    Special Double Prose-Fiction Issue.

229    *Adeline: A Short Play.* In *Second Coming Anthology: Ten Years in Retrospect*. A. D. Winans, editor. San Francisco: Second Coming Press, 1984.

    This anthology also serves as volume 10, numbers 1 and 2 of *Second Coming Magazine*. Purdy's play is on pages 170-182.

230    *Adeline* and *Wonderful Happy Days. Conjunctions* 2 (spring/summer 1982):  60-83.

    Two plays.  Published in both a paperback edition and a hardback edition.  Edited by Bradford Morrow.

231    *Band Music. City Lights Review* 9 (1990):103-113.

    An international annual of contemporary fiction, poetry, essays, and political commentary edited by Nancy J.

Peters and Lawrence Ferlinghetti. Purdy's one-act play "Band Music" was performed by Theater for the New City in 1990 with Sheila Dabney and Crystal Field. Contains two photographs of the performance.

232    *The Berry-Picker*. *New Directions in Prose and Poetry* 45 (1982):157-165.

233    *Bright Summer Stars*. In *Lord John Ten: 10: A Celebration*. Edited by Dennis Etchison. Northridge, California: Lord John Press, 1988.

A collection of twenty-six short stories, essays, poems, photographs and a play by contemporary authors. Purdy's play is on pages 13-22.

234    *Clearing in the Forest*. *New Directions in Prose and Poetry* 40 (1980): 83-90.

One-act play.

235    *Cracks*. *Cosmopolitan* 153 (August 1962): 64-69.

One-act play. Has photographic illustrations by Erwin Blumenfeld.

236    *A Day After the Fair*. *The Texas Arts Journal* 1 (1977): 51-70.

A play in five scenes. Journal edited by Cameron Northouse.

237    *Heatstroke*. *Dirty Bum: A Magazine* 1 (fall 1987): 14-26.

One-act play.

238    *Heatstroke*. *Antaeus* 66 (spring 1991): 395-400.

Contained in an issue devoted to one-act plays.

239    *Immaculate Housekeeping*. *Dirty Bum: A Magazine* 2 (winter 1987/1988): 22-25.

One-act play.

240    *Joker in the Pack*. *Red Bass* 13 (1988): 7-9.

One-act play.

241    *Mr. Cough Syrup and the Phantom Sex. december* 8.1
       (1966):175-177.

      A short one-act play.

242    *Now. New Directions in Prose and Poetry* 41 (1980): 98-
       105.

      One-act play.

243    *Now. European Gay Review* 3 (1988): 24-35.

      One-act play.

244    *Souvenirs. City Lights Review* 2 (1988): 64-70.

      A one-act play.

245    *True. New Directions in Prose and Poetry* 34 (1977):
       140-145.

      One act-play.

246    *Wedding Finger. New Directions in Prose and Poetry* 28
       (1974): 77-98.

      One-act play.

247    *What Is It, Zach? New Directions in Prose and Poetry* 43
       (1981): 171-179.

      One-act play.

248    *Wonderful Happy Days. Conjunctions* 2 (spring/summer
       1982): 72-83.

      One-act play.


## 3. Poetry

249    "Are You in the Wintertree?" Utrecht: Sub Signo Libelli,
       1987.

250    "The Black Boy I Met Half A Year Ago." *Lactuca* 12
       (February 1989): 44.

251    "Blossoms." *Contact/II* 9 (summer/fall 1989): 30.

252    "The Brooklyn Branding Parlors." *Niagara Magazine* 12/13 (fall 1980): 51.

First appearance of this poem.

253    "The Brooklyn Branding Parlors." *New Directions in Prose and Poetry* 44 (1982): 182.

254    "The Brooklyn Branding Parlors" and "Solitary in Brooklyn." In *A New Geography of Poets*. Compiled and edited by Edward Field, Gerald Locklin and Charles Stetler. Introduction by Marge Piercy. Fayetteville, Arkansas: The University of Arkansas Press, 1992.

An anthology of one hundred and eighty three contemporary poets exploring the world they live in. The arrangement is by geographical location and the two poems by Purdy on pages 118-119 are under New York City.

255    "Do You Wonder Why I Am Sleepy?" *Lactuca* 12 (February 1989): 45.

256    "Eight Poems." *Contact/II* 9 (summer/fall 1989): 29-32.

Includes: "White Yellow Orange," "In a Deep Slumber," "Fighting in a Wood," "Blossoms," "Untitled." "From Rivers, and from the Earth Itself," "White Sheep," and "Men of Bangladesh."

257    "4 Poems." In *The Two Worlds of Vassilis Voglis*. Edited by Arthur Lambert. New York: Saurus Productions, Midco Printing & Publishing, 1988.

Contains: "I'll Mail Lilacs & Lilies," "My Greatest Pain," "Jan Erik Said:" and "Jan Erik, Alone." Poems are on pages 46-53.

258    "Four Poems." *Botteghe Oscure* 23 (28 February 1959): 299-302.

Four poems are: "Merry-Go-Round Horses and Carrousel," "An Ode to Godwin Dwight," "Vendrá," "What." These poems are contained in this volume, edited by Marguerite Caetani.

259  "He Watched Me." *Bomb* 9 (spring/summer 1984): 63.

260  "He Watched Me" and "The Brooklyn Branding Parlors." In *Best Minds: A Tribute to Allen Ginsberg*. Edited by Bill Morgan and Bob Rosenthal. New York: Lospecchio Press, 1986.

> An anthology of two hundred and four friends contributed their writing to celebrate Allen Ginsberg's sixtieth birthday. Purdy's two poems are on pages 231-232.

261  "I Have Told You Your Hands Are Salt." In *Poets for Life: Seventy-six Poets Respond to AIDS*. Edited with an introduction by Michael Klein. Preface by Rt. Rev. Paul Moore, Jr. Foreword by Joseph Papp. Essay by Carol Muske. New York: Persea Books, 1989.

> A collection of poems written by seventy-six of the best contemporary poets—gay and straight, male and female, black and white. The poems "express the complex depths, the whirlpools of despair, the agony of feeling betrayed, the passion, the nostalgia for youth, the holocaust of dying, the mysterious quality of gay and lesbian love." Purdy's poem is on page 200.

262  "I Will Arrest the Bird That Has No Light." *New Directions in Prose and Poetry* 36 (1978): 11.

263  "In the Event of." *New Directions in Prose and Poetry* 17 (1961): 224.

264  "Jan Erik." *Exquisite Corpse* 7 (January/May 1989): 15.

265  "Jan Erik Speaks." *Lactuca* 11 (October 1988): 41.

266  "Jan Erik Said:" *Art: Mag* 11(spring/summer 1989): 10.

266a  "Jan Erik Said:" *Gypsy* 12-13 (1989): 54.

267  "Men of Bangladesh." *Lactuca* 12 (February 1989): 45-46.

268      "Merman." *Contact/II* 7 (fall 1985): 31.

269      "My Dear This Is a Dreadful Coming Out." *New Directions in Prose and Poetry* 24 (1972): 175.

270      "My Greatest Pain." *Conspiracy Charges* 15 (1991): 11.

271      "The Peacock Beyond Garden Walls." *New Directions in Prose and Poetry* 17 (1961): 310.

272      "Poems." *december* 9 (1967): 100.

> Includes three poems: "The Lovely Listless Wind Has Sighed," "Whenever You Pee," and "Carl Van Vechten."

273      "Seven Poems." *Focus Midwest* 4 (1966): 33.

> Seven very short poems ranging from two to four lines each. Notes indicates the "seven poems are from a work in progress which now bears the tentative title: "Poems for Children Away From Home," to be published by Farrar, Straus, & Giroux.

274      "The Thick Residuum of Night." *Conspiracy Charges* 16 (1991): 12.

275      "Water Bird." *New Directions in Prose and Poetry* 20 (1968): 44.

276      "Water Bird." In *Man in the Poetic Mode*. Edited by Joy Zweigler. Evanston, Illinois: McDougal, Littell & Company, 1970.

277      "White Sheep." *Lactuca* 12. (February 1989): 44.


## 4. Essays

278      "Aspects of Self: A Bowles Collage." *Twentieth Century Literature* 32 (fall/winter 1986): 259-300.

> This issue of *Twentieth Century Literature* is devoted to Paul Bowles. The article entitled "Aspects of Self:

A Bowles Collage" consists of fourteen replies in answer to a request to "critics, friends of Bowles, and novelists who may have been influenced by his work." Purdy's reply on pages 288-289 recalls his first meeting Bowles at Carl Van Vechten's "elegant suite of rooms on Central Park West." Purdy writes "That evening I found Mr. Bowles a very quiet, extremely receptive man, and though deep and inscrutable, kind and amicable."

279    "James Purdy on Denton Welch." *Little Caesar* 12 (1981): 131.

Purdy's essay on fellow author Denton Welch. This issue of the poetry magazine is entitled: "Overlooked and Underrated: Essays on Some 20th Century Writers." Edited by Ian Young.

280    "Notes on Recognition." *Nimrod* 22 (spring/summer 1978): 69.

A short essay or "informal remarks" on being a writer. Purdy writes "To be a writer, you have to be on your knees to experience; you have to be open to everything. Sometimes we resist material for a long time because it is too painful. But writing is part of nature too. It has, like the birth of a child, a gestation period. So you have to let it happen; you can't force it. On the other hand, you do have to give it every chance of happening by putting yourself in the position for writing, by exercising writing anything that comes to mind for at least fifteen minutes every day, to get the flow going. You are a vessel."

281    "A Statement and Anonymous/Anomalous Letters." *Conjunctions* 1 (winter 1981/82): 175-185.

Purdy's statement praises James Laughlin as "One of the very few writers in America today who has any literary taste or insight." And Purdy notes that "His contribution to American culture is incalculable." Also contains Purdy's short story. This is an Inaugural Double-Issue in both hard and paperback editions. Anthology is edited by Bradford Morrow.

282     "Success Story." *New York Times Book Review* (6 June 1971): 24, 26.

> Humorous and satirical article with subtitle "Boogie Broome in the Big Time" on how to write and publish a best seller. Ends with "As Boogie said while on tour with Mogul Wimminsare: 'It's not so much what you can do for money in this grand old U.S.A.—you can't do a thing without it.' "

## 5. Reviews

283     "Dame Edith Sitwell's Sad, Witty, Farewell." *Life* 58 (30 April 1965): 8, 12.

> A book review of *Taken Care of: The Autobiography of Edith Sitwell*. Purdy begins the review by describing his only meeting with Dame Sitwell in "New York, on St. Patrick's Day, 1957, at the St. Regis Hotel." Purdy was living in a small Pennsylvania town at the time. Purdy writes "This elegant autobiography—one of her best books—as witty, as her *English Eccentrics*, as original as her *Facade*—is a dazzling reflection of her own larger than life personality. Brief and concentrated, it fully recreates the atmosphere and the people of her life."

284     "Lunacy Among the Teacups." *New York Times Book Review* (7 September 1986): 27.

> A very positive review of Kate Grenville's first novel, *Lillian's Story*.

## 6. Introductions, Forewords, Afterwords and Tributes

285     "Afterword." *Antioch Review* 37 (winter 1979): 34-35.

> A typical Purdy denouncement against American publishers, editors, and book reviewers. Purdy writes "My stories have been translated into over thirty foreign languages and many of the stories from my books *Color of Darkness* and *Children is All* have been

anthologized over fifty times and taught in universities and high schools."

286    "Introduction." In *Weymouth Sands* by John Cowper Powys. New York: Harper & Row, 1984.

Purdy ends this fine tribute to Powys with "Most of the popular novelists of Powys's day are today forgotten. But his own books, read only by a 'happy few' when he lived, go on being reprinted for a new and devoted audience, an audience as unusual and persistent as the writer himself. If may be he will outlast all the other English novelists of this century."

287    "Vassilis Voglis." In *Two Worlds of Vassilis Voglis*. New York: Saurus Productions, Midco Printing & Publishing, 1988.

A short tribute to the artist, Vassilis Voglis. Purdy writes "Vassilis has no competitor, no real equal. If one would choose music for the man and his paintings one might select Liszt's 'Nocturnal Procession.' " Tribute is on page 14.

## 7. Interviews

288    Aletti, Vince. "American Gothic: James Purdy's Divine Madness." *Village Voice Literary Supplement* 31 (9 September 1986): 18-20.

An intelligent and penetrating article/interview on Purdy's writing with emphasis on his latest novel, *In the Hollow of His Hand*. Also includes many important quotes from Purdy including the information that "his parents were divorced when he was eleven and then he was shunted from father to mother to grandmother in various Ohio villages." Also noted that "he ran away to Chicago at sixteen and had an adventurous 'nightmare' time (I guess I didn't know any better or I would have been frightened) until he joined the army." One of the more informative and important articles/interviews on Purdy. It includes a large photograph of Purdy.

289    Barron, Frank. "James Purdy: Penthouse Interview."
       *Penthouse: The International Magazine for Men* 5 (July
       1974): 89-93.

       A standard interview in which Purdy expresses his
       views on writing, his career, New York establishment,
       and background.  Purdy notes he went to Chicago at the
       age of sixteen and attended the University of Chicago
       before joining the Air Force during World War II.  Has
       four photographs of Purdy by Ed Galluci including one of
       his Brooklyn apartment.

290    *Conversations with Writers II*. Volume 3. Detroit,
       Michigan: Gale Research Company, 1978.

       A collection of eleven individual interviews of
       contemporary writers including Stanley Ellin, James T.
       Farrell, Anita Loos, James A. Michener, William
       Styron, and Eudora Welty.  The long, informative
       interview of James Purdy by Cameron Northouse
       provides little autobiographical material.  The questions
       and answers dwell heavily on Purdy's writing, his
       philosophy on writing and life, his negative reception by
       critics, his views on writers (current and past), his
       experience in writing for the theatre and his writing of
       his latest novel, *Narrow Rooms*.  Interview contains an
       excellent photograph of Purdy.

291    Cuomo, Joseph. "An Interview with James Purdy." *A
       Shout in the Street: A Journal of Literary & Visual Art* 2
       (1979): 76-92.

       This interview is preceded by Purdy's short story
       "Some of These Days."  Cuomo compares this story
       with *Eustace Chisholm and the Works* because both
       have a homosexual landlord as a main character.  Purdy
       points out that both are about "a man who runs away
       from himself."  Again, Purdy emphasizes that all of his
       stories are based on real people.  Purdy also discusses
       his problems getting published and the "so-called
       literary establishment's" problems with accepting his
       writings.  Briefly mentioned are *The Nephew*, *In a
       Shallow Grave*, *Malcolm*, *I Am Elijah Thrush*, and *A
       Day At The Fair*.  Noted throughout is the misspelling

of Eustace Chisholm as Chisolm.  Contains a small photograph of Purdy.

292    Dahlin, Robert. "PW Interviews: James Purdy." *Publishers' Weekly* 219 (19 June 1981): 12-14.

A typical interview with Purdy which stresses that he writes about family and real people in his books.  He reviews Purdy's first publishing efforts and his early supporters.  He states his continuous dislike of most critics and the New York Establishment.  Purdy talks about his use of language in which he tries "to use the speech of a person."  And he states "Language is like our blood.  It's such an intimate part of us.  Our language is us.  When I write my fiction, which is about souls, I have to use their language.  Language is the soul, the soul coming out."  Purdy notes that "people have said, 'He has such a special vision, it's not valid.'  That's absurd.  Any vision, no matter how cracked, is valid.  I usually write about a person in crisis because that's the time we tell the truth."

293    DeStefano, George. "The Purdy Principle." *Outweek* 50 (June 13, 1990): 50-52.

An article based on an interview with Purdy.  Novels discussed include *Garments the Living Wear*, *Eustace Chisholm and the Works* and *Narrow Rooms*.  DeStefano writes that "Although Purdy is gay, and homosexuality has figured in his work since *63: Dream Palace*, he does not consider himself a gay writer."  DeStefano notes that "Purdy's work has met with outraged condemnation as well as extravagant praise.  The explicit gay sexuality and the sometimes extreme sexual violence depicted in his novels has turned off more than a few squeamish, middlebrow, heterosexist critics.  Perhaps even worse for a writer than being savaged, though, is being ignored, which has too often been Purdy's undeserved fate."  Article has a full-page photograph of Purdy by Michael Wakefield.

294    Frame, Allen. "James Purdy, Interview." *Bomb* 5 (1983): 20-21.

This interview took place after the production of three of Purdy's one-act plays, *What Is It Zach?*, *True*, and *The Berry-Picker* by Nightshift, a New York theatre group working out of the Laight Again Club in New York's East Village during October and November, 1982. The majority of the questions and answers are about the plays and the production. Interview contains a photograph of Purdy by Allen Frame.

295    Gavron, Donald J. "An Interview With James Purdy." *Art: Mag* 11 (spring/summer 1989): 3-9.

A standard question and answer interview. Purdy's novels *Garments the Living Wear*, *Malcolm*, *Cabot Wright Begins*, *On Glory's Course*, *In the Hollow of His Hand*, *I Am Elijah Thrush*, *Eustace Chisholm and the Works*, *Narrow Rooms* and *In a Shallow Grave* are all noted and remarked upon. Purdy's problems with finding people in the United States to publish his works are discussed. Purdy notes that his work has been translated into "about 32, 35 languages. But in some of the cases, like in South Korea, there's just one story published, and in Israel there's just one story, published in Hebrew. In France, I think everything has been published, and in Italy a great many, in Holland many. They even have published some of my stories in Estonia, which now is part of Russia, unwillingly part of Russia."

296    Huizenga, Chris. "James Purdy: A Voyage of Discovery." *After Dark* 9 (July 1976): 70-73.

A wonderful interview with Purdy written at the time of the publication of Purdy's latest novel, *In a Shallow Grave*. Many of the questions and answers focus on an in-depth study of the novel's plot, characters and Purdy's own analysis of this work. Purdy discusses *I Am Elijah Thrush*, *The House of the Solitary Maggot*, *Jeremy's Version* and *Cabot Wright Begins*. This is one of the best interviews because it provides insight into Purdy's writing and self. Positive reference is made to The Trinity Square Repertory Company's (Providence, Rhode Island) translation and production of *Eustace*

*Chisholm and the Works.* The play was directed by Adrian Hall and presented at the Lederer Playhouse in April, 1976. Huizenga ends his interview with "readers unfamiliar with Purdy's work are well-advised to start with *In a Shallow Grave*, a contemporary classic of immense and quiet power that breaks like thunder on a sunny day, and then read back to the early books. It's a voyage of discovery." Article contains two photographs of Purdy by Jack Mitchell. The full-page photography is the best this compiler has seen. Also included are four photographs of scenes from the play, *Eustace Chisholm and the Works* by William L. Smith.

297    Lear, Patricia. "Interview with James Purdy." *StoryQuarterly* 26 (1989): 55-76.

A long interview in which Purdy comments on many of his novels. Purdy noted that *63: Dream Palace* is his favorite and that *The House of the Solitary Maggot* "is very important among my books." Purdy identifies Amos in *Eustace Chisholm and the Works* and Cliff in *The Nephew* as himself "in a way." He talks about Edith Sitwell, Tennessee Williams, Dorothy Parker, Flannery O'Connor, Clifton Fadiman, Gordon Lish, Henry Chupack, and Stephen Adams. Contains a photograph of Purdy.

298    Link, James. "James Purdy." *Interview* 11, nos. 6-7 (1981): 62-63.

An interview which discusses Purdy's early writing and his very negative feelings about the 'First Circle' of fame and his New York publishing scene. Purdy said he was first published in his early twenties by "a tiny magazine in Chicago run by a conscientious objector who took 'A Good Woman.' " This was followed by the publication of "You Reach for Your Hat" and "Sound of Talking" after World War II. Contains a photograph of Purdy by Giuseppe Pino.

299    Midwood, Barton. "Short Visit with Five Authors and One Friend." *Esquire* 74 (November 1970): 150-153.

The five writers are Russell Edson, James Purdy,
Grace Paley, I. B. Singer, Frank Conroy, and Maurice is
the friend. The interview states that Purdy lives in a
small apartment in Brooklyn Heights on Henry Street.
He is 47 and lives alone. Just finished *Jeremy's
Version*. Indicates Purdy's dislike of *New York Times
Book Review*. Notes he has been translated into 25
different languages, including Chinese and Turkish and
has been praised by George Stein, a critic of some
acuity and considerable affluence. First novel,
*Malcolm*, sold about 4500 copies in hardback and
250,000 copies in paperback. From the paperback sale
he made $800. He said that he is supported mainly by
grants. Midwood is a novelist.

300      Morrow, Bradford. "An Interview with James Purdy."
*Conjunctions* 3 (autumn 1982): 97-111.

A long, in depth, and important interview. Morrow
begins by asking what authors Purdy read and who had
an early influence on him. Purdy lists Unamuno,
Hemingway, Anderson, Melville, and Hardy. Purdy
discusses his daily writing routine and thinks *Malcolm*
and *The House of the Solitary Maggot* are among his
best books. Purdy lists "Some of These Days,"
"Eventide," "You Reach for Your Hat," "Cutting
Edge," "Man and Wife," "Sleep Tight," "Daddy
Wolf," "Goodnight Sweetheart," and "Summer
Tidings" as the short stories he would select for a
collection of his works. Biographical information
relates that he went to Chicago after high school; joined
the army in 1941 and was based at Scott Field,
Belleville, Illinois; after the service, he taught in Cuba
for one year and had a short story published in *Prairie
Schooner*. After Cuba, he taught at Lawrence College;
he lived in Spain for a time; he wrote *Malcolm* while
living with a friend, Jorma Jules Sjoblom, in
Pennsylvania near Quakertown; moved from
Pennsylvania to Brooklyn in 1962. Purdy emphasizes:
"Communication is life. We are only human as long as
we have communication with other human beings. If
man lived totally alone, he wouldn't be human.... This is

the whole reason for art, and for life. Only by being next to other people are we human. And in our culture this happens less and less and less. That's why we have all kinds of strange behavioral anomalies." Also published in a paperback edition.

301    Niel, Jean-Baptiste. *La Maison Niel*. Paris, France: Gallimard, 1995

A brief interview with James Purdy in French on pages 98-99.

302    Real, Jere. "Interview With James Purdy." *Blueboy* 25 (October 1978): 25-28.

An interview which discusses Purdy's writings, *Malcolm, The Nephew, Cabot Wright Begins, The House of the Solitary Maggot, I Am Elijah Thrush, In a Shallow Grave* and *Narrow Rooms*. This interview was published at the time of Purdy's Narrow Rooms. Emphasis is placed on the homosexual aspects of Purdy's work. Purdy is quoted as saying, "My point is that if we don't face ourselves, we face violence. If we really don't know ourselves, then our lives may end in such violence." The article has a photograph of Purdy by Thomas Victor.

303    Swift, Edward. "Brooklyn." *New York Native* (18 November 1984): 37, 39.

This article is based on a telephone interview with Purdy which occurred on September 17, 1984, "when Purdy was recovering from minor surgery in Eclectic, Alabama." The majority of the questions and answers are about *Eustace Chisholm and the Works*. The interview contains Purdy's usual diatribe on publishers, reviewers, and critics. Of special interest is Purdy's reply to the statement by Swift that "I am always being asked if you're a black writer." Purdy's answer: "when my first book appeared, *63: Dream Palace*, which was published in England the first time, people thought I was black. A black novelist, I won't mention his name, but he said to me once, 'you're the last of the niggers,' and I liked that very much. Yes, I think it's the highest compliment. To me the black experience, which is so similar to that of the artist, was that you could never belong, you could never fit in, you could never be anything but black, you could never be anything but an outcast. And I loved that, and in a way I rejoice that blacks are becoming not an outside group but I also regret, just as I do with homosexuals, that once one joins the rest you lose something. You lose something very precious. In the gay movement, not all but many seem to think that if they can be accepted by the Great Society they will reach the apogee of their dreams. But to me, I don't think I ever want to be accepted by the Great Majority. If they did accept us, they would accept us because our books were selling; they wouldn't care what was in the books." Contains a photograph of Purdy by Ken Fuch.

304    Varble, Stephen. "I Am James Purdy." *Interview* 3 (December 1972): 28-29.

    A wonderful interview with Purdy which takes place in his Brooklyn apartment at the time of the publication of *I Am Elijah Thrush*. The usual negative comments about the New York critics and television are here besides a glimpse into Purdy's writing and early background. Varble precedes the interview with: "James Purdy is one of the heroes of modern literature, and perhaps the greatest writer of fiction in America today. His books differ greatly in style and subject matter but they are all charged with divine comedy and human possibility. They are visionary even when they go in the disguise of ordinary subject matter." Contains a large photograph of Purdy by Fabian Bachrach.

## 8.  Letters and Responses to Editors

305    "Malcolm, Mr. Cough Syrup, and The American People."
       *The Harvard Advocate* 100 (March 1966): 29.

    This is a response by Purdy to a number of critics
    praising and criticizing his work, most notably *Malcolm.*

306    "Purdy's Purge." *Saturday Review* (14 November 1960):
       31.

    A letter to the editor by Purdy in response to Granville
    Hicks's "nonreview of my novel *Malcolm* in the
    September 26, 1960 issue of *Saturday Review*." Purdy
    writes, "As to Granville Hicks and his ilk, sitting in
    their chairs of retirement and spouting guff about
    'reality,' the quicker they leave the literary scene the
    better."


## 9.  Correspondence

307    Bowles, Paul. *In Touch:  The Letters of Paul Bowles.*
       Edited by Jeffrey Miller.  New York: Farrar, Straus and
       Giroux, 1994.

    A collection of more than four hundred letters written
    by Bowles over a sixty-three year period, 1928 to 1991.
    Twelve of these letters were written between January,
    1960 and February, 1978 and are either to Purdy (3) or
    about Purdy or one of his novels (9).  On June 1, 1967,
    Bowles writes to Purdy, "*Eustace Chisholm* arrived.
    Thank you.  I found it exciting to read; it seemed to go
    back to the world of *Dream Palace*, which I've always
    loved."  On September 4, 1967 Bowles writes to James
    Leo Herlihy, "A letter today from James Purdy makes
    me feel he is not in a very good way.  He feels *Eustace
    Chisholm* was a failure.  And he adds that the reason is
    that he is not Jewish or Negro or a 'taker of LSD.'
    What can you gather from that?"  The next sentence
    reads, "This whole country is a dried pool of shit.  Is it
    a non sequitur, or something graver?  Strange man."

308 Sitwell, Dame Edith. *Selected Letters, 1919-1964*. Edited by John Lehmann and Derek Parker. New York: Vanguard Press, 1970.

> A collection of five letters Ms. Sitwell wrote to James Purdy between 1956 and 1959, plus a letter to Sir Malcolm Bullock on October 13, 1959 in which she writes, "I am convinced that in the future he will be regarded as the greatest American prose writer of our time."

## 10. Miscellaneous

309 "Baked Chicken and Sausage." In *The Great American Writers' Cookbook*. Edited by Dean Faulkner Wells with an introduction by Craig Claiborne. Oxford, Mississippi: Yoknapatawpha Press, 1981.

> Purdy's recipe is on page 79.

310 Bartlett, Paul Alexander. *Spokes for Memory*. Baltimore, Maryland: Icarus Press, 1979.

> A collection of poems by Bartlett. Purdy writes on the back cover, "I find great pleasure in his work. Really beautiful and most distinguished."

311 "A Books Survey: Critics Influence on the Novelists." *Books* 4 (February 1967): 1.

> Twelve contemporary authors were asked if "critics influence the novelist?" Purdy replied "I don't like critics. It's not that they're critical, but irrelevant. They set up an intellectual rule which cannot measure the essentially human product, which is the book. They have the wrong measuring stick. Critics are especially bad in this country. They assume that you're doing what you didn't intend to do—and didn't do. European critics respect your vision. They've had more serious intellectual training and are not members of a personality cult."

312 *Lord John Signatures.* With an introduction by Stephen
King. Northridge, California: Lord John Press, 1991.

A collection of full-page black and white photographs
accompanied by the individual signatures of important
people with the emphasis on contemporary American
authors including John Barth, Ray Bradbury, Elmore
Leonard, Joyce Carol Oates and James Purdy. The last
part of the book includes signatures of important
historical figures, e.g., John Q. Adams, James Monroe,
Calvin Coolidge, Theodore Roosevelt, and Ronald
Reagan. This is a limited edition of four hundred
numbered copies, one hundred fifty deluxe copies and
26 lettered copies, all of which have been signed by
each of the participants.

313 "The Professional Viewpoint." *Twentieth Century Studies*
2 (November 1969): 123.

This issue of *Twentieth Century Studies* is devoted to
"The Treatment of Sexual Themes in the Modern
Novel." Included is Tony Tanner's article "Sex and
Identity in *Cabot Wright Begins.*" Also included are
twenty-five authors' personal statements on the topic
of sex in the modern novel. Purdy's statement is
typical Purdy providing ten separate and individual
statements. For example: "Sex in America is an
undesired commodity, which is one's wish to conform
forces one to purchase." And, "Even 'homosexuality'
is now respectable, welcomed by the 'cured'
heterosexual film and book reviewers, so long, that is,
that love of one's own sex is as unfelt as
heterosexuality, and is a fashion plate."

314 "A Question of Commitment." *New York Times Book
Review* 73 (June 2, 1968): 2-3, 14.

The *New York Times* asked 13 prominent novelists and
critics "to address themselves once more to the old but
lively question of 'engagement' because of the summer
of 1968 promised or threatens—to be a critical one in
American life." Purdy answered by saying "This is an
age of exhibitionists, not souls. The press and the
public primarily recognize only writers who give them

'doctored' current events as truth. The more unimportant and popular the writer, the more he is vocal on issues, the more he is on view, strikes attitudes, is partisan on 'noble' movements of the hour or day. For me, the only 'engagement' or cause a 'called' writer can have (as opposed to a public writer) is his own vision and work. It is an irrevocable decision: he can march only in his own parade. On the other hand, how easy it is to be 'engaged' in any one of the issues of today (even if the writer hasn't taken the time to understand it or the men behind it), march and testify, expose himself and howl before the cameras, rather face the solitary and grueling ordeal of telling the one truth it is given him to know and which is his work." Other responses were from James Baldwin, Hortense Calisher, Malcolm Cowley, Leslie Fiedler, William H. Gass, Maryn Mannes, Joyce Carol Oates, Norman Podhoretz, Reynolds Price, John Simon, John A. Williams, and Gore Vidal.

315    "Reading Your Own." *New York Times Book Review* 72 (4 June 1967): 6-7, 32-33.

The *New York Times* asked 13 distinguished novelists around the world "If you were to set aside some reflective summer hours to reread one of your own novels, which one do you imagine you would give your particular pleasure?" Purdy answered "Out of all my books I would probably try to reread my short novel *63: Dream Palace* with most interest today. This story of a boy's unwilling murder of his brother was my first major effort, and the work which cost me the most care and pain. If I were to begin leafing through its pages now, I think I would be most struck by the sound of its special idiom and rhythm, for the language comes out of my own hoarded remembrance of the speech of West Virginia and Illinois.... I don't doubt, however, that I would soon come to a halt in my rereading. I know 'Dream Palace' too well to go far in it. Indeed, I am it, and at the same time I no longer feel at home with its drifting cadences." Other responses were from Kurt Vonnegut, Jr., John Barth, Anthony Burgess, Herbert

Gold, Nathalie Sarraute, Isaac Bashevis Singer, C. P. Snow, John Updike, Chester Himes, John Hawkes, Georges Simenon, and Peter DeVries.

316   "Rereading: Not for Pleasure Alone." *Antaeus* 59 (autumn 1987): 69.

    This is a commentary by Purdy on rereading certain books under the chapter heading "Literature as Pleasure."

317   Rexer, Lyle. "Brooklyn, Borough of Writers." *New York Times Book Review* (8 May 1983): 12-13, 31.

    Mr. Rexer asked a number of writers currently living in Brooklyn why the borough had been important. Writers included James Purdy, June Jordan, Daniel Fuchs, Paula Fox, Alfred Kazin, Joe Flanery, Isaac Bashevis Singer, Hubert Selby Jr., Maurice Sendak, Pete Hamill, Bernard Malamud, Wallace Markfield, Mark Helprin, and Gilbert Sorrentino. Purdy writes, "You might think that I chose Brooklyn. I didn't. I moved here because I was desperate to find a room. But one reason I stay here is to be near where everything is supposed to be going on and at the same time not be exposed to the pressure that so many of my friends suffer."

318   "Self Portrait." In *Self-Portrait: Book People Picture Themselves, from the Collection of Burt Britton*. New York: Random House, 1976.

    This is a drawing of how Purdy sees himself. Drawing is on page 18.

319   "Talking About Angus Wilson." *Twentieth Century Literature* 29 (summer 1983): 115-150.

    Part of a longer article in which D. P. Walker, Hortense Calisher, Nadine Gordimer, Patrick White, Vance Bourjaily, John Leggett, Peter Conradi, Clive Sinclair, Lorna Martyn Goff, David Plante and Philip Collins discuss their recollections of Wilson. Purdy relates a 1961 visit of Wilson to New York—Wilson, Powys, and Sitwell championed Purdy's first book, *63: Dream Palace*.

320     Woolf, Cecil and John Bagguley, editors. *Authors Take Sides on Vietnam: Two Questions on the War in Vietnam Answered by the Authors of Several Nations*. New York: Simon and Schuster, 1967.

> Over 500 authors were asked to respond to a questionnaire about the intervention of the United States in Vietnam. This volume contains the responses from 168 authors. James Purdy responded: "I am opposed to intervention by the United States of America in Vietnam, but such mass massacres seem to me inescapable as long as the content of the American mind is cigarette and liquor ads, its religion dope-sex, its people millionaire movie and baseball stars.... Vietnam is atrocious for the dead and maimed innocent, but it's probably sadder to be a live American with only Madison Avenue for a homeland and a God."

321     Woolf, Cecil and Jean Moorcroft Wilson, editors. *Authors Take Sides on the Falklands: Two Questions on the Falklands Conflict Answered by More Than a Hundred Mainly British Authors*. London, England: Cecil Woolf, 1982.

> James Purdy wrote, "I believe that Britain and Argentina should have settled the matter of the Falkland Islands peacefully many years ago. The United States has constantly fostered regimes which are cruel, tyrannical and genocidal in Latin America, and I am afraid the events in the Falkland Islands will make cooperation and understanding between the English-speaking world and Latin America still more difficult."

# C.  Translations of James Purdy's Works

322    "Alba." *Nuovi Argomenti* Terza Serie,12 (Ottobre-Dicembre 1984): 54-56.

     Italian translation by Luciano Perego of the short story "Dawn."

323    *Aruma no oi*. Tokyo: Kawade Shobo Shinsha, 1970.

     Japanese translation of *The Nephew* by Suzuki Kenzo.

324    "Bonnie." *Nuovi Argomenti* Terza Serie, 45 (Gennaio-Marzo 1993): 76-79.

     Short story.  Italian translation by Luciano Perego.

325    *Børn Og Bestier*. Fredensborg, Denmark: Arena, 1964.

     Danish translation of *Children is All* by Elsa Gress.

326    "Brawith." *Nuovi Argomenti* Quarta Serie 3 (Aprile-Guigno 1995): 29-34.

     Italian translation by Luciano Perego of "Brawith."

327    *Brorsonen*. Stockholm: Bonnier, 1963.

     Swedish translation of *The Nephew* by Hakan Norlén.

328    *Brorsonen*. Oslo: Gyldendal, 1964.

     Norwegian translation of *The Nephew* by Torborg Nedreaas.

329    *Cabot Wright Begyndes*. Kobenhawn: Gylendals Bekkasinbogen, 1967.

     Danish translation of *Cabot Wright Begins* by Poul Borum.

330    *Cabot Wright Legt Los*. Reinbeck, Germany: Rowohlt, 1967.

     German translation of *Cabot Wright Begins* by Gisela Stege.

331     *Cabot Wright Sätter Igang.* Stockholm: Bonnier, 1969.
Swedish translation of *Cabot Wright Begins* by Olov
Jonason.

332     *Cabot Wright Begins.* Japan: Novels Now, 1971.
Japanese translation of *Cabot Wright Begins.*

333     *Cabot Wright Legt Los.* Hamburg: Sammlung Luchterhand,
1992.
German translation of *Cabot Wright Begins* by Gisela
Stege.

334     *Cabot Wright ci Riprova.* Torino: Giulio Einaudi, 1994.
Italian translation of *Cabot Wright Begins* by Floriana
Bossi. First published in 1968 as "Un Ignobile
Individuo." This edition contains a note by Purdy.

335     *Cambres Estretes.* Barcelona: Edicions 62, 1988.
Spanish translation of *Narrow Rooms* by Jordi Arbonès.

336     *Camino de la Gloria.* Barcelona: Versal, 1985.
Spanish translation of *On Glory's Course* by Susana
Constante.

337     *Ce que Raconta Jeremy: Roman.* Paris: A. Michel, 1973.
French translation of *Jeremy's Version* by Marie Tadié.

338     *Color de Oscuridad.* Barcelona: Seix Barral, 1963.
Spanish translation of *Color of Darkness* by Juan Godó
Costa.

339     "Color of Darkness." In *A Pound of Prose: Een Bundel
Engelse en Amerikaanse Verhalen Voor de Bovenbouw.*
Edited by Cornelis Buddingh. Amsterdam: Meulenhoff
Educatief, 1977.

       A collection of eighteen short stories including Purdy's
"Color of Darkness" on pages 127-138. Each selection
is preceded by a photograph of the writer, a brief
biographical sketch and a short, select bibliography. In

addition, each story has a black and white illustration. Mariet Numan illustrated the Purdy story.

340    "Come Divenni un'Ombra." *Nuovi Argomenti* Terza Serie 30 (Aprile - Giugno 1989): 8-9.

Italian translation by Luciano Perego of Purdy's short story.

341    *Come in una Tomba*. Milano: SE, 1990.

Italian translation of *In a Shallow Grave* by Maria Pia Tosti Croce.

342    *Comienza Cabot Wright*. Mexico: Joaquin Mortiz, 1968.

Spanish translation of *Cabot Wright Begins* by José Agustín and Juan Tovar.

343    Couleur de Ténèbres. Paris: Gallimard, 1966.

French translation of *Color of Darkness* by Jacqueline Péry and Pierre Chevrillon. Preface by Dame Edith Sitwell.

344    "Coup de Chaler." *Le Journal Litteraire* 25 (December 1987/January 1988): 36-38.

French translation by Alain Wagneur of "Color of Darkness."

345    *Os Crimes de Cabot Wright*. Rio de Janeiro: Civiliza Brasileira, 1967.

Portuguese translation of *Cabot Wright Begins* by Luís César Barroso.

346    *Dans le Creux de sa Main*. Paris: Librairie Artheme Fayard, 1988.

French translation of *In the Hollow of His Hand* by Léo Dilé.

347    "Donna Attende." *Nuovi Argomenti* Terza Serie 42 (1992): 101.

Italian translation by Luciano Perego.

348    "Dormi In Pace." *Nuovi Argomenti* Terza Serie 7 (Luglio-Settembre 1983): 26-30.

Italian translation of "Rest in Peace" by Luciano Perego.

349    *Les Enfants, C'est Tout*. Paris: Gallimard, 1967.

French translation of *Children is All* by Yvonne Davet.

350    *Enge Räume*. Berlin, Germany: Albino, 1982.

German translation of *Narrow Rooms* by Wolfgang Eisermann.

351    "Estasi." *Nuovi Argomenti* Terza Serie 16 (Ottobre-Dicembre 1985): 15-19.

Italian Translation by Luciano Perego.

352    *Eustace Chisholm and the Works*. Tokyo: Farrar, Straus and Giroux, Inc. and Japan Uni Agency, 1972.

Japanese translation by Chuji Kunitaka.

353    *Eustace Chisholm & Consorten*. Amsterdam: Athenaeum-Polak & Van Gennap, 1979.

Dutch translation by Thomas Graftdijk.

353a    *Eustace Chisholm & Consorten*. Amsterdam: Athenaeum-Polak & Van Gennap, 1990.

Dutch translation by Thomas Graftdijk. "2e dr."

354    *Die Farbe der Dunkelheit: Elf Stories und eine Novelle:* Hamburg: Rowohlt Verlag, 1959.

German translation of *Color of Darkness: Eleven Stories and a Novella*, translated by Helene Henze. Back cover contains an early photograph of James Purdy and praise for the collection by Angus Wilson, Edith Sitwell, Marianne Moore, James T. Farrell, John Cowper Powys, Langston Hughes and Paul Bowles.

355    "From Rivers, and From the Earth Itself" and "The Axles Creaking Under the Wagons." *Art Mag* 10 (1988): 33.

Two poems from *Collected Poems*, Dutch edition.

356    *Der Gesang des Blutes*. Berlin: Albino, 1995.

    German translation of *In a Shallow Grave* by Dino Heicker and Michael Sollorz. Edited by Gerhard Hoffmann.

357    *De Gewaden der Levenden*. Amsterdam: Athenaeum-Polak & Van Gennep, 1990.

    Dutch translation of *Garments the Living Wear* by Graa Boomsma.

358    *Habitaciones Exiguas*. Barcelona: Montesinos, 1985.

    Spanish translation of *Narrow Rooms* by Marcelo Cohen.

359    *I Figli Sono Tutto*. Torino: Einaudi, 1971.

    Italian translation of *Children is All* and *Color of Darkness* by Floriana Bossi.

360    "I Saloni di Brooklyn." *Nuovi Argomenti*, Terza Serie 4 (Ottobre-Dicembre 1982): 151.

    Italian translation by Luciano Perego of Purdy's poem "The Brooklyn Branding Parlors."

361    *Un Ignobile Individuo*. Torino: Einaudi, 1968.

    Italian translation of *Cabot Wright Begins* by Floriana Bossi.

362    *Ik ben Elijah Thrush*. Amsterdam: Athenaeum-Polak & Van Gennep, 1994.

    Danish translation of *I Am Elijah Thrush* by Harm Damsma.

363    *In een Ondiep Graf*. Amsterdam: Athenaeum-Polak & Van Gennep, 1986.

    Dutch translation of *In a Shallow Grave* by Graa Boomsma.

364    *In een Ondiep Graf*. Amsterdam: Athenaeum-Polak & Van Gennep, 1989.

Dutch translation of *In a Shallow Grave* by Graa Boomsma. "3e dr."

365    *Les Inconsolés*. Paris: Albin Michel, 1984.

French translation of *Mourners Below* by Claire Malroux.

366    *Je Suis Vivant Dans Ma Tombe*. Paris: Editions Albin Michel, 1979.

French translation of *In a Shallow Grave* by François Xavier Jaujard.

367    *Junto a las Estrellas*. Barcelona: Península, 1995.

Spanish translation of *Out With the Stars* by Roser Berdagué.

368    *Kleur van Duisternis*. Amsterdam: Athenaeum-Polak & Van Gennep, 1973.

Dutch translation of *Color of Darkness* by Hans Plomp.

368a    *Kleur van Duisternis*. Amsterdam: Athenaeum-Polak & Van Gennep, 1989.

Dutch translation of *Color of Darkness* by Hans Plomp. "2e dr."

368b    *Kleur van Duisternis*. Amsterdam: Athenaeum-Polak & Van Gennep, 1989.

Dutch translation of *Color of Darkness* by Hans Plomp. "3e dr."

369    *Kyabotto Raito Biginzu*. Tokyo: Kawade Shobo Shinsha, 1971.

Japanese translation of *Cabot Wright Begins* by Suzuki Kenzo.

370    *Malcolm*. Amsterdam: Uitgeverij Contact, 1967.

Dutch translation by Katja Vranken.

371    *Malcolm*. Paris: Gallimard, 1961.

French translation by Anne Canavaggia.

372    *Malcolm.* Fredensborg, Denmark: Arena, 1962.
Danish translation by Elsa Gress Wright.

373    *Malcolm.* Buenos Aires: n.p., 1963.
Spanish translation by Luis Tobío.

374    *Malcolm.* Reinbeck, Germany: Rowohlt, 1963.
German translation by Erwin Duncker.

375    *Malcolm.* Torino: Einaudi, 1965.
Italian Translation by Floriana Bossi.

376    *Malcolm.* Helsinki: Arena, 1966.
Finnish translation by Juhani Niskanen.

377    *Malcolm.* Oslo: Gyldendal Norsk Forlag, 1966.
Norwegian translation by Colbjørn Helander.

378    *Malcolm.* Stockholm: Bonnier, 1966.
Swedish translation by Olov Jonason.

379    *Marukomu no Henreki.* Tokyo: Hakusuisha, 1966.
Japanese translation of *Malcolm* by Suzuki Kenzo.

380    *Malcolm.* Paris: Gallimard, 1991.
French translation by Marie Canavaggia.

381    *Malcolm.* Amsterdam: Pranger, 1980.
Dutch translation by Katja Vranken.

382    *Malcolm.* Barcelona: Editorial Anagrama, 1984.
Spanish translation by Luis Echávarri.

383    *Malcolm.* Hamburg: Luchterhand Literaturverlag, 1992.
German translation by Erwin Duncker.

384    *Malcolm.* São Paulo: Siciliano, 1995.
Portuguese translation by Joana Angelica d'Avila
Melo.

385      "Mi Chiedi Sempre." *Nuovi Argomenti* Terza Serie 22 (Luglio-Settembre 1987): 96, 105.

        Italian translation of the poem "You Always Ask Me."

386      *Die Millionärin auf der Wendeltreppe Kannibalischer Beziehungen*. Berlin: Albino, 1984.

        German translation of *I Am Elijah Thrush* by Wolfgang Eisermann.

387      *Mister Evening*. Stockholm: Carlssons, 1992.

        A collection of several stories in Swedish; translation by Jan Broberg.

388      *Nauwe ruimten*. Amsterdam: Athenaeum-Polak & Van Gennep, 1991.

        Dutch translation of *Narrow Rooms* by Graa Boomsma.

389      *Der Neffe*. Hamburg: Roman Rowohlt, 1964.

        German translation of *The Nephew* by Erwin Duncker.

390      *Der Neffe*. Hamburg: Luchterhand Literaturverlag, 1992.

        German translation of *The Nephew* by Erwin Duncker.

391      *Nel Palmo Dello Mano*. Rome: Gremese Editore, 1989.

        Italian translation of *In the Hollow of His Hand* by Virginia Teodori.

392      *The Nephew*. Tokyo: Novels Now, 1970.

        Japanese translation of *The Nephew*.

393      *Le Neveu*. Paris: Gallimard, 1964.

        French translation of *The Nephew* by Renée Villoteau.

394      *Nevøen*. Fredensborg, Denmark: Arena, 1961.

        Danish translation of *The Nephew* by Elsa Gress Wright.

395      *Il Nipote*. Torino: Einaudi, 1963.

Italian translation of *The Nephew* by Floriana Bossi.

396    *Il Nipote*. Milano: Longanesi, 1969.

Italian translation of *The Nephew* by Floriana Bossi.

397    *Les Oeuvres d'Eustace*. Paris: Gallimard, 1969.

French translation of *Eustace Chisholm and the Works* by Suzanne Mayoux.

398    *El Papa Llop i Deu Contes Més: Relats Escollits (1956-1987)*. Barcelona: Edicions Proa, S. A., 1996.

Catalan edition of eleven short stories selected and translated by Ferrán Toutain from *63: Dream Palace* and *The Candles of Your Eyes and Thirteen Other Stories*.

399    "De Pest." In *Dit Verval: Verhalen Rond een Grote Ziekte Met een Kleine Naam*. Edited by Ron Mooser. Amsterdam: De Woelrat, 1988.

Purdy's story "The Pest" is on pages 117-131.

400    "Poesia." *Nuovi Argomenti* Terza Serie 49 (Gennaio-Marzo 1994): 75-76.

Italian translation by Cesare Maoli of Purdy's poem "They Say the Frankincense Tree."

401    "Por Que No Pueden Decirte El Porque?" In *Crónicas de Norteamerica* Buenos Aires: Editorial Jorge Alvarez, 1967.

A short story anthology of twelve contemporary authors inclucing Capote, Baldwin, Algren, Faulkner, Wolfe, Hemingway, and Updike. This is a translation of Purdy's short story "Why Can't They Tell You Why?" by Juan Godó Costa. Includes a biographical description of Purdy by Ricardo Piglia.

402    *Die Preisgabe: Roman*. Hamburg: Rowohlt, 1970.

German translation of *Eustace Chisholm and the Works* by Kai Molvig.

403    *Die Preisgabe: Roman*  Berlin:  Albino, 1996.

German translation of *Eustace Chisholm and the Works* by Kai Molvig.

404    *Rose e Cenere.*  Torino: Einaudi, 1970.

Italian translation of *Eustace Chisholm and the Works* by Attilio Veraldi.

405    *Le Satyre.*  Paris: Gallimard, 1967.

French translation of *Cabot Wright Begins* by Suzanne Mayoux.

406    Shijin Yusutisu Chizamu no Nakama.  Tokyo: Shinchosha, 1972.

Japanese translation of *Eustace Chisholm and the Works* by Chuji Kunitaka.

407    *63, Drømmeslottet.*  Fredensborg, Denmark: Arena Forfatternes, 1960.

Danish translation of *Color of Darkness* by Elsa Gress Wright.

408    *63: Palazzo del Sogno.*  Torino: Einaudi, 1960.

Italian translation of *Color of Darkness* by Floriana Bossi.

409    *El Sobrino.*  Buenos Aires: Editorial Sudamericana, 1962.

Spanish translation by Luis Tobío of *The Nephew*.

410    "3 Poesie."  *Nuovi Argomenti* Terza Serie 42 (Aprile-Giugno 1992): 100-101.

Italian translation by Luciano Perego of "Men of Bangladesh," "Swarthy and Melancholy Men," and "A Lady Is Waiting in Gardens and Paths."

411    *La Tunique de Nessus: Roman.*  Paris: Librairie Artheme Fayard, 1990.

French translation of *Garments the Living Wear* by Léo Dilé.

412 *La Version de Jeremy*. Buenos Aires: Ediciones Corregidor, 1977.

Spanish translation of *Jeremy's Version*.

413 *La Versione di Geremia*. Torino: Einaudi, 1973.

Italian translation of *Jeremy's Version*.by Bruno Oddera.

414 "La Voragine." *Nuovi Argomenti* Terza Serie 39 (Luglio-Settembre 1991): 45-50.

Italian translation by Cesare Maoli.

415 "Weiss Nicht Warum: Eine." *Erzahlung* 11 (1958): 55-58.

German translation of Purdy's "Why Can't They Tell You Why?" by Helene Henze.

416 *Zartliche Kannibalen*. Hamburg: Mannerschwarm, 1995.

German translation by Jürgen Abel of three short stories from *The Candles of Your Eyes* collection including "The Candles of Your Eyes," "Rapture," and "Mud Toe the Cannibal," and three stories from *63: Dream Palace* (1991 edition), including "Mr. Evening," "Everything Under the Sun," and "Some of These Days."

# D. Adaptations of James Purdy's Works

417 Albee, Edward. *Malcolm*. New York: Atheneum, 1966. New York: Dramatist's Play Service, 1966. London: Jonathan Cape with Secker & Warburg, 1967.

A play adapted from the novel by Purdy.

418 Bose, Hans-Jurgen von. *63 Dream Palace = Traumpalast '63*. Mainz, Germany: Schott, 1990.

Opera based on the novella by James Purdy.

419 Helps, Robert. "Gossamer Noons." Conductor, Gunther Schuller; Soprano, Bethany Beardslee; American Composers Orchestra. Composers Recordings, 1978.

Music based on poems by James Purdy.

420    Hundley, Richard. "Come Ready and See Me: Medium Voice and Piano." New York: n.p., 1971.

A musical score based on a poem by Purdy.

421    ———. "Eight Songs: Voice and Piano." New York: Boosey and Hawkes, 1981.

A collection of eight songs for voice and piano which includes three songs based on poems by James Purdy. "Birds, U.S.A." and "Come Ready and See Me," are from his work *Mr. Evening: A Story & Nine Poems* and "I Do" from *The Running Sun*.

422    ———. "Octaves and Sweet Sounds: for Voice and Piano." New York: Boosey and Hawkes, 1993.

A collection of five songs based on work by James Joyce ("Strings in the Earth and Air"); e. e. Cummings ("Seashore Girls"); Jose Garcia Villa ("Moonlight's Watermelon"); James Purdy ("Straightway Beauty on Me Waits"); and Gertrude Stein ("Well Welcome"). These songs were commissioned in the winter of 1989 by Art Song Minnesota. "The work was written for mezzo-soprano Glenda Maurice and pianist Ruth Palmer, who gave the premiere performance at the McKnight Theatre in The Ordway in St. Paul on June 9, 1990. Mr. Hundley notes "Straightway Beauty on Me Waits" is a love song whose music is as rapturous as its subject."

423    ———. "Straightway Beauty on Me Waits." New York: Boosey and Hawkes, 1993.

424    *In a Shallow Grave.* Burbank, California: Warner Home Video, 1989.

A videocassette from the American Playhouse Films. A Skouras Picture Release, produced and directed by Kenneth Bowser. Starring Michael Biehn and Patrick Dempsey. Based on Purdy's novel.

425     Reaux, Angelina. *Celebrating America: A Celebration of 20th Century American Composers and Poets (1895-1991).* Boston, Massachusetts: Boston Conservatory, 1992.

> Contains twenty-four songs including Richard Hundley's work based on James Purdy's "Come Ready and See Me."

# E. Media Recordings by and about James Purdy

426     *Eventide and Other Stories.* New Rochell, N.Y.: Spoken Arts, 1970.

> Four-record set of Purdy short stories, read by the author.

427     "James Purdy." New York: Full Track Press, 1979.

> A cassette in which Purdy's reads his short story "Some of These Days." Includes an interview of Purdy by Joe Cuomo.

428     *Malcolm.* Deland, Florida: Everett/Edwards, 1970.

> A cassette recording of Warren French's discussion of *Malcolm.*

429     *63: Dream Palace.* New York: Spoken Arts, 1968.

> A sound recording (33 1/3 rpm) of Purdy reading his novella.

# Works about James Purdy

## A. Critical Books, Book Chapters and Essays in Collections

430     Adams, Stephen D. *The Homosexual as Hero in Contemporary Fiction*. Totowa, N.J.: Barnes & Noble Books, 1980.

> A study of homosexual themes in contemporary fiction which focuses on a selection of writers whose work "marks the emergence of the male homosexual's quest for selfhood from the literary landscape of the compulsory villainy and tortured ambiguity." Chapter three, entitled "Gothic Love," deals with Truman Capote, Carson McCullers, and James Purdy. Adams writes that Purdy "sees the world around him as essentially gothic and escapist in character, a chamber of horrors which he dramatizes in symbolic form."

431     ———. *James Purdy*. London: Vision Press, 1976.

> Adams writes, "This book seeks to define the steady progress of Purdy's art and to explore his evolving themes and preoccupations. Although he has been widely acclaimed as one of America's major contemporary writers, there is as yet no clear consensus of opinion with regard to the nature of his fiction. The primary intention, then, is to provide an account of that unfolding imagination, by a close reading

of his work." Adams succeeds beautifully in his intention. He carefully analyzes Purdy's body of works through 1976. Adams's understanding of Purdy's writing is one of the best published. The book contains a bibliography of Purdy's works, introductions, selected criticism (eighteen references), and a list of three interviews.

432    Aldridge, John W. *Time to Murder and Create: The Contemporary Novel in Crisis*. New York: David McKay, 1966.

A discussion of the novels of John O'Hara, William Styron, Mary McCarthy, John Updike, Katherine Anne Porter, and others. James Purdy is referred to as one member of the "serious younger novelists [who] are minting a fresh currency of the creative imagination." This group includes Bellow, Baldwin, Malamud, Salinger, and Roth.

433    Allen, Mary. *The Necessary Blankness: Women in Major American Fiction of the Sixties*. Urbana: University of Illinois Press, 1976.

A study of how women are treated by authors identified by Allen as "the best writers to have come of age in the sixties and who deal significantly with women or a concept of the feminine." Chapter one is entitled "Women of the Fabulators: Barth, Pynchon, Purdy, Kesey." These writers are grouped together because their writing shares the characteristic of showing a delight in the fantastic. In discussing women in Purdy's writing, Allen refers to *Cabot Wright Begins*, *Malcolm*, *The Nephew*, *63: Dream Palace*, "Don't Call Me by My Right Name," and "Why Can't They Tell You Why?"

434    Austen, Roger. *Playing the Game: The Homosexual Novel in America*. Indianapolis: Bobbs-Merrill Company, 1977.

A study of the "relevant male fiction—veiled or unveiled—that has appeared in this country over the past hundred years placed in simple chronological order

71

with bits of background on the author and gay life as it seems to have been lived at the time." Purdy is represented with a discussion of *Color of Darkness*, *Malcolm*, and *Eustace Chisholm and the Works*.

435    Bernard, Andre, editor. *Rotten Rejections: A Literary Companion*. Wainscott, N.Y.: Pushcart Press, 1990.

In this compilation of literary rejections, a 1960 rejection of Purdy's *Malcolm* is noted as "incomprehensible."

436    Bier, Jesse. *The Rise and Fall of American Humor*. New York: Holt, Rinehart and Winston, 1968.

A critical and historical study of American humor. In the chapter entitled "Modern American Humor," Purdy is mentioned along with his novel *Cabot Wright Begins*.

437    Bradbury, Malcolm. *The Modern American Novel*. New York: Oxford University Press, 1983.

A history of the American novel from the 1890's. Chapter seven, "Postmoderns and Other: the 1960's and 1970's," refers to Purdy, Hawkes and Bowles as writers linked together by "a fiction of extreme new grotesque in [their] work." Bradbury also groups Purdy and Southern as writers of "black humour, a humour derived from historical and existential despair." The appendix includes a list of American novelists "whose work seems to me [the author] most significant." Purdy is listed.

438    ——. *The Modern American Novel*. New edition. New York: Viking, 1992.

A very substantial revision of Bradbury's 1983 work. The author notes that "the whole text has been fundamentally reworked and enlarged and two extended new chapters have been added, to bring the story up to the immediate present." Purdy is mentioned four times in the list of major American novels since 1890. *63: Dream Palace*, *Color of Darkness*, *Malcolm*, *Cabot Wright Begins*, and *On Glory's Course* are cited.

439     Bungert, Hans, editor. *Die Americanische Short Story:
        Theorie und Entwicklung*. Darmstadt: Wissenschaftliche
        Buchgesellschaft, 1972.

>       A collection of articles on the American short story
>       reprinted from various literary journals. Includes
>       "Notes on the American Short Story Today" by
>       Richard Kostelanetz.

440     Burgess, Anthony. *The Novel Now: A Student's Guide to
        Contemporary Fiction*. London: Faber and Faber, 1971.

>       Burgess writes, "The fantastic inner country of the self
>       is the theme of much of James Purdy's writing—
>       *Malcolm, The Nephew*, and *63: Dream Palace*.
>       *Malcolm* may be read as an allegory of growing up in an
>       era, our own, which offers nothing; but the child's image
>       of its corruption is derived from within, from fantasies
>       begotten by his own mind."

441     Chupack, Henry. *James Purdy*. Boston, Massachusetts:
        Twayne, 1975.

>       The first monographic study of James Purdy and his
>       work. Five chapters are devoted to analyses of
>       Purdy's fiction. "The first chapter introduces the
>       pertinent facts of Purdy's life, the major themes
>       pervading his fiction, and related literary matters." The
>       last chapter ends with: "All told, Purdy is a writer of
>       marvelous powers, who has made us think deeply and
>       seriously about the human condition, which he regards
>       woefully. In short, Purdy's power and style are two
>       positive virtues in a period when many writers simply
>       lack one or another of these ingredients in their
>       works." The book contains a chronology and a
>       selected bibliography.

442     Davis, Douglas M, editor. *The World of Black Humor: An
        Introductory Anthology of Selections and Criticism*. New
        York: E. P. Dutton, 1967.

>       Davis attributes the naming of the current "Black
>       Humor" literature to Conrad Knickerbocker's 1964
>       article, "Humor With a Mortal Sting." Davis, in part
>       III of his study, entitled "Four Endings", has chosen

four selections which he says are examples of "Black Humor ... three of which reach a particularly raucous pitch and, for contrast, a fourth that is almost effeminate in tone." Purdy's conclusion to *Cabot Wright Begins*, Charles Wright's *The Wig* and William Burrough's *Nova Express* are the first three selections followed by John Barth's *The Floating Opera*. Also included in this anthology is a reprint of Conrad Knickerbocker's "Humor with a Mortal String" from the *New York Times Book Review* and a reprint of Richard Kostelanetz's article on "The American Absurd Novel," also published originally in the *New York Times Book Review*.

443    Donald, Miles. *The American Novel in the Twentieth Century*. London: David & Charles, 1978.

A study of the American novel from Fitzgerald, Hemingway, Wolfe, Dos Passos and Steinbeck to popular science and detective fiction. In chapter four, "The Minorities - Black Fiction, The Jewish-American Novel" Purdy's writing is given as an illustration of the 1960s development of "bringing into the open the erstwhile suppressed question of homosexuals as a minority group." *Malcolm*, *Cabot Wright Begins* and *Eustace Chisholm and the Works* are noted. Donald writes that "Purdy is certainly an impressively stylish writer in the main and odiferous stream of black comedy."

444    Fiedler, Leslie A. *The Return of the Vanishing American*. New York: Stein and Day, 1968.

This is the third volume in Fiedler's "venture in literary anthropology." He briefly refers to Purdy's *Cabot Wright Begins* as an example of the use of a black character ("Winters Hart") in literature.

445    Finkelstein, Sidney. *Existentialism and Alienation in American Literature*. New York: International Publishers, 1965.

Finkelstein has written a "study of existentialism, first in its rise as a philosophy in Europe and then in its

74

influence on literature, particularly that of the United States today." Chapter thirteen, entitled "Alienated Expression and Existentialist Answers," has a section dealing with the works of John Updike and James Purdy. *Malcolm* and *The Nephew* are discussed in depth. Finkelstein refers to Purdy as a "brilliant and honest young writer."

446    Freese, Peter. *Die Amerikanische Kurzgeschichte nach 1945: Salinger, Malamud, Baldwin, Purdy, Barth.* Frankfurt am Main: Athenaum Verlag, 1974.

A scholarly study written in German of five American authors. Chapter 5 discusses James Purdy's life and works. Numerous references are made to the important Purdy studies.

447    French, Warren. "The Quaking World of James Purdy." In *Essays in Modern American Literature.* Edited by Richard E. Langford. Deland, Florida: Stetson University Press, 1963.

This essay is revised and greatly expanded from an introduction to Purdy written by French for the first issue of *Scope*, the University of Florida literary magazine. In this essay French discusses and reviews *Color of Darkness*, *63: Dream Palace*, *Malcolm* and *The Nephew*. French notes that "an indication of Purdy's stature is his refusal to stop experimenting. Few experimental novels are popular enough to become inexpensive paperbacks, and success might have tempted Purdy—as it has other recent writers—to keep expressing over and over his irrefutable points about society's destruction of youth." French ends his insightful study of Purdy's work with: "There is a dream world even in *The Nephew*, but the dream is no longer all nightmare as in Purdy's earlier works. This dream, though, is neither pointless weeping over what may have never been nor fatuous promise of pie in the sky. It is the kind of dream that those who cannot ignore the degeneracy of the contemporary world may be able to accept when they must reject worn-out banalities paraded as ideals—the kind of dream that cannot stop a world of unremitting change from quaking, but that might have prevented its shattering by giving people the vision to move with it."

448 ———. *Season of Promise: Spring Fiction, 1967.* Columbia, Missouri: University of Missouri Press, 1968.

A reprint of five book reviews from the Kansas City Star during April and May, 1967. Included are reviews of James Purdy's *Eustace Chisholm and the Works*, Thornton Wilder's *The Eight Day*, R. K. Narayan's *The Vendor of Sweets*, William Goldman's *The Thing of It Is*, and Don Asher's *Don't the Moon Look Lonesome*. The long, very positive review of *Eustace Chisholm* reveals French's clear understanding of Purdy's novel. French notes: "Purdy is an extremely serious, but never a pompous artist. He has forged from colloquial American speech a language of unique compression and power, and he has the extraordinary ability to treat the most unpleasant subject matter with a deftness of touch that fascinates the reader even as it appalls him." French dedicated this volume to James Purdy "to thank him for his exciting contribution to the native tradition of American fiction." This is the Missouri Literary Frontiers Series, Number 2.

449 Friedman, Melvin J. and John B. Vickery, editors. *The Shaken Realist: Essays in Modern Literature in Honor of Frederick J. Hoffman.* Baton Rouge: Louisiana State University Press, 1970.

Contains Nathan A. Scott's essay, "The Conscience of the New Literature." Scott mentions Purdy along with Pynchon, Barth, Stern, Friedman, Heller and Hawkes as writers in whom "we can discern a particular current of sensibility, a kind of highly stylized vision, which establishes these novelists as constituting a distinctive force on the present scene."

450 Glicksberg, Charles I. *The Sexual Revolution in Modern American Literature.* The Hague: Martinus Nijhoff, 1971.

A detailed history of the development of the sexual revolution that took place in twentieth-century

American literature. This study traces literature from William Dean Howells and the group of literary naturalists such as Dreiser, Anderson, Hemingway, Fitzgerald, Faulkner and O'Neill to contemporary writers including Purdy, Miller, Mailer, Kerouac, Porter, Barth, Nabakov, and Jones. The chapter on "The Death of Love" includes a study of Purdy's *Cabot Wright Begins* and ends: "In the course of spinning this tour de force of a fable, James Purdy deliberately uses rape as a shocking symbolic device to unmask the sex mystique that is current in America."

451    Harris, Charles. *Contemporary American Novelists of the Absurd*. New Haven, Connecticut: College & University Press, 1971.

A study of four novelists—Heller, Vonnegut, Pynchon, Barth—whose writings "treat absurdist themes with what we may call absurdist techniques. Their vision of an absurd universe not only constitutes the theme of their novels but is reflected as well by the ways they manage incident, characterization, and language." In the epilogue Purdy's *Malcolm* is discussed and compared to Barthelme's novel, *Snow White*. Harris notes: "Purdy and Barthelme are representative of most contemporary absurdist novelists in the special ways they use artifice to convey themes that are quite serious."

452    Hassan, Ihab. *Contemporary American Literature, 1945-1972: An Introduction*. New York: Frederick Ungar, 1973.

A modest and brief introduction which covers fiction, poetry and drama. The chapter on fiction discusses two major novelists, Saul Bellow and Norman Mailer, and ten prominent novelists: James Purdy, Wright Morris, John Hawkes, William Styron, Bernard Malamud, J. D. Salinger, Kurt Vonnegut, Truman Capote, John Barth, and John Updike. The author presents a very favorable discussion of Purdy's *Color of Darkness*, *Children is All*, *Malcolm*, *The Nephew*, *Jeremy's Version*, and *Eustace Chisolm and the Works*. In summary, the author notes that "Purdy's voice can be querulous; his

77

world can be too cramped, its blackness almost willed; and women seldom bring life or grace into it. But he understands the inner chaos of men too well, the archetypal night of their souls. Like some absurd lapidary or icy expressionist, he cuts the lineaments of dread and innocence into the gross matter of existence." Under the chapter on drama, Purdy's short play *Cracks* is mentioned as "a work with Brechtian overtones."

453    ——. *Radical Innocence: Studies in the Contemporary American Novel*. Princeton, New Jersey: Princeton University Press, 1961.

A work which is divided into three major sections: 1. The Hero and the World: A historical perspective of the changing image of the hero in the modern novel; 2. The Forms of Fiction: A formal analysis of the way the novel, as a genre, responds to the shifting vision of man in contemporary American fiction; 3. The Individual Talent: An exemplary view of four writers. Though Purdy is not one of the four writers, he is mentioned along with Philip Roth and John Updike as "promising newcomers." There is also an analysis of *63: Dream Palace* in which Hassan states that "Purdy's work cultivates a dream-like literalness, a quiet, blood-chilling use of irrelevance, and a sense of human need so desperate and extreme that no cause is adequate to explain the agony we perceive."

454    Hilfer, Anthony. *American Fiction Since 1940*. London: Longman, 1992.

One of a series of volumes which gives a critical introduction to the major genres in their historical and cultural context. In chapter one, "From Social Protest to Solipsism," the author notes: "James Purdy's novels of the 1960's and John Rechy's *City of Night* (1962) ran original variations on homosexual themes but their work was not supplemented by enough writers to form the critical mass of a sub-genre, a movement."

455 Hipkiss, Robert A. *Jack Kerouac, Prophet of the New Romanticism: A Critical Study of the Published Works of Kerouac and a Comparison of Them to Those of J.D. Salinger, James Purdy, John Knowles, and Ken Kesey.* Lawrence: The Regents Press of Kansas, 1976.

"A critical study of Kerouac's published works to discover the essential themes, the nature of their treatment, and the reasons for their development." And, "to set Kerouac in perspective among the postwar Romantic writers by examining the works of four authors who represent different points of view concerning the problems of how to effect love and self-realization in our technologized, nuclear age." Hipkiss notes "James Purdy is the most versatile of the writers chosen." Hipkiss discusses and compares Purdy's *Malcolm, 63: Dream Palace, Jeremy's Version, Cabot Wright Begins, Eustace Chisholm and the Works,* and *The Nephew* to Kerouac's writing. Thematic comparisons include: youthful heroes, sex as a release from boredom, strong aversion to commercial values of society, distrust of the spoken word for communicating honest feeling, and style.

456 Hyman, Stanley Edgar. *Standards: A Chronicle of Books for Our Time.* New York: Horizon Press, 1966.

In the chapter, "The Correction of Opinion," Hyman gives a scathing review of Purdy's writing. He takes issue with writers such as James T. Farrell, Winfield Townley Scott, Katherine Anne Porter, Horace Gregory, Dudley Fitts, Dorothy Parker, Angus Wilson, John Cowper Powys, Kenneth Rexroth, R. W. B. Lewis, David Daiches, William Carlos Williams, Susan Sontag, and Theodore Solotaroff, all of whom praised Purdy's writings.

457 Johnson, Ira D., and Christiane Johnson, editors. *Les Americanistes: New French Criticism on Modern American Fiction.* Port Washington, New York: Kennikat Press, 1978.

A collection of eleven essays on contemporary American fiction by French critics—all of whom were born and educated in France, lived in the United States, and are specialists in American Literature. Chapter six, "New Modes of Story-Telling: Dismantling Contemporary Fiction," by Andre Le Vot, deals in "general terms with postmodern fiction." Purdy is discussed in context with Burroughs, Percy, Hawkes, O'Connor, Brautigan, Barthelme, Coover, and Heller.

458    Karl, Frederick R. *American Fictions, 1940-1980: A Contemporary History and Critical Evaluation*. New York: Harper & Row, 1983.

As the title implies, this is a comprehensive study of 40 years of American fiction. "Although *American Fictions* is primarily an interpretation of key American fiction in the four decades since the 1940's, it is, also, a reading of the culture from which the novels and writers derived." Karl begins his study of Purdy: "The neglect of James Purdy by both general readers and critics cannot be explained easily.... I think the reason for his neglect lies in his lack of give, his failure to cheer on, his bottom-line reality, his refusal to provide guidelines for behavior, his painful, often masochistic obsessions; taste, no question of that; but he deserves wider critical response. For if nothing else, he has fitted himself perfectly into a kind of washed-out American." Karl discusses and analyzes *63: Dream Palace*, *Malcolm*, *The Nephew*, *Cabot Wright Begins*, *Eustace Chisholm and the Works*, and *In a Shallow Grave*.

459    Kiernan, Robert F. *American Writing Since 1945: A Critical Survey*. New York: Frederick Ungar, 1983.

An introduction to "the wealth of American literature written since World War II. The work of some three hundred novelists, playwrights, and poets is chronicled." In the section on Fiction—Metafiction, James Purdy is compared to Jerzy Kosinski. Kiernan writes that Purdy's "narrators tend to be memorists who impose the discipline of their narration on stories of violent and traumatic loss, and they tend, like Kosinski's spokesmen, to focus on a situation at its moment of maximum horror. The perversions of

Purdy's characters range from incest to sadomasochism to vampirism, and his minor characters often seem dream figures, born not of women but of psychological needs. His prose, sparing of adjectives and adverbs, also recalls Kosinski's, especially when it describes the surrealistically lurid worlds of *Malcolm* and *I Am Elijah Thrush*." Also noted are Purdy's *The House of the Solitary Maggot*, *In a Shallow Grave* and *Narrow Rooms* as "darkly fantastical allegories of eternal children lost in a nightmare universe."

460    Kennard, Jean E. *Number and Nightmare: Forms of Fantasy in Contemporary Fiction*. Hamden, Connecticut: Archon Books, 1975.

"This book is a study of the fantasy techniques of some British and American novelists who gained their reputations in the sixties.... [It] is also an attempt to define two major forms of fantasy in contemporary fiction, number and nightmare, on the basis of the novelists' response to a post-existential world view." James Purdy, Joseph Heller, John Barth, and Kurt Vonnegut, Jr. are noted as writers who "accept a post-existential world view." Chapter three, entitled "James Purdy: Fidelity to Failure," is devoted to a discussion of the characters in *63: Dream Palace*, *Malcolm*, *The Nephew*, *Cabot Wright Begins*, *Eustace Chisholm and the Works*, and *Jeremy's Version*.

461    Kostelanetz, Richard, editor. *The New American Arts*. New York: Horizon Press, 1965.

A collection of essays by young writers, all under 35, who define and evaluate new trends in film, theater, painting, poetry, dance, fiction and music. In addition to editing the volume, Kostelanetz wrote the chapter on the new American fiction. He discusses Purdy's *Malcolm* and notes Purdy "employs a wispy, low-keyed style, keen psychological and emotional sensitivity, a knack for creating the telling moment and the resonant line—in general, a greater artistic control—to produce a more pruned absurd novel." Kostelanetz also mentions *The Nephew* and two short stories, "Goodnight, Sweetheart" and "Don't Call Me by My Right Name."

462 ——, editor. *On Contemporary Literature: An Anthology of Critical Essays on the Major Movements and Writers of Contemporary Literature*. New York: Avon Books, 1964.

The first third of this study includes chapters on the fiction, theater, and poetry of American, British, Canadian, French, German, Italian, Russian, and Spanish writers. The last two-thirds includes individual essays on thirty-six writers including Purdy, Agee, Baldwin, Durrell, Golding, Lessing, Lowry, Malamud, Pynchon, Roth, Singer, and Warren. The chapter on Purdy entitled, "The Damaged Cosmos" by Jonathan Cott, is an analysis of *The Nephew*, *Cracks*, and *Malcolm*. Cott notes: "What makes Purdy's stories so vital is the hard esthetic veneer in which he freezes the violent emotions his stories contain."

463 Kumar, Anil. *Alienation in the Fiction of Carson McCullers, J.D. Salinger, and James Purdy*. Amritsar: Guru Nanak Dev University, 1991.

An insightful textual analysis of three major contemporary American writers, McCullers, Salinger, and Purdy. The "nucleus of this comparative study is the theme of alienation in its various manifestations, such as alienation from self, from others, from God and from nature." Kumar analyzed Purdy's *Color of Darkness, 63: Dream Palace*, *Malcolm*, *The Nephew*, *Cabot Wright Begins*, *Eustace Chisholm and the Works*, and *Jeremy's Version*.

464 Ludwig, Jack. *Recent American Novelists*. Minneapolis: University of Minnesota Press, 1962.

A brief study of the works of Saul Bellows, James Baldwin, Ralph Ellison, Norman Mailer, William Styron, and others. Purdy's *Malcolm* and *The Nephew* are mentioned. This is Number 22 in a series from the University of Minnesota Pamphlets on American Writers.

465    Malin, Irving. *New American Gothic*. Carbondale: Southern Illinois University Press, 1962.

A detailed examination of six representative "Gothic" authors and their work. Studied are Purdy, Salinger, Hawkes, McCullers, Capote, and O'Connor. Malin points out that the metaphors of the new American Gothic writers are love, narcissism, family, dream-like quality, silence, and the breakdown of communication. Malin writes: "New American Gothic depends to a great extent on image, not idea. Because it deals with limitations of personality and wars in the family, it seeks not to be expansive but intensive. It presents a vertical world." Discussed are Purdy's *Color of Darkness*, *Malcolm*, "Man and Wife" (short story), "Sound of Talking" (short story), *The Nephew*, "Why Can't They Tell You Why?" (short story) and *63: Dream Palace*. Malin summarizes Purdy's writing with: "Purdy, like Hawkes, writes about non-recognizable nature and city life. He spends less time on visual description. His prose is artless, highly flexible, fluid ... Purdy concentrates on incident or effect—he uses his simple style to lure us into the horror, so much so that we are not really aware of the style as instrument."

466    ——, editor. *Psychoanalysis and American Fiction*. New York: E. P. Dutton, 1965.

A collection of "fifteen essays that approach American fiction from the psychoanalytical point of view." Essay number thirteen by Malin entitled "The Gothic Family" discusses "the way contemporary Gothic novelists—McCullers, Salinger, Capote, Purdy, and so on—portray family relationships. Their Gothic family is stylized—distorted by narcissistic tendencies." Malin writes that: "James Purdy does not supply a vision of the good parent who refuses to allow their children to grow up. We are back to daily horror, not transforming visions."

467    Meindl, Dieter. "James Purdy 'Don't Call Me by My Right Name.' " In *Die Amerikanische Short Story der*

*Gegenwart*. Edited by Peter Freese. Berlin: Erich
Schmidt, 1976.

In his interpretation of James Purdy's short story
"Don't Call Me by My Right Name," Meindl defines
questioning man's ability to communicate as the central
theme in Purdy's narrative work. Juxtaposing his
analysis with interpretations of other authors, Meindl
find the complexity of the author manifested in a
symbiosis of surrealism and symbolism. According to
Meindl, the story describes a conflict situation of a
married couple, in which the woman cannot identify
with her husband's name and demands from him to
change it. The name functions as a symbol for identity,
the essence of one's very being, and as a
representation of her and her husband's character. In
the course of the story the balance between
amusement and disaster shifts to a loss of self control,
and communication finally manifests in a violent
exchange of punches.

468    Miller, James E. *Quests Surd and Absurd: Essays in
American Literature*. Chicago: University of Chicago
Press, 1967.

This is a "volume of essays loosely related by their
recurring concern with the quest theme in American
Literature." The individual essays range from the
study of early 19th Century American romantics to the
post World War II new American novelists. In the first
essay on the new American novel. Purdy is linked to
twenty-four novelists including Salinger, Morris,
Updike, Price, Roth, Mailer, Jones, Kerouac, Styron,
and others. Miller notes that Carson McCullers' *The
Ballad of the Sad Cafe*, and James Purdy's *Malcolm*
were both made into full-length dramas by Edward
Albee. Miller labels Purdy and Hawkes as Gothic
writers similar to southern writers such as McCullers,
Capote, and O'Connor. He also labels Purdy, Hawkes,
and Burroughs as surrealistic writers.

469    Moore, Harry T., editor. *Contemporary American Novelists*. Carbondale: Southern Illinois University Press, 1964.

   A collection of critical, literary essays on contemporary writers which includes Gerald Weales' "No Face and No Exit: The Fiction of James Purdy and J. P. Donleavy." Weales examines Purdy's *Children is All, Malcolm*, and *The Nephew*. Weales summarizes his essay by stating that Purdy "ranges from the dusty macabre of *63: Dream Palace* to the grotesque and sometimes funny comedy of *Malcolm* to the deceptive matter-of-factness of *The Nephew*. There is great range, too, in quality. His stories often appear to be slices, slabs cut out of something not quite perceivable. Ordinarily, he arrests his characters at a moment when drunkenness, uncontrollable garrulity, fear, some strong emotion brings a revelation which is usually oblique, suggestive, amorphous."

470    Nagel, James, editor. *American Fiction: Historical and Critical Essays*. Boston: Northeastern University Press, 1977.

   Twelve papers presented at a symposium held at Northeastern University, October 15-16, 1976. In the chapter, "Tension and Technique: The Years of Greatness," by Linda W. Wagner, Purdy is referred to as one of [Nathaniel] West's many followers of writing satire. Introduction by James Nagel.

471    Newman, Charles H. *The Post-Modern Aura: The Act of Fiction in the Age of Inflation*. Evanston: Northwestern University Press, 1985.

   This is a study and "critique of the pretensions of the literary-cultural avant-garde in the United States today. It is also a critique of the current opposition to the avant-garde—neo-realists, academic humanists, and political conservatives." Chapter 22, "Fiction as Forgetting," discusses Purdy's *Cabot Wright Begins*. This discussion is similar to his article "Beyond Omniscience." Preface by Gerald Graff.

472    O'Connor, William Van. *The Grotesque: An American Genre, and Other Essays*. Carbondale: Southern Illinois University Press, 1962.

A collection of critical essays on American Literature. In the first chapter of the book entitled "The Grotesque: An American Genre," Purdy is mentioned as "a more recent literary arrival ... [and] ... is an acute observer and creator of the grotesque." O'Connor uses *63: Dream Palace* as an excellent example and notes that, at the end of the story, "Human dignity has rarely been expressed in such an unlikely scene or human love in such unlikely language."

473    Pease, Donald. "James Purdy: Shaman in Nowhere Land." In *The Fifties: Fiction, Poetry, Drama*. Warren French, editor. Deland, Florida: Everett/Edwards, 1970.

Pease's essay is a careful study of the individual characters in Purdy's collection of short stories, *Color of Darkness*, *63: Dream Palace*, and his 1959 novel *Malcolm*. Pease notes: "While Purdy's work is involved, it is also involving ... Purdy describes America in the winter of its life—nowhere and coming to nothing." In the bibliography section, Schwarzschild's *The Not-Right House: Essays on James Purdy* is noted as the first separate publication devoted to Purdy. Also noted are references to Purdy's recordings of *63: Dream Palace* and *Color of Darkness*.

474    Peden, William. *The American Short Story: Front Line in the National Defense of Literature*. Boston: Houghton Mifflin, 1964.

A brief introduction to the development of the short story in America. The emphasis is on the major directions and achievements of the short story since the 1940's. James Purdy is grouped with John Cheever and Eudora Welty because "for all their differences, [they] possess the same interest in the problems of human loneliness, separateness, and unknowableness." Peden states: "Among the most distinguished recent American short stories concerned with mental or emotional disturbance and the grotesque or the abnormal are those by James Purdy." Peden analyzes the stories in *Children is All* and *Color of Darkness*. The author also compares Purdy's subject matter and themes to those of Jean Stafford and Tennessee Williams.

475    ——, editor. *The American Short Story: Continuity and Change, 1940-1975.* 2nd edition, revised and enlarged. Boston: Houghton Mifflin, 1975.

A thirty-five year history of the development of the American short story. Peden analyzes Purdy's two collections of short stories in detail. He notes that *Color of Darkness* and *Children is All* "usually concern people who are either emotional or physiological grotesques or both. Lonely, lost, isolated, unloved, or undesirable, they are confined within private hells that are their own making and sometimes created by forces over which they can exercise little if any control." Peden ends his discussion on Purdy by stating "Purdy's is a strange, highly individual talent. His awareness of the murky depths of human cruelty or indifference is as startling as his recognition of their opposites. He is preoccupied with the recurring themes of loneliness and isolation, and with the paradoxes he sees inherent in the human situation—love-hate, beauty-ugliness, compassion-cruelty. Out of these paradoxes and these themes, Purdy has created a fictional world uniquely his own." The appendix includes a list of the "One Hundred-Plus Notable or Representative American Short Story Writers, 1940-1975."

476    Polsgrove, Carol. *It Wasn't Pretty, Folks, But Didn't We Have Fun? Esquire in the Sixties.* New York: W. W. Norton, 1995.

A journalistic history of *Esquire Magazine* in the sixties with emphasis on Harold Hayes and the active roles he played in the development of *Esquire* during his tenure. *Esquire* published a number of Purdy's short stories. An interview by Barton Midwood was published in November 1970. The interview made

Purdy come "off as a surly simpleton." Gordon Lish, Fiction editor, wrote to Purdy to soften the blow.

477    Pondrom, Cyrena N. "Franz Kafka: His Place in World Literature." In *Comparative Literature Symposium Proceedings*. Volume 4. Lubbock, Texas: Texas Tech Press, 1971.

Report based on a symposium held January 28-29, 1971.

This symposium contains a detailed, scholarly study by Pondrom, entitled "Purdy's *Malcolm* and Kafka's *Amerika*: Analogues with a Difference." The author compares and contrasts the similarities of these two works relative to their "plot, structure, central character, action, setting, image and motif." The author concludes: "For both Kafka and Purdy there comes the withering perception of the ultimately absurd demand: initiation into a full humanity must be sought and will fail; the boy will seek the father but can never find him. For all their differences, then, there is essential similarity between Purdy and Kafka in the shared vision of the insolubly contradictory demands of the human circumstance."

478    Punter, David. *The Literature of Terror: A History of Gothic Fictions from 1765 to the Present Day*. London: Longmans, 1980.

Chapter 14 "Modern Perceptions of the Barbaric" discusses James Purdy, Mervyn Peake, John Hawkes, Joyce Carol Oates, Thomas Pynchon, J. G. Ballard, and Angela Carter. Punter singles out *Eustace Chisholm and the Works* as the example of Purdy's gothic writing. Punter's analysis of the novel is very negative on all accounts—characters, language, and prose style.

479    Raban, Jonathan. *The Technique of Modern Fiction: Essays in Practical Criticism*. London: Edward Arnold, 1968.

A collection of fifteen essays in which chapter twelve, "Registers in the Language of Fiction," discusses and compares the language in Purdy's short story,

"Sermon," to Jonathan Edward's famous eighteenth-century sermon, "Sinners in the Hands of an Angry God." Raban concludes: "One could, I think, link the two pieces together so that it would be extremely hard to detect where Purdy left off and Edwards began."

480    Saltzman, Arthur M. *Designs of Darkness in Contemporary American Fiction*. Philadelphia: University of Pennsylvania Press, 1990.

A study which tries "to portray the variety and scope of responses to the disqualification of epiphanic faith." Saltzman has chosen representative works by authors "who dominate discussions of Postmodern fiction, which is to say, those whose works are frequently used to suggest the justifiability of speaking of a distinctive new period in American fiction." John Barth, Donald Barthelme, Thomas Berger, Robert Coover, Don De Lillo, E. L. Doctorow, John Hawkes and James Purdy are a few of the authors whose works he analyzes. *Cabot Wright Begins* and *Malcolm* are the two Purdy novels Saltzman discusses.

481    Sarotte, Georges Michel. *Like a Brother, Like a Lover: Male Homosexuality in the American Novel and Theatre from Herman Melville to James Baldwin*. Translated from the French by Richard Miller. New York, Anchor Press, Doubleday, 1978.

Originally appearing in French, this study is a "systematic analysis of male homosexuality in American theater and fiction." Purdy's *Eustace Chisholm and the Works*, *Malcolm*, and *The Nephew* are discussed in detail.

482    Scholes, Robert E. *Fabulation and Metafiction*. Urbana: University of Illinois Press, 1979.

This study contains only brief mention of Purdy as a writer of black humor. Purdy is listed with other "exciting young writers of black humor such as Albee, Barth, Donleavy, Friedman, Hawkes, Heller, Pynchon, Southern, and Vonnegut."

483      ——. *The Fabulators*. New York: Oxford University Press, 1967.

>The author defines fabulation as fiction writing that is "less realistic and more artistic kind of narrative: more shapely, more evocative; more concerned with ideas and ideals; less concerned with things." This study deals with Lawrence Durrell, Iris Murdoch, Kurt Vonnegut, Jr., Terry Southern, John Hawkes, and John Barth. James Purdy is mentioned in a discussion of "Black Humor" in fiction.

484      Schulz, Max F. *Black Humor Fiction of the Sixties: A Pluralistic Definition of Man and his World*. Athens, Ohio: Ohio University Press, 1973.

>A study of novels written mainly in the 1960's in which the author attempts to define "Black Humor" by establishing guidelines "preliminary to our coming to terms with the cultural and literary achievement of this period." The author notes: "Friedman inadvertently gave literary respectability and philosophical cohesion to the group, when he patched together thirteen pieces ... for Bantam Books in 1965 and nonchalantly entitled them 'Black Humor.' " James Purdy is included in this volume.

485      Schwarzschild, Bettina. *The Not-Right House: Essays on James Purdy*. Columbia, Missouri: University of Missouri Press, 1968.

>One of the best writers on Purdy and his writings. William Peden writes in the introduction that "Schwarzschild's essays help us see this strange world afresh. She has read Purdy with wisdom and insight. She understands his exiled wanderers perhaps more thoroughly than any one else who has written on them, knows that to love them means to be shaken with pity and terror. So, of course, does their creator." This collection of eight essays, of which three have appeared earlier in literary journals, covers Purdy's writing to 1968. In her essay, "Love in the Twentieth Century: *Cabot Wright Begins*," Ms. Schwarzschild beautifully demonstrates her understanding of Purdy's

writing. "James Purdy's work is about love. Love between mother and child, brother and brother or sister, husband and wife, aunt and nephew, friends, neighbors, strangers, people stumbling, groping towards each other, and failing, always failing, cruelly, tragically, when the very survival of the beloved depends on love."

486    Scott, Nathan A., editor. *Adversity and Grace: Studies in Recent American Literature*. Chicago: University of Chicago Press, 1968.

A collection of nine essays which relates theology and literature in order to provide "a convincing demonstration of the possibility for a new kind of understanding and mutual enrichment between religion and culture." In his introduction, "Theology and Literary Imagination," Scott mentions the numerous highly gifted novelists who have entered American literary life in the years since World War II, and who were not written about in these essays, including James Purdy and John Hawkes, who he calls "two brilliant artists."

487    ———. *The Broken Center: Studies in the Theological Horizon of Modern Literature*. New Haven: Yale University Press, 1966.

Mentions Purdy along with R. W. B. Lewis, Ralph Ellison, J. D. Salinger, John Knowles and William Styron as representative figures in American literature of the time who express in their novels what a character in Purdy's *Malcolm* says "keep your hands off my soul."

488    Skaggs, Calvin. "The Sexual Nightmare of 'Why Can't They Tell You Why?' " In *The Process of Fiction: Contemporary Stories and Criticism*. Edited by Barbara McKenzie. New York: Harcourt, Brace & World, 1969.

A detailed analysis of Purdy's short story "Why Can't They Tell You Why?" Skaggs notes that "Purdy's is a nightmare world dominated by the surrealistic illogic of dreams; events occur in a two-dimensional dreamscape

in which Purdy fails to make human behavior make
sense."

489    Solotaroff, Theodore. *The Red Hot Vacuum and Other
       Places on the Writing of the Sixties*. New York:
       Atheneum, 1970.

   A collection of essays and reviews devoted mainly to
   contemporary writers including Purdy, Golden,
   Malamud, Chester, Selby, O'Connor, Goodman,
   Burroughs, Bowles, Bellow and Roth.  The chapter on
   James Purdy entitled "The Deadly James Purdy" is an
   analysis of the short story, "Eventide," and the novel,
   *Cabot Wright Begins*.  Solotaroff writes "Purdy is a
   naturalist of unusual subtlety and a fantasist of unusual
   clarity.  These two strains cross repeatedly in his
   fiction, for his subject is most often the enigmatic
   borderland between innocence and depravity, and his
   characters are generally people who are cut off from the
   more or less normal life of humanity—orphans, invalids,
   Negroes, spinsters, homosexuals, failed artists, and
   other lost souls who retreated into the weird logic of
   their illusions and privations, their pain and cruelty."

490    Spiller, Robert E., editor. *A Time of Harvest: American
       Literature, 1910-1960*. New York: Hill and Wang, 1962.

   A collection of fifteen essays covering fifty years of
   American literary history.  The chapter by R. W. B.
   Lewis entitled "Recent Fiction: Picaro and Pilgrim"
   singles out Purdy, Bellows, Salinger, Ellison, Kerouac,
   and Mailer as writers that "represent what is best in
   postwar American fiction."  And, names who have
   "kept the art of fiction alive in America during hard
   artistic times."  Lewis compares Purdy's *Malcolm* and
   Ellison's *The Invisible Man* and writes "Both Purdy
   and Ellison (in their exceedingly different ways)
   introduce their comically ill-equipped young heroes nor
   merely to assorted individuals and situations, but
   rather to individuals and situations that are clearly
   representative of the great sources of power and
   control in our epoch.  In the case of *Malcolm*—a
   startlingly original novel that verges on ironic

allegory—the persons encountered stand, respectively, for Art, Money, Religion (or, better, Religiosity), Sex, Fate, and Death."

491    Tanner, Tony. *City of Words: American Fiction 1950-1970*. New York: Harper & Row, 1971.

An insightful and detailed study of eighty-seven novels by twenty-nine authors in which each author succeeds in his aim "to try to understand the American imagination as it has expressed itself in fictional forms during this period." Tanner believes "A close study of the literature of the present can help us to arrive at a clearer perception of some of the plights and privileges of our own inescapable modernity." Chapter four, "Frames Without Pictures," is devoted to an analysis of Purdy's *63: Dream Palace*, *Color of Darkness*, *Malcolm*, *Cabot Wright Begins*, *The Nephew* and *Eustace Chisholm and the Works*. In his discussion of *Cabot Wright*, Tanner writes that Purdy "gathers together all the themes opened up or touched on in Purdy's earlier work and explores them with a subtlety and humour and power which makes this, to my mind, not only Purdy's most profound novel but one of the most important American novels since the war."

492    Tuttleton, James W. *The Novel of Manners in America*. Chapel Hill: University of North Carolina Press, 1972.

"The most exciting writers today, which is to say those writers nearest the happy condition of genius, are preoccupied with forms other then the novel of manners," so states the author in chapter eleven, entitled "The Way We Love Now." Tuttleton cites the fiction of Purdy, Nabakov, Hawkes and Bowles as examples of writing about "a world that is oriented inward, reflecting the inner eye, the private vision, the subjective self. Alienated from the social order—even from the role of critic of that order, such writers create their visions out of dreams, fantasy and nightmare." Mentions Albee's adaptation of Purdy's *Malcolm* in a chapter devoted to Edward Albee's work.

493    Wager, Willis. *American Literature: A World View*. New York: New York University Press, 1968.

A history of American literature from Columbus and Franklin to Eliot, O'Neill, Faulkner, Wilbur, Albee and Morris. The chapter on Wilbur, Albee, and Morris mentions Albee's dramatization of Purdy's *Malcolm*. Also the author notes Purdy's *Color of Darkness*, *Children is All*, *Malcolm*, *The Nephew*, *Cabot Wright Begins* and *Eustace Chisholm and the Works* and Nabokov's *Lolita* as examples of "black humor."

494    Waldmeir, Joseph J., editor. *Recent American Fiction: Some Critical Views*. Boston: Houghton Mifflin Company, 1963.

A collection of reprints of some of the best literary criticism devoted to American novelists who have come to prominence since the end of World War II. Each selection was chosen because of its extensive treatment of the novelists and their work. Paul Herr's "The Small, Sad World of James Purdy" from the *Chicago Review* is included on pages 246-251.

495    Wallace, Ronald. *The Last Laugh: Form and Affirmation in the Contemporary American Comic Novel*. Columbia, Missouri: University of Missouri Press, 1979.

Referring to the work of a variety of postwar novelists, among them Purdy, Heller, Donleavy, Elkin, and Wallace, the author examines patterns of character, plot, and style in their recent comic fiction. Special emphasis is placed on Purdy's *Cabot Wright Begins*.

496    Weales, Gerald. *The Jumping-Off Place: American Drama in the 1960's*. New York: Macmillan, 1969.

A critical description of American plays with emphasis on plays produced off-Broadway. Weales gives Purdy's two plays, *Cracks* and *Children Is All*, a negative review. Weales writes, "For an author who uses dialogue so tellingly in his novels and stories, James Purdy is strangely inept in his two plays, published in *Children is All*." *Cracks* was performed off-Broadway in 1963 on a bill with Ellen Violett's adaptations of four Purdy stories.

497   Weaver, Gordon, editor. *The American Short Story, 1945 - 1980: A Critical History*. Boston: Twayne, 1983.

A collection of essays dealing with the development of the short story in three separate periods: 1945-1956: Post-World War II Manners and Mores; 1957-1968: Toward Diversity of Form; 1969-1980: Experiment and Tradition. Purdy's two collections of short stories, *Color of Darkness* and *Children is All,* are briefly analyzed in the second essay "Toward Diversity of Form" by E. P. Walkiewicz.

498   West, Paul. *The Modern Novel: The United States and Other Countries*. London: Hutchinson and Company, 1963.

A work which sketches the present day novel by comparing one national tradition with another. This study covers the novel in England, France, United States, Germany, Italy, Soviet Russia and Spain. In volume two, part three, chapter two, "Time, South and Identity," Purdy's *The Nephew, Colour of Darkness* and *Malcolm* are noted and compared to Agee's *A Death in the Family* and to Nabokov, Capote, and McCullers.

499   Witham, W. Tasker *The Adolescent in the American Novel: 1920-1960*. New York: Frederick Ungar, 1964.

This study is based on the author's Ph.D. dissertation. Witham surveyed over five hundred novels having an adolescent as a major character. The author picked novels of "greatest literary value" for this study. The work includes a discussion of Purdy's *Malcolm* and *63: Dream Palace* and noted that: "fantasy and realism are combined, with fascinating originality" in these works.

# B. Critical Journal and Periodical Articles

500      Albee, Edward. "Who Is James Purdy? Edward Albee Tells." *New York Times*, 9 January 1966, sec. 2, pp. 1, 3.

>Two days before Albee's adaptation of Purdy's novel, *Malcolm*, opened on Broadway, Albee wrote this article about Purdy and his writing. Albee writes "There is, right now, living in Brooklyn—deep in Brooklyn—a wonderful, cheerful, softspoken man who, unlike most writers, wears a hat when he goes out, and whose telephone is almost always either busy or disconnected. His name is James Purdy, and he is widely reputed to be one of our few fine serio-comic novelists." About the novel *Malcolm*, Albee writes, "the book is deeply sad and terribly funny."

501      Alou, Damia. "James Purdy en Castellano: Una Aproximacion." *Pasajes* 7 (1987): 75-83.

>A discussion in Spanish of Purdy's *Color of Darkness*, *Malcolm*, *63: Dream Palace*, and *On Glory's Course*.

502      Austen, Roger. "But for Fate and Ban: Homosexual Villains and Victims in the Military." *College English* 36 (November 1974): 352-359.

>The entire issue is devoted to the homosexual imagination. An insightful study of five works whose theme is "an attachment between a military officer and his subordinates." Compared and contrasted are Melville's *Billy Budd*, Lawrence's *The Prussian Officer*, McCullers' *Reflections in a Golden Eye*, Murphy's *The Sergeant*, and Purdy's *Eustace Chisholm and the Works*. Austen ends his excellent article: "Most writers using this theme, however, place enough barriers between the two men to assure a sad ending, and the only comfort that gay readers have is that, once in awhile, we come across the tremulous Southern tenderness of a Carson McCullers or the stifled cry of compassion of a James Purdy."

503    Baldanza, Frank. "James Purdy on the Corruption of Innocents." *Contemporary Literature* 15 (summer 1974): 315-330.

A study of Purdy's theme of "the relationship between a young innocent and the corrupt adult world in which he must make his way" is explored by comparing Purdy's writing to a "number of picaresque works dealing with roughly the same theme." Fernando de Rojas' *La Celestina*, Stevenson's *Treasure Island* and *Kidnapped* and John Meade Falkner's *Moonfleet* are compared to Purdy's "Everything Under the Sun," *Eustace Chisholm and the Works*, and *63: Dream Palace*. Baldanza refers to *63: Dream Palace* as Purdy's "masterful novella."

504    ——. "James Purdy's Half-Orphans." *Centennial Review* 18 (summer 1974): 255-272.

A very positive review of Purdy's writing. Baldanza described Purdy's characters as half-orphans in his collections of short stories, *Color of Darkness* and *Children is All*, and his novel, *Jeremy's Version*. Baldanza states that his "brief examination of the half-orphan stories reveals the failure of human love in a pattern of reciprocal paradoxes: feminine sexuality is biased by all the paradoxes of creation, because the immense sacrifices and devotion exacted by conceiving and nurturing offspring eventuate in a possessiveness which in turn distorts and cripples the masculinity of the son. His distorted sexuality renders him a grotesque who, as an adult, grants the same legacy to the next generation. Purdy's vision is somber and frightening and it is to our peril that we continue to ignore it."

505    ——. "Northern Gothic." *Southern Review* 10 (July 1974): 566-582.

An excellent article comparing and contrasting the writings of James Purdy and Sherwood Anderson. Baldanza selects these midwestern authors (Ohioans) in order "to analyze common subject matter, characters, techniques, and themes." Purdy's *63:*

*Dream Palace, Jeremy's Version, Eustace Chisholm and the Works*, and *The Nephew* are analyzed. Baldanza notes that "Purdy and Anderson, however, are writers of vastly different quality. Purdy is an assured artist who writes with clarity, control, and direction; every speech, every word, every detail repays whatever amount of attention the reader wished to give it." Baldanza uses the term "Northern Gothic" primarily to indicate the strong resemblances to an older tradition of southern writing, running from Poe to Flannery O'Connor, "although Purdy resembles Carson McCullers more nearly than other members."

506    ——. "The Paradoxes of Patronage in Purdy." *American Literature* 46 (November 1974): 347-356.

Baldanza identifies one of the basic themes in Purdy's writing as that of the relationship between a patron and a protégé. He analyzes this relationship in *Malcolm, The Nephew, Cabot Wright Begins, Eustace Chisholm and the Works, Jeremy's Version, I Am Elijah Thrush* and the short story "Mr. Evening." Baldanza concentrates on "Mr. Evening" to demonstrate "the rich complexity of this un-theme in all of Purdy's work."

507    ——. "Playing House for Keeps with James Purdy." *Contemporary Literature* 11 (autumn 1970): 488-510.

The theme of the outsider is examined in a study of Purdy's four major novels—*Malcolm, The Nephew, Cabot Wright Begins* and *Eustace Chisholm and the Works*. Baldanza provides a positive, complex, detailed and comparative analysis of the individual characters found in these four novels.

508    Bolling, Douglass. "The World Upstaged in James Purdy's *I Am Elijah Thrush*." *The University of Dayton Review* 10 (summer 1974): 75-83.

Bolling begins this detailed study of *I Am Elijah Thrush* with "The unexpected appearance of *I Am Elijah Thrush* in the midst of James Purdy's ambitious 'Sleepers in Moon-Crowned Valleys' project evidences the writer's vitality and abundance. Where *Jeremy's*

*Version*, the first volume of the project, reminds chiefly of *The Nephew* and *Eustace Chisholm and the Works*, *I Am Elijah Thrush* takes us back more nearly to *63: Dream Palace* and *Malcolm*; clearly Purdy's genius demands expression in more than a single direction.... The thematic center of the novella lies in its evocation of the sterility and vacuity inherent in false mythologizing and self-dramatizing ploys of those unable or unwilling to relate themselves authentically to 'reality'—to the sheer otherness and indifference of the world beyond the human." Bolling ends: "Purdy's magic in *I Am Elijah Thrush* is such that we cannot exhaust the fullness and presence of the whole through any easy attachments of constituents.... Once again James Purdy has demonstrated a remarkable ability to fuse philosophical perception, a richly ironic and engaging texture, and stylistic subtlety without sacrificing readability."

509    Bowen, Robert O. "Idiot's Delight Versus a Solid Product." *Northwest Review* 1 (spring 1958): 69-73.

A review of *Color of Darkness* and Robie Macauley's *The End of Pity*. Bowen gives *Color* a very negative review (idiot's delight) criticizing Purdy's rhetorical skills, character development and subject matter. Bowen ends by noting: "Ultimately we are forced to conclude that the statement of the collection as a whole is that people are aberrational and that there is no pattern of order in the world except the pattern and shock rising from the aberration."

510    Brantlinger, Patrick. "Missing Corpses: The Deconstructive Mysteries of James Purdy and Franz Kafka." *Novel: A Forum on Fiction* 20 (fall 1986): 24-40.

Brantlinger's theory is that "modern novelists have often experimented with mystery conventions, seeking to reinvest them with question marks, to render them truly mysterious. Two significant examples which display a complex awareness of the structural features of mysteries are James Purdy's *The Nephew* and Franz Kafka's *The Trial*." The author provides a long, detailed, careful analysis of *The Nephew* and compares the complex structural features of both novels.

511    Bryson, Norman. "Orgy, hors-je, hors-jeu: A Note on the Work of James Purdy." *Granta: New American Writing* (autumn 1979): 77-85.

A complex, scholarly analysis of *In a Shallow Grave.* After a brief account of the plot of the novel, Bryson writes: "Beside this bare account of the book's violent and mysterious plot, I want to mention certain details which, as the novel develops, come to establish a synchronic lyrical order that at times all but displaces the diachronic narrative order just outlined."

512    Burris, Shirley W. "The Emergency in Purdy's 'Daddy Wolf.' " *Renascence* 20 (winter 1968): 94-98, 103.

A detailed study of Purdy's short story "Daddy Wolf" from his collection *Children is All.* She notes that Purdy's story becomes "a poignant, deliberately ungrammatical and deceptively subtle verbalization of man's sense of emptiness and alienation."

513    Cami, Ben. "James Purdy, een Amerikaanse Swift." *De Vlaamse Gids* 50 (January-February 1966): 53-55.

An article in Danish discussing Purdy's *Cabot Wright Begins.*

514    Curley, Thomas F. "The Quarrel With Time in American Fiction." *American Scholar* 29 (autumn 1960): 552, 554, 556, 558, 560.

A review of six current publications including Purdy's *Color of Darkness*, Baldwin's *Giovanni's Room*, Bowles' *The Spider's House*, Mailer's *Advertisements for Myself* and Styron's *Set This House on Fire.* The premise of this essay is that "man cannot forget. When he tries to, he demeans himself; if he succeeds, he destroys himself." In this context Curley gives a favorable review of *Color of Darkness*, noting "any intelligent man can write a criticism of life; it is the novelist's distinction to recreate it."

515    Davis, Douglas M. "The New Mood: An Obsession With
the Absurd." *National Observer* 4 (15 February 1965):
22.

A positive discussion of the current black humorists in
American Literature. Discussed are: John Hawkes,
James Purdy, Joseph Heller, William S. Burroughs, John
Barth, J. P. Donleavy and Terry Southern. Interesting
note is these writers' ages range from 38 to 50. Davis
writes: "James Purdy, 41, seems to many the brightest
star in the new galaxy." He notes: "Unmarried, Mr.
Purdy lives alone in Brooklyn Heights, New York,
supported entirely by his writing and occasional help
from foundations (he has won one Ford and two
Guggenheim grants). He reads a little Greek and Latin
every day, he says, then goes out spying on the
universe." Article is well illustrated with drawings of
each author by David Seavey.

516    Denniston, Constance. "The American Romance-Parody:
A Study of Purdy's *Malcolm* and Heller's *Catch-22*."
*Emporia State Research Studies* 14 (December 1965): 42-
59, 63-64.

A three-part study of "The American Romance-
Parody." The first section deals with the structure of
"American Romance-Parody," referring to Hawthorne,
Melville and Henry James. The second section uses
Purdy's *Malcolm* as an example of a love-parody and
the third section uses Heller's *Catch-22* as a parody of
love. Denniston states: "The meaning and structure of
the book [*Malcolm*], however, becomes clean when one
treats it as a parody of the romance."

517    Fick, Thomas H. "Reading a Dummy: James Purdy's
'Plan Now to Attend.' " *Studies in Short Fiction* 25
(winter 1988): 13-19.

A very detailed discussion of Purdy's short story "Plan
Now to Attend," which was published in *Color of
Darkness*. The author notes that the story "is
deceptively simple and unjustly neglected." The author
says that because this helps one "to understand the
multiple self-deceptions that form the subject of

Purdy's first novel *Malcolm*." The essay concludes: "Purdy's 'Plan Now to Attend' should be recognized for the graceful, humorous and, above all, compact way it describes and enacts the self-deception such figures encourage."

518    Fink, Guido. "James Purdy e le Gaie Esequie del Romanzo Americano." *Paragone: Letteratura* 21 (October 1970): 82-98.

This article is more like a dinner party conversation about American literature than it is an in-depth, scholarly analysis of the work of James Purdy. The article has a promising beginning in Fink's assertion that the work of Purdy "is the middle way between the terrain of the experimentalists and the ruins of Tradition." Unfortunately, Fink does not elucidate his interesting, but nebulous and sometimes misleading assertions about the body of American literature. Rather than pursuing a particular theme or characteristic of Purdy's work, Fink makes as many intertextual references from a litany of unrelated American novels as Purdy's work will bear. This article would be best suited to the interests of an Italian scholar seeking a brief overview of American Literature with references to James Purdy rather than being useful to a scholar of the work of James Purdy in particular.

519    Foster, Richard. "What is Fiction For?" *Hudson Review* 14 (spring 1961): 142-149.

A review essay on eight novels including Purdy's *The Nephew*, Spencer's *The Light in the Piazza* and Updike's *Rabbit, Run*. A very negative review of *The Nephew* in which he compares Purdy to Hawthorne by writing, "He (Purdy) reminds one of Hawthorne inevitably. But he is a toneless Hawthorne, a mechanical Hawthorne, and thus a Hawthorne only on the surface—lacking the icy passion for debauches of moral confrontation that made Hawthorne's genius."

520    French, Warren. "James Purdy, Will Moses: Against the Wilderness." *Kansas Quarterly* 14 (spring 1982): 81-92.

This issue of the *Kansas Quarterly* is devoted to William R. Moses, Midwest poet. Warren French is a former colleague of Will Moses and authority on James Purdy. He has written an excellent study of these two men and their work. Both authors express "displeasure with the twentieth century; but [Moses's] reactions are passive, whereas Purdy's are dynamic." French discusses, compares and reviews Purdy's *63: Dream Palace*, *Malcolm*, *Cabot Wright Begins*, *Eustace Chisholm and the Works*, *I am Elijah Thrush*, *In a Shallow Grave*, *The Nephew*, *Narrow Rooms*, *Mourners Below*, *Jeremy's Version* and *The House of the Solitary Maggot*. Most of the emphasis is focused on *Jeremy's Version* and the *The House of the Solitary Maggot*.

521    ———. "The Quaking World of James Purdy." *Scope* 1 (spring 1961): 45-47.

This essay is an introduction to Purdy for the University of Florida literary magazine. In this essay French discusses and reviews *Color of Darkness*, *63: Dream Palace*, *Malcolm* and *The Nephew*. French notes: "An indication of Purdy's stature is his refusal to stop experimenting. Few experimental novels are popular enough to become inexpensive paperbacks, and success might have tempted Purdy—as it has other recent writers—to keep expressing over and over his irrefutable points about society's destruction of youth." French ends his insightful study of Purdy's work: "There is a dream world even in *The Nephew*, but the dream is no longer all nightmare as in Purdy's earlier works. This dream, though, is neither pointless weeping over what may have never been nor fatuous promise of pie in the sky. It is the kind of dream that those who cannot ignore the degeneracy of the contemporary world may be able to accept when they must reject worn-out banalities paraded as ideals—the kind of dream that cannot stop a world of unremitting change from quaking, but that might have prevented its shattering by giving people the vision to move with it."

522    ——, and Marc Rosenberg. "The Beast That Devours Its Young." *CCC: College Composition and Communication* 13 (May 1962): 4-8.

One of the most unusual and creative articles on Purdy's *Malcolm*. Warren French is a professor of English and Marc Rosenberg was his undergraduate student. The analysis of *Malcolm* is written as a conversation between the two, professor and student. Both are positive and enthusiastic about the novel and bring different viewpoints and understanding. However, it is the student's comments that add dimension to the article. As part of the conversation the student reads his paper on *Malcolm* and concludes: "Because *Malcolm* is the kind of book that makes us laugh and say, 'this is ridiculous,' and after having done that, makes us realize that it is ourselves at whom we are laughing, it speaks for today's youth as does *The Catcher in the Rye*. Before *Catcher* was legitimized by the academic priests, it was the delightful literary mistress of many a college student. It seems that *Malcolm* will follow the same pattern."

523    Galloway, David D. "Clown and Saint: The Hero in Current American Fiction." *Critique: Studies in Modern Fiction* 7 (spring/summer 1965): 46-65.

A discussion of literary characters found in contemporary American fiction. The author has divided his essay into clown and saint-like characters. He identifies Purdy's *Malcolm* as a "child saint." Other authors discussed are J. D. Salinger, Jack Kerouac, John Updike, and Edward Lewis Wallant.

524    Gavron, Donald J. "Off the Strip: James Purdy and His Work." *Art: Mag* 11 (spring/summer 1989): 1-2.

A tribute to Purdy. Gavron writes that "the people presented to us in James Purdy's fiction are not the spoiled, self-absorbed Holdens or Rabbits of affluent suburbia, but the unloved, neglected and dispossessed who haunt the streets and small towns, walking through life invisible, overwhelmed by the absurdity of their condition yet still grasping for love, acceptance, peace. Purdy is a master not only of what people say to each other, but what they keep hidden. Hidden truths so terrible that revealing them invokes violence and tragedy."

525    Gorlier, Claudio. "La Trappola dell' American Gothic." *L'Approdo Letterario* Nuova serie (September-December 1974): 208-210.

This article, "The Trap of the American Gothic," revolves tightly around the essay by Frank Baldanza entitled "Northern Gothic." Gorlier begins the article by presenting a limited cultural/literary background for the American Gothic as a whole and makes intertextual, thematic links between Purdy's work and that of Frank O'Connor and William Faulkner. Gorlier contends that the "Faulknerian gothic" is a fulcrum on which the Purdy work operates. Gorlier then refers back to the work of Baldanza, who points out defining characteristics of Purdy's work as "the grotesque, alienation, and most of all, the eccentric." Baldanza's assertion that "the fear of having lost control over the stimuli of ... 'black humor' or of 'light nihilism' " is the principle around which the rest of the article develops. Gorlier refers to themes in Purdy's work only as they pertain to the article written by Baldanza, or to critical or creative works about Purdy, so this article is more of a point of reference for other sources on Purdy's work than it is an in-depth analysis of Purdy's writing.

526    Grinnell, James W. "Who's Afraid of 'Daddy Wolf'?" *Journal of Popular Culture* 3 (spring 1990): 750-752.

An interesting explication of Purdy's short story, "Daddy Wolf," in which the author compares Benny's eating of Cream of Wheat to Li'l Abner (cartoon character) by Al Capp doing the same, the eating of the Cream of Wheat symbolizing hope and future success.

527　Hassan, Ihab. "The Dismemberment of Orpheus:
　　　Reflections on Modern Culture, Language and Literature."
　　　*American Scholar* 32 (summer 1963): 463-484.

> Contains only a brief mention of James Purdy in a
> comparison with John Hawkes, William S. Burroughs,
> and J. D. Salinger.

528　———. "Laughter in the Dark: The New Voice in American
　　　Fiction." *American Scholar* 33 (autumn 1964): 636-640.

> The author contests that the works of Bellow's
> *Henderson, the Rain King*, Ellison's *The Invisible
> Man*, Capote's *Breakfast at Tiffany's*, Cheever's *The
> Wapshot Chronicle*, Purdy's *Malcolm* and Salinger's
> *The Catcher in the Rye* all illustrate dark laughter in
> their works and contains "a good deal of bitterness and
> some madness, too."

529　———. "The Novels of Outrage: A Minority Voice in
　　　Postwar American Fiction." *American Scholar* 34 (spring
　　　1965): 239-253.

> Outrage, as defined by Mr. Hassan, Professor at
> Wesleyan University, "is an irrational dialectic of
> violence threatening the human form, the very nature of
> man." The author uses nine novels to make his point:
> "This is to say that in the nearer reaches of terror or
> violence, the old novel of protest and the new novel of
> outrage are not always sharply distinct." Novels
> discussed included: William Styron's *Set This House
> on Fire*; James Baldwin's *Another Country*; Ralph
> Ellison's *The Invisible Man*; Paul Bowles's *The
> Sheltering Sky*; James Purdy's *63: Dream Palace*;
> Flannery O'Connor's *Wise Blood*; Norman Mailer's
> *The Naked and the Dead*; John Hawkes' *The Cannibal*;
> and William Burroughs' trilogy *Naked Lunch*, *The Soft
> Machine*, and *The Ticket That Explodes*.

530　Herr, Paul. "The Small, Sad World of James Purdy."
　　　*Chicago Review* 14 (autumn/winter 1960): 19-25.

> A very positive appreciation of Purdy as writer, artist,
> creator of "a world of his own. It is a small, sad world,
> but it is also very close to an accurate image of life in

America today." This study provides a careful analysis of *Malcolm* and relates Purdy's short story "Why Can't They Tell You Why?" to *Malcolm*. Herr states that Purdy "is a writer of integrity with a voice of his own [and] has a highly personal vision of his own—bitter, ironic and grotesque." Herr compares Purdy's writing to that of Nathaniel West and Samuel Beckett.

531    Hjorth, Daniel. "Saknad Ach Oskuld - James Purdy's Forfattarskap." *Bonniers Litteraera Magasin* 31 (summer 1962): 473-476.

An article written in Swedish which deals with Purdy's early writings—*Malcolm, 63: Dream Palace, Children is All*, and *The Nephew*.

532    Knickerbocker, Conrad. "Humor With a Moral Sting." *New York Times Book Review* (27 September 1964): 3, 60-61.

Knickerbocker believes that since World War II serious American fiction can be divided into two camps, white and black. Knickerbocker places Purdy along with Southern, Donleavy, Burroughs, Friedman, Pynchon, Gaddis, Barth and others on the black humorists list. Knickerbocker quotes Purdy as saying "I am in the position of liking the roots, somehow, of America and loathing everything it stands for today.... We live in the stupidest cultural era of American history. It is so stupid it inspires me." Knickerbocker refers to *Malcolm* and the short story "Daddy Wolf" as examples of Purdy's black humor.

533    Kostelanetz, Richard. "Notes on the American Short Story Today." *Minnesota Review* 5, nos.3-4 (1965): 214-221.

Points to writers such as James Purdy, Kenneth Koch, Tillie Olsen, and Thomas Pynchon as "model practitioners of the short story." He praises "Goodnight, Sweetheart," "Don't Call Me by My Right Name" and "63: Dream Palace." The article also contains a brief mention of *Malcolm* which, he says, "is a minor masterpiece in the absurd tradition—

taut, resonant, and almost European in its strong
control of every element."

534    ——. "The Point Is That Life Doesn't Have Any Point."
*New York Times Book Review* (6 June 1965): 3, 28, 30.

Kostelanetz discusses "absurd literature" written by
Beckett, Ionesco, Heller, Barth, Pynchon, Malamud and
Gaddis. He refers to James Purdy as one of the
authors in the 1960's whose work can be labeled
"absurd fiction."

535    ——, editor. "The New American Fiction." *Ramparts* 3
(January/February 1965): 57-60, 62.

Excerpt from *The New American Arts*, edited by
Richard Kostelanetz. Kostelanetz considers John
Barth, James Purdy, Vladimir Nabokov, and William
Burroughs as "The most interesting recent novelists."
Kostelanetz writes that "Absurdity and madness are
themes especially explored by the new novelists" and
"Purdy employs a wispy, low-key style, more
psychological and emotional sensitivity, and a knack for
creating the telling moment and resonant line—in
general, a greater artistic control—to produce a more
pruned absurd novel."

536    Krummel, Regina Pomeranz. "Two Quests in Two
Societies." *English Record* 17 (April 1967): 28-32.

Krummel compares and contrasts Purdy's *Malcolm* to
Raskolnikov of Dostoyevsky's *Crime and Punishment*.
Krummel notes that both Malcolm and Raskolnikov are
searching for their fathers; both are searching for a
"meaning in life by the absence of a link to a design for
a purpose in the world;" both authors "cast gloomy
gazes across an entire culture." Krummel concludes by
noting, "Purdy's world, unlike Dostoyevsky's, has
neither divine guidance nor the love of an earthly
father."

537    Levine, Paul. "The Intemperate Zone: The Climate of
Contemporary American Fiction." *The Massachusetts
Review* 8 (summer 1967): 505-523.

This essay is a discussion of contemporary fiction writers as Purdy, Friedman, Brossard, O'Connor, Capote, Burroughs, Barth, Mailer and others. Purdy's *Cabot Wright Begins* is used as one example of a writer whose main character "discovers that his identity as a human being lies outside the corrupting confines of contemporary society."

538    Lewis, R. W. B. "American Letters: A Projection." *Yale Review* 51 (autumn 1961): 211-226.

James Purdy is one of "the names I make out for honor in the postwar generation." Included also are Ralph Ellison, Saul Bellow, William Styron, Norman Mailer, and J. D. Salinger. Includes a discussion of *Malcolm*.

539    Lorch, Thomas M. "Purdy's *Malcolm*: A Unique Vision of Radical Emptiness." *Wisconsin Studies in Contemporary Literature* 6 (summer 1965): 204-213.

A detailed, careful analysis of Purdy's *Malcolm* in an attempt "to understand his [Purdy's] dark, perverse interpretation of contemporary life." Lorch begins his essay: "*Malcolm* is an important novel.... James Purdy not only ranks among the finest American novelists writing today; he has also established a radically original fictional voice.... Purdy's dislocated, grotesque world has a distinct quality all its own." Lorch writes: "In *Malcolm*, Purdy has created a world turned upside down, one in which everything is dislocated, disjointed and askew. The novel incorporates a number of recurrent patterns in American literature: the initiation of youth, the search for a father, the quest for identity, and the innocent victimized by society." Lorch concludes: "In *Malcolm*, Purdy presents a beautiful but terrifying portrait of man on the brink of non-being or perhaps having already passed over the edge."

540    Maloff, Saul. "James Purdy's Fictions: The Quality of Despair." *Critique* 6 (spring 1963): 106-112.

Maloff considers Purdy's writing, found in *Color of Darkness* and *Children is All* as the "real thing—a book that will stand alone, an authentic instance of the art of narrative." The author finds echoes in Purdy's writing to Kafka, Nathaniel West and Beckett. "Sound of Talking," "Mrs. Benson," "Daddy Wolf," "Sermon," "63: Dream Palace," "Cutting Edge," "Why Can't You Tell Me Why?" "Man and Wife," and "You Reach for Hat" are discussed. Maloff considers the end of Purdy's finest fiction, "63: Dream Palace" as "one of the perfect (and most moving) moments in modern fiction."

541  McNamara, Eugene. "The Absurd Style in Contemporary American Literature." *Humanities Association Review* 19 (spring 1968): 44-49.

A brief discussion of the absurd style in Purdy's *Malcolm*, Heller's *Catch-22*, and Pynchon's *V* and *The Crying of Lot 49*.

542  ——. "The Post Modern American Novel." *Queens Quarterly* 69 (summer 1962): 265-275.

Analyzes and compares Purdy's *Malcolm*, Styron's *The Long March* and *Lie Down in Darkness*, Gaddis's *The Recognitions*, and Griffin's *The Devil Rides Outside*. The author believes these four are the only writers of the post-modern American period who are "carefully going their own individual ways, seeking to perfect their aloof form, in spite of the vicious conditions of publishing in the United States." The author notes that the four are "technically innovative, impressively original and important in style ... and have thematic similarities. All are involved with the theme of violated love in our modern and the ultimate death of self because of that rejection. And all are concerned with the theme of the search for a father—both a literal father, a home, a source of creative love and life, and a symbolic father, a source of certitudes." He states that the style in *Malcolm* is "wild, burbling, heightened, extravagant" and the writing is a "unique work of art."

543  Miller, Paul W. "James Purdy's Early Years in Ohio and His Early Short Stories." *Midamerica: The Yearbook of*

*the Society for the Study of Midwestern Literature.* 11
(1984): 108-116.

An excellent analysis of the eleven short stories in
*Color of Darkness* in which he points out that they deal
with three "stages of conjugal or family disintegration
that must also have afflicted the Purdy family." The
first stage is "an early stage of declining expectations
from marriage, focused on the loss of love's mutuality
and of young romance" as seen in "Man and Wife,"
and "A Good Woman." The second is "of a later
stage of alienation of husband and wife, separated by
the death of love, symbolically portrayed, by ferocious
hatred for one another, or by literal, welcome death of
one partner in marriage" as noted in "Sound of
Talking," "Don't Call Me by My Right Name," and
"You Reach for Your Hat." The third stage consists
"of family disintegration, when the alienation of
husband and wife is reenacted in the next generation
through the alienation of child from parent and parent
from child as in "Why Can't They Tell You Why?,"
"Color of Darkness," and "Cutting Edge." This article
is of special importance because it provides some of the
most detailed biographical material found on Purdy's
family. Miller writes that William (Purdy's father),
Vera (Purdy's mother), and James and his two
brothers "suffered between 1908, the year the boys'
parents were married, and the dissolution of the Purdy
marriage through divorce twenty-two years later." In
the "Notes," Miller identifies James' older brother
Richard (1909-67) who became a professional actor,
and Robert (1921-  ) the youngest brother who served
as a coach and athletic director in Ohio schools up to
the time of his retirement.

544    ———. "James Purdy's Fiction as Shaped by the American
Midwest: The Chicago Novels." *Costerus.* New Series.
66 (1988): 149-161.

A remarkable study of Purdy's three novels set in
Chicago: *63: Dream Palace, Malcolm,* and *Eustace
Chisholm and the Works.* Miller notes: "the sustained
contrast between Purdy's Midwestern town novels and

his city novels is apparent. Whereas in the town novels Purdy repeatedly, some would say obsessively, portrays and analyzes various stages in the decline of the American family, in the city novels, taking the demise of the traditional family as a given, he shows the catastrophic impact of urban society on deracinated youth." Of very special importance in this study is Miller's identification in the Chicago novels of the characters to those in real life. He says Eloisa Brace and her husband Jerome in *Malcolm* are based on Gertrude Abercrombie and her husband Frank Sandiford in real life and Maureen O'Dell, the painter in *Eustace Chisholm*, is also Gertrude Abercrombie. He states the author Wendell Wilcox is Parkhearst Cratty of *63: Dream Palace* and he is Mr. Cox in *Malcolm* and Eustace Chisholm in *Eustace Chisholm*. In addition, Chicagoan Miriam Bomberger Bard Andreas and her husband Osborn appear in *63: Dream Palace* as Grainger the great woman and in *Malcolm*, "along with her husband Osborn, as Madame and Girard. Later Osborn Andreas appears as Reuben Masterson in *Eustace Chisholm*." Miller also concludes that Fenton Riddleway in *63: Dream Palace*, Malcolm in *Malcolm* and Amos Ratcliffe in *Eustace Chisholm* are portraits of Purdy himself. The majority of this fascinating essay is devoted to an analysis of *Eustace Chisholm*. In summary, Miller writes, "In retrospect one sees that Purdy's three urban novels give an artistic reflection of the lives and experiences of Purdy himself and some of his Chicago contemporaries from the 1930's to 50's, and more important, reveal increasing depth and complexity in their treatment of social problems and of the problem of evil."

545      ——."The Limits of Realism in James Purdy's First Ohio Novel *The Nephew." Midamerica: The Yearbook of the Society for the Study of Midwestern Literature*. 12 (1985): 83-96.

A careful analysis of *The Nephew*, in which Miller identifies Rainbow Center as "modeled on Bowling Green, Ohio," Boyd Mason as Purdy's divorced father, and Alma Mason as Purdy's Aunt Cora, his father's sister. He also identifies many of the other characters as neighbors to actual people living in Bowling Green. Listed under "Sources" is the note that "Miss Cora Purdy, Ex-Teacher, Dies" in December, 1966 and "William Purdy, 86, Realtor, Dies" in February, 1964.

546 Moore, Harry T. "The Present-Day American Novel." *Essays by Diverse Hands: Being the Transaction of the Royal Society of Literature*. New Series. 31 (1962): 123-142.

Professor Moore's essay was read at the Royal Society of Literature meeting on June 16, 1960. The essay covers the gambit of American fiction writers, touching on Fitzgerald, Faulkner, Hemingway, O'Hara, Nabokov, Donleavy, Styron, Jones, Purdy, and others.

547 Newman, Charles. "Beyond Omniscience: Notes Toward a Future for the Novel." *TriQuarterly*, No. 10 (fall 1967): 37-52.

In a study of the development of the modern novel, Newman discusses Bellow's *Herzog*, Capote's *In Cold Blood* and Purdy's *Cabot Wright Begins*. The major part of the article deals with the characters, plot and writing style of this novel. Newman states: "In many respects, Purdy is that last novelist. He carries Gide's ideas of the 'pure' novel—one which would leave the greatest amount possible to the reader's imagination—to its logical if absurd conclusion. He exemplifies Joyce's implicit assumption that originality in literature derives initially from waiving all literary conventions. He is Tolstoy's noble narrator who can 'explain' nothing of what he has seen. He exemplifies the new novelists' concern with art as criticism as much as creation. And he is Ortega's ultimate novelist for certainly he has forgotten enough. In short, he has given up every conceivable prop of omniscience. There is no conflict between imaginary and scientific psychology, because there is no longer any distinction between them. Purdy certifies that if a novel is to mean anything in our day, it must have as its central proposition the question of its own existence."

548    Numasawa, Koji. "Black Humor: An American Aspect." *Studies in English Literature* 44 (1968): 177-193.

A scholarly article on black humor as written by American authors. Discussed are: West's *A Cool Million*, Donleavy's *The Ginger Man*, Albee's *The American Dream* and *The Zoo Story*, Gelber's *The Connection*, Friedman's *Far From the City of Class*, Heller's *Catch-22*, Southern's *The Magic Christian*, and Purdy's *Malcolm*. Concerning *Malcolm*, Numasawa writes, "complete with the rumored resurrection of the hero, *Malcolm* once more is an example of the mock-religious black comedy."

549    Pease, Donald. "False Starts and Wounded Allegories in the Abandoned House of Fiction of James Purdy." *Twentieth Century Literature* 28 (fall 1982): 335-349.

A study of the characters in Purdy's works. Pease noted that the people in Purdy's novels are "orphans, abandoned children, foundlings and outcasts, who share a common inability to be salvaged by the world that pre-exists them." *Malcolm*, *The Nephew*, *Eustace Chisholm and the Works*, and *I Am Elijah Thrush* are analyzed in detail. A keen, unique observation made by Pease is that "The houses in Purdy's novels are not distinct from the paradisiacal settings, but wall in horticulture gardens where plants are displayed, animals stuffed and people dismembered. Images of the horticultural gardens reappear as shadowy backdrops in all of Purdy's novels: the park in *63: Dream Palace*, the wedding tavern in *Cabot Wright Begins*, Mrs. Maelstrom's greenhouse in *Eustace Chisholm and the Works*, Mrs. Barrington's lawn in *The Nephew*, the Arctury's Gardens in *I Am Elijah Thrush*, and the pastoral settings of *Jeremy's Version*, *The House of the Solitary Maggot*, and *In a Shallow Grave*."

550    Peden, Donald. "Out of Contrasts: Two Fictional
       Worlds." *Virginia Quarterly Review* 39 (spring 1963):
       346-348.

       Peden writes: "James Purdy is among the most
       distinguished members of a group of gifted American
       fiction writers including Jean Stafford and Flannery
       O'Connor, whose particular domain is the grotesque,
       the sick, and the abnormal—what in recent years has
       with increasing frequency been labeled American
       Gothic." Mentions work being published in "Prairie
       Schooner" and the "Black Mountain Review" and how,
       in 1956, "A group of his admirers—Chicago
       businessmen incidentally—subsidized and privately
       distributed his collection of new strange and haunting
       stories 'Don't Call Me by My Right Name.' "
       Discusses *Children is All* and notes that Purdy "writes
       without pretension using almost laconic dialogue
       reminiscent of Hemingway and O'Hara without being in
       any way imitative." Peden stresses Purdy's unusual
       talent, his uniqueness and his "concerns with
       loneliness, separateness, withdrawal and
       unknowableness." He concludes the article by
       discussing some of the works of Hortense Calisher,
       whose short stories are similar to Purdy's.

551    Pomeranz, Regina. "The Hell of Not Loving: Purdy's
       Modern Tragedy." *Renascence* 16 (spring 1964): 149-153.

       An excellent analysis of *Malcolm*, *The Nephew*, and
       the short stories in *Color of Darkness*—stresses
       Purdy's need to love someone at all costs. "When
       man has not found his 'self' he reaches out to death
       and frequently preys upon another calling at love.
       Dostoyevsky said that hell is the suffering of being
       unable to love. In his two novels and his short stories,
       Purdy sees loss of self and loss of human love and
       identity as Man's greatest tragedy." Briefly compares
       Purdy to Carson McCullers and J. D. Salinger and notes
       the resemblance of community life to that of
       Waynesburg, Ohio.

552    Profit, Marie-Claude. "Lecture(s) de Malcolm." *Revue Francaise D'Etudes Americaines* (Avril 1976): 135-143.

An article in French which "first analyzes the novel [*Malcolm*] with a view to showing its obvious structure.... The first time, to start a linear development, characterized by the repetition of abortive attempts at including Malcolm in some sort of plot: an open structure. The second time, to start a vectorial development. Malcolm is included in the plot, the character is irreversibly projected from one episode into the next and deteriorates to his and the novel's speedy end: a closed structure. The analysis reveals a number of anomalies. They lead me to suggest an altogether different, less immediate reading of the book: *Malcolm* as a work in progress, the characters as 'writer' and 'character,' the second part as a demonstration—and denouncing—of conventional fiction writing."

553    Renner, Stanley. " 'Why Can't They Tell You Why?': A Clarifying Echo of the Turn of the Screw." *Studies in American Fiction* 14 (autumn 1986): 205-213.

An excellent study and comparison of Purdy's "Why Can't They Tell You Why?" to Henry James's *The Turn of the Screw*. The author concludes with: " 'Why Can't They Tell You Why?' exposes the true story of *The Turn of the Screw*: the dramatization of the terrible developmental damage done to children by the Victorian sexual squeamishness in which they are brought up by the angel in the house, the great governess, the era, guardian of its moral and spiritual purity."

554    Ryan, Marjorie. "Four Contemporary Satires and the Problem of Norms." *Satire Newsletter* 6 (spring 1969): 40-46.

A discussion of Purdy's *Cabot Wright Begins*, Heller's *Catch -22*, Berger's *Reinhart in Love* and Barth's *Floating Opera*. Ryan compares and contrasts each novel with the others.

555    Schott, Webster. "James Purdy: American Dreams." *The Nation* 198 (23 March 1964): 300-302.

A study of Purdy's writings with emphasis on the characters in his novels and short stories. Of special importance are the many quotes from Purdy's letters, including the following: "all of my work is a criticism of the United States, implicit not explicit. This is a culture based on money and competition, is inhuman, terrified of love, sexual or other, obsessed with homosexuality and brutality. Our entire moral life is pestiferous and we live in a completely immoral atmosphere.... I am not even writing novels, I am writing me. I go on writing to tell myself at least what I have been through.... All of my work is, I believe, poetry, and therefore to be spoken. I write it spoken. I am only incidentally a story teller.... There don't seem to be any men or women in America; there are those who are young and have everything before them—and then there are the others, mostly dead.... I suppose one of the themes of my work is you must accept yourself and others, whatever they are.... I don't see despair in my writing, because I think my work is the truth.... We live in the stupidest cultural era of American history. It is so stupid it inspires me." This evaluation of Purdy's writings states: "Intensely private and as fixed in focus as a dime-store telescope, Purdy's work thus far constitutes the most arresting description of disassociation and human transgression to be found in American literature. It cannot be accounted for except in terms of naive genius and personal torment of the kind that would drive a man to self-destruction if he couldn't write."

556    Schwarzschild, Bettina. "Aunt Alma: James Purdy's *The Nephew*." *University of Windsor Review* 3 (fall 1967): 80-87.

A detailed discussion of Purdy's *The Nephew* with emphasis on the main character, Alma Mason. The article ends: "Cliff may not have had the gift to write of love, but this is James Purdy's greatest gift of all. Alma said of her nephew 'I never knew him, I only loved him.' Purdy shows us that in her act of love, nonetheless, she knew all that one can know of anyone."

557 ———. "Fenton Riddleway: 63: Dream Palace." *december* 8 (1966): 178-182.

A perceptive essay analyzing Purdy's *63: Dream Palace*. Ms. Schwarzschild examines the main character, Fenton Riddleway, and concludes: "Fenton Riddleway is himself with every fiber of his being, with every breath he takes and every word he says. And being himself he transcends and becomes us. That is his hold on our imagination."

558 ———. "The Forsaken: An Interpretive Essay on James Purdy's *Malcolm*." *Texas Quarterly* 10 (spring 1967): 170-177.

A detailed analysis of *Malcolm* using many quotations from the novels. Ms. Schwarzschild states: "The most despairing line of the book and perhaps in all of James Purdy's work is Mrs. Cox's prognostication of Kermit's doom, 'Kermit will never be able to say yes to anything again.' It is final and inevitable." The author compares Madame Gerard to "Isis and Other Great Mothers." The study notes: "In *Malcolm*, James Purdy has told us the eternal story of the child in the vocabulary of our time. It will have to be told again and again to remind us of our childhood and of the eternal bewildered child within us that needs the love and care and guidance toward self-realization that no one gave Malcolm."

559 Skerrett, Joseph Taylor, Jr. "Dostoievsky, Nathaniel West and Some Contemporary American Fiction." *The University of Dayton Review* 4 (winter 1967): 23-35.

The contemporary American novelists studied and compared to Nathaniel West are James Purdy, Bruce Jay Friedman, Joseph Heller, J. P. Donleavy, John Barth, and Thomas Pynchon. Skerrett labels these writers as the "Black Humorists." He notes that: "the works of the Black Humorists tend to be stylized and mannered in form, as was the poetry of the earlier half of the century." He states: "Among the Black Humorists, it is Purdy who most felicitously shares West's enthusiasm for the surreal techniques." The majority of the essay compares the main characters in West's *Miss Lonelyhearts* and *A Cool Million*; Purdy's *Malcolm* and *63: Dream Palace*, Barth's *The Sot-Weed Factor*, Friedman's *Stern* and Pynchon's *V*. Skerrett writes that: "the main characters of each of these novels learns, if anything is learned at all, that his grand conception of his own being and essence cannot be supported in reality. If there is any unifying common denominator to the Black Humorists' thought, it is the belief in the necessity of living life on a human scale, not in terms of impossible and absurd concepts and false importances. And this also they share with Nathaniel West."

560 ——. "James Purdy and the Works: Love and Tragedy in Five Novels." *Twentieth Century Literature* 15 (April 1969): 25-33.

A positive discussion of *63: Dream Palace*, *The Nephew*, *Malcolm*, *Cabot Wright Begins*, and *Eustace Chisholm and the Works*. Skerrett notes: "The vision of life presented by James Purdy in his five novels is a tragic one.... The world of theses novels is the world in the evening at the point of diminishment and loss.... The tragic action of each novel is played out against a background of more than vaguely symbolic chaos in the natural order and/or disruption of the social order."

561 ——. "James Purdy and the Black Mask of Humanity." *Melus* 6 (summer 1979): 79-89.

Discusses the images of black men and women in the writings of Purdy. Skerrett explores Joel Ullay in *Cabot Wright Begins*, Beaufort Vance and Luwana Edwards in *Eustace Chisholm and the Works*, Estel Blanc, George Leeds and Gus in *Malcolm*, Mahala in "Eventide," Naomi Green in "Scrap of Paper," Galway in "Summer Tidings," Burleigh Jordan in "On the Rebound," James de Salles in "Some of These Days," and Albert Peggs in *I Am Elijah Thrush*. Skerrett ends his fine essay with: "I do not know of another white American author who has created so satisfying a gallery of black portraits without resorting to history or sociology. Purdy's blacks do not merely illustrate in racial disguise conflicts dealt with elsewhere in his work, nor do they rehash traditional images uncritically. Perhaps this is the reason his critics and reviewers have not noticed the high incidences of black figures in his work, his black characters are so thoroughly integrated."

562    Spiegel, Alan. "A Theory of the Grotesque in Southern Fiction." *Georgia Review* 26 (winter 1972): 426-437.

Comments "that in the work of 'Northern' writers such as Nathaniel West, Nelson Algren, Ralph Ellison, John Hawkes, Joseph Heller and James Purdy we find the true modern expression of the Gothic perspective; that is, the world viewed as nightmare fantasy." The author uses an excerpt from Purdy's *Malcolm* to demonstrate this point.

563    Stetler, Charles. "Purdy's Malcolm: Allegory of No Man." *Critique: Studies in Modern Fiction* 14.3 (1973): 91-99.

A long, detailed analysis of Purdy's first novel, *Malcolm*. Stetler begins his essay: "Purdy has not written merely another novel of adolescence in a century already overstocked. Instead, he has offered up a sport on that type, using the genre to satirize it, with a wry approach to form as well as content. Viewed this way, the satire of an already cheerless book is deepened, and the blackness of its humor becomes more pervasive, more complete and more grim." Stetler ends: "Instead of the novel being an allegory of a young everyman, it is more an allegory of no man—the way Purdy sees modern man ... perhaps that is the way we must look at *Malcolm*, as ceremony, a texture with the substance deliberately removed. In a way the novel is like a whopping practical joke, because we are not supposed to hunt for meaning in a practical joke. Like life in the modern world, only the human is important."

564     Tanner, Tony. "Birdsong: I Am Elijah Thrush." *Partisan Review* 39 (fall 1972): 609-614.

> A long, positive analysis of *I Am Elijah Thrush*. Tanner takes the opposite view from his contemporary critics and sees this novel as a "hauntingly serious and beautifully written book." Tanner notes that one of its serious themes is "people living off each other without loving each other—as serious in Purdy as in Hawthorne and James." The review concludes, "Looked at another way, the book accepts that man, like a Beckett character, will go on muttering to the end, dreaming of a birdsong lost and a silence yet to be reached. But then this book does so many things, finally resisting demystification through its inexhaustible magic." Reprinted as "James Purdy's *I Am Elijah Thrush*." in *New Directions in Prose and Poetry* 26 (1973): 62-69.

565     ——. "My Life in American Literature." *TriQuarterly* 30 (1974): 83-108.

> Tony Tanner is an English critic of American fiction and a strong supporter of Purdy's writing. Tanner writes in this informal, autobiographical essay: "The result is a piece which is discursive, ambulatory and discontinuous." A small portion of the article compares his very positive review of Purdy's *I Am Elijah Thrush* (*Partisan Review*, fall 1972) to Margaret Drabble's negative review in which she found Purdy's novel "totally meaningless," while Tanner found it "both enjoyable and full of meaning."

566     ——. "Sex and Identity in *Cabot Wright Begins*." *Twentieth Century Studies* 2 (November 1969): 89-102.

> A very careful, detailed and positive analysis of *Cabot Wright Begins*. Tanner writes, "To my mind, not only Purdy's most profound novel but one of the most important novels since the war." This article was later published in Tanner's *The City of Words*.

568     Wilkinson, Jane. "James Purdy's Short Stories." *Studi Americani* Volume 23/24 (1977/1978): 345-364.

An excellent, detailed study of the short stories in
*Color of Darkness* and *Children is All*. Ms. Wilkinson
writes: "In the analysis of the topography of Purdy's
world it becomes evident that in all its features, its
space relationships, its sounds and silences, its
objects, plants and animals, its light, colour and
darkness, contribute, each in its specific way, to the
general sense of void and desolation." Many of the
stories are related to each other by themes, plots and
characters. Ms. Wilkinson notes: "In 'Sermon,' Purdy
gives us his most explicit illustration of his view of the
human condition 'by being infinitely repulsive you have
continued continuity and what more could any speaker
ask. What if you had become while I was talking. The
whole world would have changed, of course. You
would have all become alive. But the truth of the
continuum is that it is continuous. You have not failed
History. You have gone on with it, by continuing' but
all of his stories are pervaded by the feeling of
continuity, by a timeless flux, expressed in a series of
images and situations."

# C. Reviews

## *Cabot Wright Begins*

569     "The Black Humorists." *Time* 85 (12 February 1965): 94-
96.

A review article about a "new group of U. S. novelists"
including Purdy, Heller, Friedman, Barth and Donleavy.
The reviewer writes: "None of these recent writers has
yet stamped a unique signature on the times. They are
rogue talents, unpredictable, disturbing, and powerful
individuals. Thus, they form no cohesive school or even
a wave. Nonetheless, critics of late have taken to
calling them 'black humorists.' " A review of Purdy's
*Cabot Wright Begins* notes "On the surface, Purdy's
books seem simple, easy to read. In fact, they are only

easy to misread, and when approached carefully they turn out to be the blackest of all." Contains a photograph of Purdy.

570 "Books." "Age of Poop." *Newsweek* 64 (2 November 1964): 107-108.

A mixed review of *Cabot Wright Begins*. the reviewer writes, "James Purdy is absolutely infuriatingly real. He seems to have created out of the clay of colloquial American speech an entirely new language, precisely suited to his purposes.... At its best *Cabot Wright Begins* is furiously funny, but it is not wholly successful. No Swift, Purdy is unable to contrive the form adequate to contain the full fury of his feeling. Uncontained by formal control, disgust can become merely nasty, merely petulant."

571 Brophy, Brigid. "Native Sons." *New Statesman* 69 (4 June 1965): 886-887.

A review of six recent novels published in Great Britain which includes Purdy's *Cabot Wright Begins* along with Nadine Gordimer's *Not for Publication* and Richard Wright's *Lawd Today*. A short, mixed review which calls the novel a "black-comedic idea."

572 Clinton, F[arley]. "Books in Brief." *National Review* 17 (4 May 1965): 387.

A very negative review of *Cabot Wright Begins*. The reviewer writes, "James Purdy's reputation as a writer of special distinction seems to be a complete hoax, and he handles his delicate pathetic theme with every degree of falseness, clumsiness and bad taste."

573 Crews, Frederick C. "Review." *New York Review of Books* 3 (5 November 1964): 13-15.

A review of four novels including Purdy's *Cabot Wright Begins*. A mixed review in which the reviewer dislikes most of what Purdy has written. He ends his review: "The book explodes in a truly spectacular display of random aggression. Purdy sets up his argument so

that this debacle appears as a noble gesture of
refutation."

574    Darack, Arthur. "James Purdy's Humor At Its Best
Against American Hypocrisy." *Ohioana* 8 (spring 1965):
26-27.

A very positive review of *Cabot Wright Begins*. The
review details the plot and the characters in the novel.
Darack writes, "James Purdy is a novelist in the
tradition of Nathaniel West, with that author's savage
power, wild humor and the toughness to be tender
when every false human relationship has been stripped
away.... *Cabot Wright Begins* is aimed at exposing the
falseness Purdy detects in us, with his almost exultant
wildness of humor, his relentless attack, his racy
characters, and his sitting-duck targets." Contains a
photograph of Purdy by Fabian Bachrach and refers to
Purdy as a native of Fremont.

575    Donadio, Stephen. "The In Way Out." *Partisan Review*
32 (spring 1965): 299-303.

A review of six novels including Purdy's *Cabot Wright
Begins*. Donadio gives *Cabot* a negative review: "Mr.
Purdy, in the past, has shown himself to be a writer of
some competence, and for that reason his performance
here seems somewhat inappropriate, unless his only
purpose is to try one's patience."

576    Furbank, P. N. "Opting Out." *Encounter* 25 (October
1965): 80-84.

A review essay of Purdy's *Cabot Wright Begins*, Boll's
*The Clown* and Bassani's *The Garden of the Finzi-
Continis*. Furbank writes very favorably about *Cabot
Wright* and notes that "Purdy's high-camp black
humour is certainly one of the most authentic things in
American writing today. It is extraordinary the speed
and precision, the zestful ferocity with which, in a
sentence or a brief exchange of dialogue, he compasses
extremes of absurdity and violence." Compares
Purdy's writings to those of Angus Wilson.

577    Gloag, Julian. "One Weary Savage." *Saturday Review* 47 (12 December 1964): 50-51.

A mixed review of *Cabot Wright Begins*. Gloag notes, "Mr. Purdy loses all his cleverness and all his wit, and, wildly lambasting everything in sight, merely serves up a froth of the staggeringly obvious. Nevertheless, more than half of *Cabot Wright Begins* comes off." Gloag notes: "He [Purdy] has enough originality and (albeit specialized) talent to outlast most critics."

578    Goran, Lester. "Burlesque and Sarcasm." *Chicago Tribune Books Today* (15 November 1964): 8.

A mixed review of *Cabot Wright Begins*. Goran writes, "The point of *Cabot Wright Begins*, I think, is that the American people have been driven into sex as the only method by which they can assert their humanity, and even this has been taken away from them. As black humorists go, Purdy has suffered the fate of all men of great vision; he has lived to observe his techniques for distorting the face of humanity into rubberoid Halloween masks adopted by lesser men, his shocks become ritualized, his funny pop flight of dialog and comment out of soap opera become whole novels."

579    Hatch, Robert. "Peering In with the Outsiders." *Harper's Magazine* 230 (January 1965): 90-91.

A positive review of *Cabot Wright Begins*. Hatch also reviews Genet's *The Thief's Journal* and Burroughs' *Nova Express*, and consider all three writers as "Outsiders."

580    Howard, Elizabeth Jane. "The Strange Adventure." *The Spectator* 214 (4 June 1965): 727-728.

A review of five current novels which includes a short positive review of *Cabot Wright Begins*. Howard writes, "but in the sense that this is a nasty story told by a grown-up to nasty children, I suspect that it's characteristic of his [Purdy's] powers."

581    Hyman, Stanley Edgar. "The Conviction of Opinion." *New Leader* 47 (23 November 1964): 19-20.

A very negative review of *Cabot Wright Begins*, in which it is noted that "Purdy is neither a novelist nor a fiction writer. He is a social satirist, and at times a funny and effective one." Hyman takes to task much of Purdy's earlier praise by prominent literary figures as Sitwell, Dauches, Rexroth, Southern, Parker and Porter.

582     Laut, Stephen J. "Book Review." *Best Sellers* 24 (1 November 1964): 315.

A negative review of *Cabot Wright Begins*. The reviewer notes, "The chief voice Purdy finds in modern life is phoniness, the phoniness of writers, publishers, literary critics, the phoniness of family relationships, of marriage, of modern love and passion." Laut further states that the novel is not good satirical writing because "it is not enough to reveal the madness, confusion and non-sequiturs of life. There must be a pity, a love of men, despite his foibles. This book is clever, too clever for its own good."

583     Malin, Irving. "Melange a Trois." *Ramparts* 3 (March 1965): 79-80.

A positive review of *Cabot Wright Begins*, which concludes, "Despite the repetitious incidents and cluttered sermons, *Cabot Wright Begins* is brilliantly effective when Purdy allows his images to live in his characters. Cabot 'ticks' as do his clocks and pulse, especially when he says HA! to the world itself. HA! helps him to be more than another grotesque image; it makes him defiantly human."

584     Moon, Eric. "Fiction." *Library Journal* 89 (15 October 1964): 3973-3974.

Review of *Cabot Wright Begins*. A very positive review that notes, "It is a wildly funny book, beautifully written, and with a deadly serious underlay."

585     Mudrick, Marvin. "All That Prose." *Hudson Review* 18 (spring 1965): 110-123.

A long review essay on seventeen current works including Purdy's *Cabot Wright Begins*, Pritchet's *The Key to My Heart* and Lessing's *Children of Violence*. Cabot receives a very positive review and Mudrick writes, "It is a relief to turn to so professional a purveyor of Grand Guignol as James Purdy, who takes the new freedom for his very Muse."

586    "Notes on Current Books." *Virginia Quarterly Review* 41 (winter 1965): 8.

A very positive review of *Cabot Wright Begins* which states, "His book is a passionate plea for sanity at a moment when it is later than we think, phrased in idiomatic terms comprehensible even to dullards; as such it deserves wide recognition for its pertinence and importance at a critical point both in the history of literature and that of Western culture."

587    Oates, Joyce Carol. "Notions Good and Bad." *Kenyon Review* 27 (winter 1965): 175-180.

A review of Purdy's *Cabot Wright Begins*, Kesey's *Sometimes a Great Notion*, and Stafford's *Bad Characters*. Oates' dislike of *Cabot* is evident when she writes, "at its worst, however, Purdy's satire is noisy and tedious and inexplicably commonplace."

588    O'Conner, Patricia T. "New & Noteworthy." *New York Times*, 19 January 1986, sec. 7, p. 32.

A brief review of the 1986 paperback edition of *Cabot Wright Begins* which quotes from Susan Sontag's earlier and very positive review when the novel was first published.

589    Petersen, Clarence. "Review." *Chicago Tribune*, 5 January 1986, arts sec., p. 30.

A brief review of the new paperback edition of *Cabot Wright Begins* in which Peterson writes that "Purdy brings off a satirical tour de force."

590    Pollock, Venetia. "New Novels." *Punch* 248 (30 June 1965): 976.

A review of Purdy's *Cabot Wright Begins* and
Buechner's *The Final Beast*. Pollock provides a very
positive review and notes, "This is a magnificent,
terse, debunking with effortless good nature, much
warm affection and light liveliness."

591    Poston, Lawrence, III. "Review." *Books Abroad* 39
       (spring 1965): 219.

A positive review of *Cabot Wright Begins*. In
summarizing the plot Poston notes that "the point here
is that Purdy, a talented and skillful moralist, is less
concerned with verisimilitude than with an explanation
of the resources of comedy."

592    Prescott, Orville. "The Waste of a Small Talent." *New
       York Times*, 19 October 1964, p. 31.

A very negative review of *Cabot Wright Begins*, which
states that the novel "is as wretched a waste of small
talent and of a reader's time as any novel published in
recent years."

593    Pryce-Jones, Alan. "3 Gifted Men Rummage Through
       Garbage Cans." *New York Herald Tribune Book Review*
       (12 November 1964): 15.

A review of three current novels: *Last Exit to Brooklyn*
by Hubert Selby Jr., *Nova Express* by William S.
Burroughs and Purdy's *Cabot Wright Begins*. Pryce-
Jones gives *Cabot Wright* a mixed review and notes,
"Mr. Purdy has much to be said for him. He can be
extremely funny; he conveys cold dislike with great
skill; he purses his lips into a beautiful retch. But he
has constructed his account of Cabot Wright the rapist,
and the book which is to be written about him, like a
set of Chinese boxes, and the boxes do not fit. Maybe
Mr. Purdy has tried to work off too much spleen; maybe
he is at best in a short story. Parts of his latest book
succeed as wry entertainment, the whole fails as a
work of art." Contains a photograph of Purdy.

594    Saal, Rollene W. "Pick of the Paperbacks." *Saturday
       Review* 48 (20 November 1965): 40.

A brief review of the Avon paperback editions of *Cabot Wright Begins*, *Color of Darkness*, and *Children is All*. Reviewer notes, "Purdy employs the Lenny Bruce frontal attack to illuminate the human experience."

595     Solotaroff, Theodore. "A Stud Farm for Horselaughs." *New York Herald Tribune Book Review* (18 October 1964): 3.

A very positive review of *Cabot Wright Begins*. The review is preceded by a positive, analytical examination of Purdy's earlier work. Solotaroff favorably compares Purdy to Welty, O'Connor, Malamud, Hawkes, Barth, McCullers and Gaddis. Solotaroff notes that "Purdy's most powerful characters are isolates who have suffered or are suffering the loss of an essential emotional tie and are thereby rendered vulnerable to the depredations of others and the ravages of their own endless sorrow and rage. Dread, anxiety, perversion, grotesqueness, obscenity—motifs of modern writing—enter Purdy's stories as naturally as they do nightmares, without particular reference to contemporary culture." Solotaroff further writes that in *Cabot Wright Begins*, "Purdy has suddenly turned away from these lonely and timeless preoccupations. *Cabot Wright Begins* strikes out at the contemporary world with a vengeance, almost as though all of Purdy's hatred of it, which he had been suppressing for the sake of his art, had suddenly boiled up and spilled over." Solotaroff notes, "Purdy is a naturalist of unusual subtlety and a fantasist of unusual clarity.... It remains to say, of course, that a writer who takes on our culture today is hard put to maintain his wits amid the witlessness of detachment and deliberateness of art still remains the best defense against the grotesqueness and biliousness that infect our minds. The main thrust of Purdy's career has been to make us aware of this truth."

596     Sontag, Susan. "Laughter in the Dark." *New York Times Book Review* (25 October 1964): 5.

A wonderful review of *Cabot Wright Begins* and an
important analysis of Purdy's writing. Sontag notes:
"There is Purdy the satirist and fantasist; Purdy the
gentle naturalist of American, particularly small-town
American life; and Purdy the writer of vignettes or
sketches, which give us a horrifying snapshot image of
helpless people destroying each other. In other words,
a Purdy that can be compared, respectively, with
Nathaniel West, with Wright Morris, with Carson
McCullers." Concerning *Cabot Wright Begins*, she
writes, "*Cabot Wright Begins* may not be Purdy's best
book, but it is one of his best. It is a fluent, immensely
readable, personal and strong work by a writer from
whom everyone who cares about literature has
expected and will continue to expect, a great deal."

597    Taylor, Griffin. "Time and the Annihilators: Five Views
       on Seeking and Finding at Mid-Century." *Sewanee
       Review* 73 (autumn 1965): 736-747.

       A long review including Purdy's *Cabot Wright Begins*,
       White's *The Burnt Ones*, Stafford's *Bad Characters*,
       Janeway's *Accident* and Gerber's *Stop Here, My
       Friend*. Taylor provides a positive review of *Cabot* and
       writes, "Mr. Purdy's invention and skill in using his
       wide knowledge are awesome. He is possessed with a
       shattering mirth at what he sees. The measure of his
       sympathy with suffering humanity is to be gauged by
       the laughter he evokes, and this book makes one laugh
       a great deal." Taylor compares this work to *The
       Ginger Man* by Donleavy and notes that Purdy "has
       much in common with the European dramatists,
       Durrenmott, Max Frisch and N. F. Simpson, for
       example, who believe that the tragic hero is no longer
       possible, because the conditions for tragedy no longer
       exist."

598    Walsh, George. "A Look Through an Honest Spyglass."
       *Cosmopolitan* 158 (January 1965): 32.

       A strong review of *Cabot Wright Begins* in which the
       reviewer writes, "James Purdy, in this magnificent,
       hilarious, incisive satire, turns the spyglass of utter

honesty on these idle, flapping gonfalons, reveling them once and for all as the tattered, tawdry ensigns they really are.... James Purdy's book is a unique novel of our times. As a slashing attack on modern values, it has no peer."

599     Weatherby , William. "The Choler of Despair." *Times Literary Supplement* (10 June 1965): 474.

A positive review of *Cabot Wright Begins* and a discussion of *The Nephew*, *Malcolm* and *63: Dream Palace*. Concerning *Cabot Wright*, the reviewer writes, "With this novel, Mr. Purdy seems to have reached an extreme in his vision: he has created (or reflected?) a world begging for destruction or at least some storm of sanity to wash it clean. What saves him from despair is his humour. *Cabot Wright Begins* is not only the most savage of satires on the American way of life or way of death, as Mr. Purdy would have it; it is also an extremely funny book. He even succeeds in making rape seem almost a Thurberish subject, and the flat, careful Ohio tone of the precise style is just right for dead-pan effects.... If the Purdy style has the tread and music of Ohio, his viewpoint is very much that of an Ohio traveller abroad. Whatever his memory of solid values and the possibility of innocence among the frame houses, he seems to be appalled by what he finds in comparison in the great world beyond. Whether in Chicago or New York, the cities he knows best as a writer, he is forever being faced by the destruction of people, physically or spiritually. Apparently finding love only in some dream of the vanished Ohio frame houses, he still searches endlessly for it, scorning no place and no character, whether among the manipulators of *Malcolm* or the victims of *Cabot Wright*." "As the tone and rhythm of the style have not changed, we suspect that Mr. Purdy has taken to satire as Swift did, and although in many ways this is his most brilliant novel, it is also his most dangerous because he is driving himself to an extreme rejection."

600    Wilson, Angus. "The Horror Game." *The Observer* (London), 30 May 1965, p. 27.

> Positive review of *Cabot Wright Begins*. Wilson writes that *Cabot* is Purdy's "funniest novel, funny in a simple, sometimes crude way, suited to its target.... Mr. Purdy has succeeded in writing a comic book in a bad taste that is quite deliberate and almost always under his control; that is not an easy feat."

## *The Candles of Your Eyes and Thirteen Other Stories*

601    Christophersen, Bill. "Reviews." *Studies in Short Fiction* 25 (fall 1988): 492-493.

> A mixed review of *The Candles of Your Eyes and Thirteen Other Stories*. Chistophersen writes, "Each of these tales showcases a different aspect of Purdy's ductile art, which ranges from realism to romance to camp to satire to soap opera ... but at their best, these stories—original, unflinching, spare—afford an unwonted glimpse into the fissures of the social bedrock and those who shelter there."

602    Eidus, Janice. "Book Review: *The Candles of Your Eyes and Thirteen Other Stories*." *Review of Contemporary Fiction* 12 (summer 1992): 202.

> A favorable review which begins, "I love all of James Purdy's work" and ends with, "This remarkable collection of stories is a showcase for Purdy's talent; he's alternately wild and campy, fierce and grim, smart and tender, and always complex and original, always extraordinary."

604    Munk, Erika. "Scares and Giggles." *New York Times Book Review* (6 September 1987): 23.

> A mixed review of *The Candles of Your Eyes*. Munk writes, "*The Candles of Your Eyes* includes fourteen pieces, many of them extremely short, covering almost twenty years of Mr. Purdy's writing; it's his third collection and, to no surprise, wildly uneven. The near-

magical delights of a thrown voice neatly caught in midflight are too often overtaken by the clacking of dummy figures crudely manipulated to give us a scare or a giggle, and the writer's compassion for his characters' naiveté can turn into a complicitous wink at the audience."

605    Nichols, Loxley F. "Book Reviews." *National Review* 40 (4 March 1988): 50-52.

A review of both *Candles of Your Eyes* and *In the Hollow of His Hand*. Nichols finds only half of the stories in *The Candles of Your Eyes* successful. The review of *In the Hollow of His Hand* is mixed with Nichols noting "The writing, especially in the first 105 pages, is luxuriant and masterly and the characters are compelling not only to the reader but to one another." However, the review ends by noting: "Purdy is rather like eating kumquats: colorful and exotic experimentation, but hardly substantial for a meal."

606    Overmyer, Janet. "Review." *Ohioana Quarterly* 31 (autumn 1988): 140-141.

A positive review of *The Candles of Your Eyes*. Overmyer notes that in these short stories "people need people, hardly an original observation, but one which Purdy demonstrates repeatedly. And they need each other even if the others are unsuitable or not to be found."

607    Schmieder, Rob. "Fiction." *Library Journal* 112 (1 May 1987): 84-85.

A very positive review of *The Candles of Your Eyes and Thirteen Other Stories*. Schmieder writes, "These stories confirm Purdy's true gift for fiction; he uses the short story form to work out the themes of sexual obsession, ecstatic love, and fathomless disillusionment familiar from his novels, but with a brusque, at times cartoon like execution."

608    Slavitt, David R. "James Purdy's Wacky but Elegant Love Stories." *Chicago Tribune*, 5 July 1987, p. 5.

A very positive review of *Candles of Your Eyes and Thirteen Other Stories.* Reviewer describes James Purdy as a marvel and notes, "These short stories would be an intolerably bleak vision of human experience, if it were not redeemed by Purdy's quirky compassion and illuminated by the virtuoso linguistic turns which he bedecks and mollifies these sad etchings."

609     Steinberg, Sybil S. "Fiction." *Publishers' Weekly* 231 (27 March 1987): 35-36.

A very positive review of *The Candles of Your Eyes* in which Steinberg writes, "This collection of fourteen stories from the veteran author of Southern gothic has a delightful freshness and vitality. As usual, Purdy, a superb storyteller, builds from small intimacies."

## Children Is All

610     Beck, Warren. "An Absorbed Commitment to a Restricted Vision." *Chicago Sunday Tribune Magazine of Books* (18 November 1962): 6.

A positive review of *Children is All.* Beck compares Purdy's writing to Conrad, Anderson and Faulkner. Beck notes that "the purity and peculiar force of Purdy's work ushers in the absorbed commitment to a restricted vision."

611     Booth, Wayne C. "Everybody's a Mistake." *New York Times Book Review* (18 November 1962): 4, 50.

A positive review of *Children is All* which states: "Of the many writers who are searching for meaning among our ruins, few conduct the search with the conviction and forte achieved by James Purdy in this collection of ten stories and two plays. By resisting the temptation to over-burden his characters with concepts, he manages, in these terse, wrenching pieces, to conduct a running battle with meaninglessness and despair, and to win the battle, without seeming to have cheated."

612     Brooke, Jocelyn. "New Fiction." *The Listener* 70 (15
        August 1963): 249.

> A review of four works including Purdy's *Children is All*
> and Brophy's *The Finishing Touch*. A very positive
> review which states: "He [Purdy] is a true original,
> and these stories seem to me quite startlingly
> effective." And, "He is also remarkably versatile, both
> in style and content; he can be witty, macabre, touching
> and whimsical (in the best sense) by turns."

613     Davenport, Guy. "Three Miscellanies." *National Review*
        14 (26 February 1963): 162-163.

> A review of recent works by Purdy, O'Hara, and
> Tomasi di Lampedusa. A positive review of *Children is
> All* which ends: "This is good writing and derives from
> discipline and understanding, but nowhere in this
> collection has Mr. Purdy found a theme worthy of his
> technique."

614     DeMott, Benjamin. "The New Books." *Harper's* 226
        (January 1963): 91-92.

> Nine short reviews including *Children is All*. DeMott
> notes that "Purdy's matter is, in large measure the
> commonplace stuff of contemporary fiction—
> exacerbation, fury, perversion, nightmare—but his
> manner is remarkable:  austere, impressive and
> impeccably controlled."

615     Hassan, Ihab. "Of Anguish and Incongruity." *Saturday
        Review*  45 (17 November 1962): 29.

> A very positive review of *Children is All*. The review
> notes, "The uncanny technical skill of Purdy brings his
> material to life because it is backed by an authentic
> vision of love, anguish and incongruity. When the
> vision falters, the work becomes fussy, nasty or
> narrow. But this so seldom occurs that we can rejoice
> again in the possession of this new work by one of
> America's best writers."

616     Horchler, Richard. "Impending Revelations."
        *Commonweal* 77 (4 January 1963): 393-395.

A negative review of *Children is All*. In summary, the reviewer writes that the collection of short stories and plays "is weak and faltering. Some of the stories in it are masterful, most of them are impressive. Even at their best, however, they add up, for me, to little more than a sudden wrench of pain, a shudder, a glimpse of the moving darkness. Brilliant and rare as these displays may be, I am afraid there is little in them to engage us very long."

617     Malin, Irving. "Occasions for Loving." *Kenyon Review* 25 (spring 1963): 348-352.

A review of four books that deal "with the supposed growth for loving." Purdy's *Children is All*, Gordimer's *Occasion for Loving*, Carter's *A Fortune in Dimes* and Updike's *The Centaur* are reviewed. A positive review which states "Purdy uses the images of imprisonment, homelessness, and parasitism in a beautifully controlled strange way."

618     Price, R. G. G. "New Novels." *Punch* 245 (14 August 1963): 247-248.

A review of four works including Purdy's *Children is All*. Price gives the collection of short stories a mixed review and states, "Mr. Purdy is good at thinking of peculiar situations but all he does with them is to stage them and go away with a shrug suggesting he has just symbolized the predicament of contemporary man or the tragic dilemma or the dangers of voting Republican or something."

619     Rama Rau, Santha. "The Limits of Miniature." *New Leader* 46 (1 April 1963): 25-26.

A positive review of *Children is All*. The reviewer notes that "Purdy creates some extraordinary moving moments and some deep insights into the lonely, troubled people about whom he writes."

620     Scott, Winfield Townley. "The Zephyrs of Death." *New Republic* 147 (17 November 1962): 25-26.

A very positive review of *Children is All*. Scott writes that Purdy is "rather complex and special" and concludes "so Purdy continues to be the exciting writer he has been from the very first."

621 Sitwell, Dame Edith. "Purdy: The Marrow of Form." *New York Herald Tribune Book Review* (18 November 1962): 6.

This is the famous review by Sitwell of *Children is All* in which she begins, "I think it undoubted that James Purdy will come to be recognized as one of the greatest living writers of fiction in our language. Perhaps the word 'fiction' is wrong: for these works are not the production of imagination alone. They are the raw material of life itself, shaped by a great artist. He pierces down to the most secret places of the heart, then brings those secret places into the light of the all-seeing, the compassionate sun, that, like the fire of Christ, loves all that lives." The review ends: "*Children is All* is, to my mind, a sublime work of pity and tenderness. It could only have been written by a great writer."

622 Taubman, Robert. "Clerical Errors." *New Statesman* 66 (16 August 1963): 66.

A review of eight recently published books in Great Britain including Purdy's *Children is All*. A positive review which states, "James Purdy's expert conversation pieces—10 stories and two short plays—use the Miss Lonelyheart's Theme in leisured class settings." The review concludes, "Mr. Purdy has more literary resourcefulness than most of the younger, American writers, and also needs it, for this material hasn't much feel of being first-hand and hard-won."

623 Zinnes, Harriet. "Review." *Books Abroad* 37 (summer 1963): 339-40.

A very positive review of *Children is All*. Zinnes writes, "Purdy's intensity lies in his power to isolate the rhythms and textures of these inner fears and to translate them into language that rolls in one's head long after the book has been closed. The dialogue (and his stories are essentially dialogue) never reveals character, it always reveals the torment of the character."

## *Color of Darkness*

624    Adelman, George. "Fiction." *Library Journal* 83 (15 January 1958): 201.

A short, negative book review of *Color of Darkness*. However, Adelman notes, "The writing is, from some points of view, very praiseworthy. Mr. Purdy's stories are presented with great subtlety, precision and even delicacy. And his ability to literally rack reader's feelings with horrifying situations is extremely skillful."

625    "American Baroque." *Times Literary Supplement* (24 March 1961): 181.

A review of three works of fiction including Purdy's *Color of Darkness* and *The Nephew*. *Color of Darkness* is "a staggering book. It has the hypnotic power over a reader that is exercised by Mr. Truman Capote and Miss Carson McCullers; but it is without the overheated atmosphere and stylistic self-intoxication into which they sometimes lapse. Also, its range of idiom is wider. It is not merely that some of the stories are comic and some macabre; what Mr. Purdy possesses is an ability to combine passionate concentration with a detached assessment of the importance of his subject matter." Concerning *The Nephew* the reviewer writes, "If it is a function of literature to extend our normal range of sympathies, then this is a novel to be reckoned with, for one cannot read it and remain indifferent to the lives of the very old."

626    Bailey, Anthony. "The Possessed." *Commonweal* 67 (17 January 1958): 415.

A very positive review of the New Directions edition of *Color of Darkness*. Bailey ends his review by writing, "Mr. Purdy, through the natural rhythm of his dialogue, the acute daring of his art, has made for a novel departure in the craft of the short-story. In fact, he has made the work of many highly skilled writers seem extremely dependent on literary convention and, in doing so, has made fresh contact with moral reality."

627    Baruch, Gertrud. "Review of *Color of Darkness*." *Bucherei und Bildung* 11 (1959): 897.

Gertrude Baruch describes Purdy's recurring theme as hopelessness and lack of contact in a world where the old value system has been deformed into its opposite. According to Baruch, Purdy uses the precision of dialogues and monologues to uncover the brink of loneliness, in which man cannot escape nothingness and friend and enemy, love and hatred, joy and agony cannot be differentiated any more because the ability to reach each other has died. Baruch suggests that *Color of Darkness*—not so much as a book to enjoy but to be admired, because it repels and gets under the skin—should be present in all libraries.

628    Bergonzi, Bernard. "Despite his Cleverness." *The Spectator* 206 (24 March 1961): 416.

A review of *Color of Darkness* and *The Nephew*. Bergonzi writes, "but in performance Mr. Purdy succeeds nearly all the time, despite his cleverness." Concerning *Colour Of Darkness* (1961 reissue) Bergonzi states, "Mr. Purdy writes with detachment that is compassionate rather than ironic, and the result is sometimes comic, sometimes pathetic and occasionally both." Concerning *The Nephew* the reviewer writes, "Mr. Purdy has all the gifts of a straightforward naturalistic writer; his characters, even the most eccentric, are firm and plausible, and his dialogue, though stylised, is authentic."

629    Bittner, William. "The State of the Story." *The Nation* 186 (11 January 1958): 34-36.

A review of twelve collections of short stories, including a short review of *Color of Darkness*. Bittner notes, "For all the variety of settings and characters in the book, the stories have a single, indeed a cumulative, effect for they all seem to reflect what a tenuous hold the human being has on dignity." "Purdy, at any rate, is that rare bird in this age of reportorial fiction, a writer who creates."

630     "The Canker of Comedy." *Time* 70 (9 December 1957): 114.

A positive review of Purdy's first collection of short stories, *Color of Darkness*, published by New Directions. The reviewer writes that "Ohio-born James Purdy, 34, writes in a manner that is all his own ... all his stories are grotesque, but caught in them, like the tremble of a bird in cupped hands, is the undeniable flutter of life."

631     Ferguson, Joe M., Jr. "Review." *New Mexico Quarterly* 28 (spring 1958): 70-71.

A positive review of *Color of Darkness* which states: "Possessor of a bizarre imagination and deft hand at dialogue, which is always frank and sometimes slightly humorous, the American writer James Purdy offers a reading experience which is not only entertaining and perturbing, but truly different."

632     Hogan, William. "A New Portrait of the Artist As a Young Man." *San Francisco Chronicle*, 20 December 1957, p. 19.

A mixed review of the American edition of *Color of Darkness*. The review compares Purdy's writing to Jack Kerouac's and Christopher Fry's. The reviewer dislikes Purdy's use of the four-letter word and writes, "the talent is too sharp to waste in gents' room walls." The reviewer concludes, "*Color of Darkness*, at the same time, may signal the approach of something big, I wish James Purdy discipline—and luck."

633     Kolve, Del. "James Purdy: An Assessment." *Time and Tide* 42 (23 March 1961): 476-477.

A very positive review of *The Nephew*, *Colour of Darkness*, which includes *63: Dream Palace* and

*Malcolm*. Kolve writes that in the three books "the surfaces are so brilliant, the fictions so apparently marginal to real life, that they can be thought merely an exorcism of dreams or an exercise in style. They are more; they build on parable, and it is on this level that the true 'substance' must be sought, the serious relationship between this novelist's art and his reader's experience of life."

634    Maddocks, Melvin. "Short Fiction in a Contemporary Pattern." *Christian Science Monitor*, 9 January 1958, p. 7.

A negative review of *Color of Darkness* which notes, "Mr. Purdy is an earnest and outspoken writer who may be afraid to paint with colors lighter than grey for fear of seeming a sold-out optimist."

635    McCarthy, Patrick J. "Book Reviews." *Arizona Quarterly* 14 (summer 1958): 169-170.

A mixed review of *Color of Darkness* which states: "The reader soon protests that this is too much. There is no denying that Purdy is a writer of talent. We may admire the skill that can rack our feeling so mercilessly, that can maintain so perfectly this somber consistency of tone. We readily concede that his powers of invention are high; these are genuinely new stories told by a distinctive, original voice ... but our admiration is given grudgingly."

636    Miller, Nolan. "The New Fiction—Summary." *Antioch Review* 17 (winter 1957): 519-524.

A review of sixteen new novels including *Color of Darkness*. Miller gives Purdy's first collection of short stories a very positive review and writes, "James Purdy in a very low key makes unforgettable the naked look of ordinary but frighteningly countless lives. His people could be anybody, are probably almost everybody; we are stunned by our look at them, caught as they are in his stories, and we will never forget them."

637     Mudrick, Marvin. "Is Fiction Human?" *Hudson Review* 11 (spring 1958): 294-301.

   A review essay of seven new short story collections by individual writers. Purdy's *Color of Darkness* received a positive review. Mudrick writes, "James Purdy has a diabolical ear for low-life dialogue, and his attitude toward the human race is that of an exterminator toward cockroaches.... Mr. Purdy's attitude is always a rather remote disgust, and his aim is always horror."

638     "Paperbacks." *Best Sellers* 30 (15 November 1970): 363.

   Just a brief mention of the Bantam edition of *Color of Darkness*. Noted, "There is about the short stories of James Purdy some of the quality of James Joyce's work in the same genre."

639     Parker, Dorothy. "Dorothy Parker on Books: Four Rousing Cheers." *Esquire* 50 (July 1958): 18, 20.

   A review of Donleavy's *The Ginger Man*, O'Connor's *Memoirs by a Public Baby*, Nicolson's *Journey to Java* and Purdy's *Color of Darkness*. A positive review of *Color of Darkness* in which Parker writes, "For here is a striking new American talent, sure and sharp and powerful. It is no cluster of sunbeams, and perhaps it is a filthy trick to Mr. Purdy, as it is to the author of any collection of short pieces—sketches, perhaps these might be called—to read his book right through at a setting. Read separately, the pieces come back to you and stay, and you realize that each one is well worth your keeping."

640     Peden, William. "And Never a Silver Lining." *New York Times Book Review* (29 December 1957): 4.

   A very positive review of *Color of Darkness* which notes, "Perhaps not since the early stories of Tennessee Williams or Angus Wilson has there been so disturbing a 'first' volume of short fiction.... *Color of Darkness* is the work of a gifted writer who appears ruthlessly honest in creating his own particular segment of a world bereft of traditional values."

641 ——. "Short Fiction as Long." *Saturday Review* 41 (25 January 1958): 17-18.

> A review of five first collections of short stories including Purdy's *Color of Darkness* and works by Godden, Farrell, Brodsky and Block, all of whom Peden considers to be "young, talented and individualistic American short-story writers." He notes that Purdy's stories are "of almost unbearable loneliness, of unhappy individuals struggling to achieve communication and understanding, but who are lost in private hells only partially of their own making." Includes a small photograph of Purdy.

642 "Pick of the Paperbacks." *Saturday Review* 48 (20 November 1965): 40.

> Notice of the Avon edition of *Color of Darkness*.

643 Ray, David. "Three Reviews." *Epoch* 11 (spring 1961): 126-130.

> Reviews of Purdy's *Color of Darkness*, Curley's *The Marriage Bed and Other Stories* and Poirier's *Stories 1961*. The short positive review of *Color of Darkness* places more emphasis on Purdy's problems of getting published than on the collection of stories.

644 Schurenberg, Walter. "An Abrund Enteang." *Neue Deutsche Hefte* 6 (August 1959): 462-463.

> A review of James Purdy's *Color of Darkness: Eleven Stories and a Novella*, that identifies the desolate condition of human communication as the common denominator of these stories. According to Walter Schurenberg, "In Purdy's work objects or symbols function as a trigger to uncover the brink of disaster along which the characters in the stories move. After two or three characters are introduced, miseries of life and anomalies are drawn to the surface during the dialogues, where the reader can recognize them while the characters involved either continue to hide them, thus maintaining their face, or it comes to an open eruption" Schurenberg's review is favorable, acknowledging Purdy's exceptional talent and

sensitivity, however not without alluding to a sense of depression and helplessness the book triggers in the reader, and questioning why Purdy writes almost exclusively in "Colors of Darkness."

645     Scott, Nathan, "Enter a Writer, Talented and Intense." *New York Herald Tribune Book Review*, (29 December 1957): 3.

A very positive review of *Color of Darkness*. Scott writes, "James Purdy can write of ordinary people with an intensity so saddening as to be terrifying. It is not easy to say how he does this. His prose is seemingly simple, direct, and yet it is (almost unanalyzably) filled with those undertones which a writer can command only instinctively—he has them by birthright or not at all. These stories bring one up close against living, breathing people as Gertrude Stein does in 'Three Lives,' and they have some of the pitying but uncompromised love that broods over Sherwood Anderson's 'Winesburg, Ohio.' They are not derivative, Purdy is his own man." Scott concludes, "Even in stories of real life, horror or terror are not, finally, enough. But the talent in *Color of Darkness* is so authoritative one expects it to do yet deeper things. It is a rich and passionate talent, already capable of memorable work, an excitement in new American writing." Contains a photography of Purdy.

646     Sundel, Alfred. "The Limp-Wrist School." *New Leader* 44 (19 June 1961): 25-26.

A very negative review of *Color of Darkness*. The review is very anti-homosexual and compares Purdy's writing to Capote and Goyen. In discussing *63: Dream Palace*, Sundel uses the term "faggot" continually to describe the characters.

## Don't Call Me by My Right Name and Other Stories

647    Bailey, Anthony. "The Uneven, Rewarding Country of the
       Short Story." *Commonweal* 65 (8 February 1957): 491.

       A very positive review of *Don't Call Me by My Right
       Name and Other Stories.* Bailey writes about Purdy's
       style as being "lucid, strong and extraordinarily
       evocative. His prose has demotic rhythms, the lilt of
       natural, American speech; and the characters spring
       forth like crops from fertile soil." The short story
       "Sound of Talking" is pointed out as an example of
       outstanding writing.


## Dream Palaces

648    Gunn, Thom. "All Pretty Much Strangers." *The
       Threepenny Review* 1 (fall 1980): 7-8.

       A positive review of a new collection, *Dream Palaces*,
       which includes the novels *63: Dream Palace*, *Malcolm*,
       and *The Nephew*. Gunn ends his review noting that
       these works "should continue to be available from now
       on, as the modern classics they are."

649    Miller, Nolan. "Books." *Antioch Review* 39 (fall 1981):
       516-517.

       A short, positive review of the 1980 edition of *Dream
       Palaces: Three Novels* by Viking Press. Reviewer
       notes "So, at last—and it's about time—Viking Press
       is to be commended for presenting Purdy's work in a
       collected, hardbound, life-long library edition."

650    Towle, Edmund. "Purdy's Parables." *Los Angeles Herald
       Examiner*, 7 September 1980.

       A positive review of Viking Press's release of *Dream
       Palaces* in 1980, which includes *Malcolm*, *The Nephew*
       and *63: Dream Palace*. Towle notes that this edition is
       "a small treasure" and that Purdy's neglect is
       "undeserved." Towle concludes, "Purdy is a

wordsmith of the first order who's vision is worth
exploring. *Dream Palaces* offers a nice start."


## *Eustace Chisholm and the Works*

651     Algren, Nelson. "It's a Gay and Dreary Life." *The Critic*
        26 (August/September 1967): 67-68.

        A very negative review of *Eustace Chisholm and the
        Works*. Algren writes, "Readers familiar with Mr.
        Purdy's previous work will have the uneasy feeling
        here that they've ridden this carousel before. Fenton
        Riddleway has become Ratcliffe; Parkhearst Cratty is
        now Ace Chisholm; Bella Cratty is Carla Chisholm; and
        Grainger the great woman is now Grandma Masterson.
        The difference in this carousel, however, is that this
        one goes off the ground and never comes down.... What
        makes the book such a deadly bore, what makes the
        reader's mind boggle, is that the author is unaware of
        anything preposterous about men who believe so firmly
        in both prayer and faggotry that they can go from sex to
        penitence without getting off their knees."

652     Barker, Paul. "Cobweb." *Times* (London), 23 March
        1968, p. 20.

        A mixed review of *Eustace Chisholm and the Works*.
        The review ends with "Sometimes, certainly, Purdy
        does cast light on the real world. But mostly he only
        casts light on language. If he had been content with
        this trap, *Eustace Chisholm* would be a much better
        novel. But the brutality of his efforts to escape wrecks
        the cobweb."

653     "Books." *Drum* 29 (March 1968): 11.

        A review of *Eustace Chisholm and the Works*. The
        reviewer notes that "the refusal to accept homosexual
        love has seldom been published more severely."

654     Coffey, Warren. "The Incompleat Novelist." *Commentary*
        44 (September 1967): 98-103.

A long, mixed review of *Eustace Chisholm and the Works*. Mr. Coffey details Purdy's background and earlier writings. Coffey writes that *Eustace* "has a good novella under a lot of fat, but it's not a novel."

655    Colimore, Vincent J. "Book Review." *Best Sellers* 27 (15 June 1967): 123.

A positive review of *Eustace Chisholm and the Works*. The review concludes: "This is not exactly pleasant reading, and yet, a genuine sense of pity is aroused for three people caught in the web of their own making, or something over which they have little or no control."

656    Cook, Roderick. "Books in Brief." *Harper's Magazine* 235 (July 1967): 94.

A positive review of *Eustace Chisholm and the Works*, which concludes, "James Purdy writes like the very devil. No matter how often one's jaw drops from stark terror or disbelief, it is still a pleasure to sell one's soul to him, for the time it takes to read his book."

657    Curley, Dorothy. "Fiction." *Library Journal* 92 (15 May 1967): 1951.

A very positive review of *Eustace Chisholm and the Works*. Curley writes, "James Purdy's new novel is remarkable for its artistic finish, for the perfection of each individual sentence, and for the completeness with which a world is created, put in action and moved to a resolution of forces."

658    Davis, Douglas M. "Blacker But Bleaker, the Latest From Some 'Black Humorists." *National Observer* 6 (19 June 1967): 19.

A review of John Hawkes' *The Innocent Party*, James Purdy's *Eustace Chisholm and the Works*, and William S. Burrough's *The Ticket That Exploded*. A negative review. [*Eustice*] "is the homosexual novel to end all homosexual novels ... is complicated, at best."

659    "Fiction." *Publishers' Weekly* 191 (27 March 1967): 59.

A negative review of *Eustace Chisholm and the Works* which states: "James Purdy's new novel will be welcome to those who are already convinced of his importance, but it is doubtful it will increase his following."

660    Freeman, Gillian. "Depressed America." *New Statesman* 75 (22 March 1968): 388.

A review of three new works of fiction which includes Purdy's *Eustace Chisholm and the Works*. A very positive review which states, "James Purdy's prose is faultless, his construction compressed, his themes of unrequited love universal. He makes the bizarre appear commonplace and the commonplace bizarre by the brilliant juxtaposition of novel ideas."

661    French, Warren. "A Horrifying Etching From Memory of Chicago." *Kansas City Star*, 21 May 1967, p. 6F.

A very positive review of *Eustace Chisholm and the Works*. French is one of the most perceptive critics of Purdy's work. For example, he writes "*Malcolm* (1959) is a dazzling surrealistic allegory of the betrayal of innocence. *The Nephew* (1960) is a frighteningly realistic portrayal of the lack of communication among families and neighbors in a small town. *Cabot Wright Begins* (1965), ostensibly the history of a rapist, is actually a vicious vendetta against the meretriciousness of New York City's literary establishment. Now *Eustace Chisholm and the Works* is a horrifying etching from memory of Chicago during the depression." And, French notes, "The distinction that entirely isolates Purdy's work from that of today's fashionable pornographers is his superb craftsmanship, his complete control of his medium. Like Swift, like Goya in 'The Disasters of War,' what Purdy is putting down hurts him; yet he feels that it must be recorded, and he steels his hand so that it will not tremble in executing the awful duty he has imposed upon it." Contains a photograph of Purdy.

662　　Gilbert, Harriett. "Family Way." *New Statesman* 107 (18 May 1984): 25.

> A review of five novels published in England. The brief and very positive review of the re-issue of Purdy's *Eustace Chisholm and the Works*, by the Gay Men's Press, new "Gay Modern Classics" series, is noted.

663　　Graham, Kenneth. "Dammable." *The Listener* 79 (21 March 1968): 383.

> A review of five works including Purdy's *Eustace Chisholm and the Works* and Vaughan's *The Seduction*. A very negative review which notes that *Eustace Chisholm* "is an autoerotic homosexual dream, enriched with sadism, but empty of imagination, humour, verbal force or vital emotion."

664　　Gross, Barry. "Pseudo-Poet and Man." *Saturday Review* 50 (5 August 1967): 37.

> A negative review of *Eustace Chisholm and the Works* in which Gross finds that, "in short, Purdy fails to surprise. The grotesqueries do not tease or tantalize; they are mechanical and predictable."

665　　"Language and Literature: English and American." *Choice* 4 (February 1968): 1383.

> A short review of *Eustace Chisholm and the Works* which notes "The writing is as brilliant as ever, often carrying the reader on in spite of himself. Even if one is repulsed by the story itself, one cannot but admire the way in which it is told."

666　　Lehan, Richard. "Fiction 1967." *Contemporary Literature* 9 (autumn 1968): 538-553.

> A long review article dealing with sixteen novels published in 1967. In a review of Purdy's *Eustace Chisholm and the Works*, Lehan notes that "caught between impulse and convention, desire and guilt, Daniel [Haws] is a prototypical twentieth-century hero—a victim of the wars that rage within him."

149

667    Lindroth, James R. "Book Reviews." *America* 117 (1 July
       1967): 20-21.

       A positive review of *Eustace Chisholm and the Works*,
       which notes, "Stylistically, Purdy presents the same
       obstacles as Gertrude Stein and Sherwood Anderson.
       Since, like them, he develops language out of the
       sensibilities of his characters, he lays himself open to
       charges of awkwardness and preciosity. Ultimately,
       however, it is communication that counts, and what
       Purdy communicates is deep moral revulsion at man's
       predilection for violence and hate."

668    Malin, Irving. "[Review]." *Commonweal* 86 (28 July
       1967): 476-477.

       A positive review of *Eustace Chisholm and the Works*,
       which notes the novel "is on one level, a study of
       economic collapse. It gives us the unemployed, the
       downtrodden, and the nondescript in Chicago of the late
       30's and early 40's. Although Purdy describes their
       hardship 'amidst the industrial whirlwind of America's
       'economic burnout,' he is less interested in naturalistic
       facts and figures than in the terrifying relationship
       between money—or the lack of it—and the will to
       power." Malin writes, "*Eustace Chisholm and the
       Works* violates our civilized sensibilities: it offers the
       painful pleasure of recognizing the incredible nature of
       love."

669    Mann, Thorpe. "Books of the Day." *Kansas City Star*, 21
       May 1967, p. 6F.

       A short introduction to two new novels, Purdy's
       *Eustace Chisholm and the Works*, and Jean Dutourd's
       *The Honors of Love*. About Purdy he writes, "He's a
       master of the satiric, the macabre, the weird, and he
       seems to be obsessed by the heart of darkness in the
       Midwest." Of special importance in this article is the
       quote by Purdy on *Eustace*: "It (*Eustace*) is a
       continuation in story form of my own version, a
       fundamental Christian one, that man has cut himself off
       from his inheritance, and has perfected his immortality

for a place in a world which is not worth the high
expense of blowing up."

670    Morris, Robert K. "James Purdy and the Works." *The
       Nation* 205 (9 October 1967): 342-344.

       A long article reviewing Purdy's writing, including
       *Malcolm, The Nephew, Cabot Wright Begins*, and
       *Eustace Chisholm and the Works*. Morris writes
       "What a Purdy character quests after in this wasteland
       is knowledge of himself. But there is an eloquence in
       Purdy that is not often found in other 'quest novels' of
       the period." And, "I count Purdy a fabulist, too, for the
       simple reason that the end toward which he writes is a
       moral one.... The important thing, however, is to
       recognize that Purdy's fables have morals, not always
       an easy task in the face of a multiplicity of themes and
       the sensational clutter of abnormal vehicles that carry
       them." In writing about *Eustace*, Morris notes
       "Purdy's anatomy of love has always been a distorted
       one. He has shown how it devours, tortures, castrates;
       he has found it crude, repulsive, destructive. His vision
       is vaguely nihilistic and at its darkest apocalyptic; but
       now and again the vision lightens. Nightmare is
       backed by reality, satire is supported by truth, black
       humor is substantiated by clear wit and, above all else,
       by logic which, in *Eustace Chisholm and the Works*, is
       pretty plain. The quest for love is hard, frustrating,
       debilitating, often nigh hopeless, but always worth it;
       for love is the only substantial timber to shore against
       our ruin."

671    "Neo-Gothic Trend." *Time* 89 (26 May 1967 ): 96-97.

       A mixed review of *Eustace Chisholm and the Works*.
       The reviewer notes the novel "is not unlike certain
       surrealistic painting in its rather surprising lack of
       effect; though an atmosphere is evoked in sharp and
       crystalline terms and though figures are intensely and
       skillfully rendered." Contains a photography of Purdy.

672    "Notes on Current Books." *Virginia Quarterly Review* 43
       (autumn 1967): 166.

A positive review of *Eustace Chisholm and the Works* which notes, "Certainly his new book enhances an already solid position in contemporary letters, forbidding content or no."

673    "Paperbacks: Fiction." *Publishers' Weekly* 193 (5 February 1968): 67.

A short review of the Bantam Books paperback edition of *Eustace Chisholm and the Works* which notes, "The beautiful and naked young man on Bantam's cover leaves the reader in no doubt that this is a novel in which homosexuality plays a large part. So do sadism and masochism and florid writing."

674    Phillips, Robert. "Stories That End With Screams." *North American Review* New series 4 (November 1967): 38-39.

A review of four new novels including Purdy's *Eustace Chisholm and the Works*. Phillips gives the novel a mixed review and writes that the novel "is an interesting failure which contains some of the best writing of a minor American author."

675    Price, R. G. G. "New Novels." *Punch* 254 (3 April 1968): 507-508.

A review of four current novels including Purdy's *Eustace Chisholm and the Works*. Price gives *Eustace Chisholm* a very negative review as he writes, "I find him only quaint and would-be winsome. His eccentrics and his preciosity don't create a grimly fairy tale world which reflects, as in a magic mirror, the human condition.... The prose is not quite as narcissistic as in the earlier books; but it lacked for me the wit and poetry better men have seen in it."

676    "Review." *Kirkus Reviews* 35 (1 April 1967): 441.

A mixed review of *Eustace Chisholm and the Works* in which Purdy is compared to Carson McCullers, Jane Bowles, and Truman Capote. The reviewer writes: "The mood elusively oscillates between the sentimental and the tragic, the comic and the grim, and the controlling commentator, Eustace, a failed

Bohemian, is a bit too gaga to give the proceedings a
telling perspective."

677     Robertson, Bryan. "Purdy & the Works." *The Spectator*
        220 (29 March 1968): 411-412.

        A long and very positive review of *Eustace Chisholm
        and the Works*,which also includes positive statements
        concerning *Colour of Darkness* and *Cabot Wright
        Begins*. Robertson compares Purdy's writing to that of
        Nathaniel West, Terry Southern, Flannery O'Connor,
        Upton Sinclair, Nelson Algren and William Burroughs
        (the last three because of their mid-west settings).
        Robertson writes: "Purdy continues the tradition with
        great gifts and the same icy stare at the disruption or
        morality of ethics."

678     Sheed, Wilfred. "An Alleged Love Story." *New York
        Times Book Review* (21 May 1967): 4, 51.

        A very negative review of *Eustace Chisholm and the
        Works*. Sheed writes, "But slowly, and one might
        guess diffidently, the book becomes a little more
        serious; and for a time, it teeter-totters between
        sentimentality and real life feeling before coming down
        surprisingly hard on the latter."

679     Trickett, Rachel. "Recent Novels: Craftsmanship in
        Violence and Sex." *Yale Review*  57 (spring 1968): 438-
        452.

        A review of eight novels including Purdy's *Eustace
        Chisholm and the Works*. A positive review in which
        Trickett writes, "Many novelists would have expanded
        the material of James Purdy's *Eustace Chisholm and
        the Works* to three times the length. But Purdy is too
        conscious an artist for this.... The discrepancy between
        extravagant action or feeling and elegantly fashioned
        form gives its characteristic quality to Purdy's work.
        Only the poise and coolness of the style make this
        nightmare vision tolerable.... His art reveals itself a
        little too consistently; the shocking elements are
        played off a little too coolly, and it isn't always easy to
        distinguish his genuine imagination from a kind of

sophisticated voyeurism not unlike Eustace's.
Nevertheless, the book has brilliance and originality."

680    "Unclaimed in a Morgue." *Times Literary Supplement* (28
       March 1968): 309.

       A negative review of *Eustace Chisholm and the Works*.
       The review begins: "American fiction gets curiouser
       and curiouser." And ends: "*Eustace Chisholm* may
       delight the converted, but it is unlikely to make new
       converts. It is as much skittish as stylish, overly
       delighted with its own eccentricities."

681    Wall, Stephen. "Romantic Love in Chicago." *The Observer*
       (London), 24 March 1968, p. 28.

       A review of three new novels including a positive
       review of *Eustace Chisholm and the Works*. Wall
       states, "The persons and predicaments of the new
       book are very clearly the products of a curious and
       individual imagination—and James Purdy is
       characteristic of the better contemporary American
       writers in his readiness to trust, even indulge, the
       imagination."

682    Wetzsteon, Ross. "Making It the Hard Way." *Book Week*
       4 (28 May 1967): 4.

       A very positive review of *Eustace Chisholm and the
       Works*. Wetzsteon summarizes and compares *Eustace
       Chisholm* to Purdy's earlier novels, *Malcolm*, *The
       Nephew*, and *Cabot Wright Begins*. He notes, "I
       should say, rather, that Purdy's novels seem to be a
       search for the proper expression of despair, that in his
       previous novels he refused to confront its source, that
       he has disguised, deflected, and dissipated its thrust—
       but that now he's found its bottom, given it its right
       name, and in so doing (not at all paradoxically) has
       sounded his first authentic note of love, hope and
       compassion."

683    Wilson, Angus. "Purdy Pushes Comedy Past Blackness."
       *Life* 62 (2 June 1967): 8.

A long, positive review of Purdy's *Eustace Chisholm and the Works*. Mr. Wilson, a long-time supporter of Purdy, calls him a "master of the mixing of the horrible, the wildly funny and the very sad." He notes, "The novel is a remarkable achievement that will outshine its slightly shaky ending."

## Garments the Living Wear

684    Duguid, Lindsay. "London's Burning." *The Observer* (London), 21 May 1989, p. 53.

A review of four new novels including a short review of *Garments the Living Wear*. Duguid notes that this is Purdy's eleventh novel and he "romanticises extremes of poverty and wealth—especially wealth—a ... Wildern burlesque, bristling with exclamation marks."

685    Harris, Bertha. "The Pest Can't Get Them Down." *New York Times Book Review* (29 October 1989): 13.

A lengthy, positive review of *Garments the Living Wear*. Harris writes, "The wit and sauce of a James Purdy drawing room extravaganza collide with the supernatural hyperbole of one of his trademark riffs on the Southern gospel tradition. The consequence is a transvestite-transsexual comedy of gay mannerism that is as reminiscent of Joan Crawford and Bette Davis in 'Whatever Happened to Baby Jane?' as it is of Wilde, Sheridan, the Book of Revelation and down-home Pentecostal awakenings."

686    Holditch, W. Kenneth. "Stylish Originals." *Times-Picayune*, 4 March 1990, sec. F, pp. 11-12.

A very positive review of *Garments the Living Wear*. Holditch notes: "James Purdy's distinguished career as an author of fiction stretches almost four decades. *Garments the Living Wear*, his fourteenth novel, is like his earlier novels and short stories, experimental and highly original. With each successive work, he has found new territory to explore, although retaining those unique characteristics that have always identified his work." In describing the novel, Holditch writes, "The novel is a satire of modern life, in which the author strikes broad and telling blows at, among other things, religion, social customs, 'the lifestyles of the rich and famous,' the sexual revolution, the feminist movement, and the hypocrisy that seems to mark every phase of human activity. Among the objects of satire, perhaps the most important is the setting itself, New York, which becomes the epitome and symbol of the corruption of the 1980's." Holditch notes that Purdy "is one of those authors who have been, for whatever reason, neglected by the critical establishment and, as a sad consequence, by many readers. He is a writer's writer, for those who love words and shape them into poetry or fiction recognize a master at work. Once again, Purdy has produced an original novel that intrigues, delights, and startles with its display of oddities." Contains a photograph of Purdy.

687    Malin, Irving. "Book Reviews: A. G. Mojtabai, *Ordinary Times* and James Purdy, *Garments the Living Wear.*" *Review of Contemporary Fiction* 10 (spring 1990): 327.

A positive review which states, "Majtabai and Purdy are two of the most interesting novelists we have." Malin notes that "the entire novel [*Garments*] is dramatic, illusory, hallucinatory."

688    Thompson, Bob. "Beastly Sojourn in the Big Rotten Apple." *San Francisco Chronicle*, 7 January 1990, Sunday Review Section, p. 10.

A negative review of *Garments the Living Wear*. Thompson writes that the novel "is a surreal convoluted tale that encompasses the decline of New York City, AIDS ('the pest'), sexual ambiguity, politics, the decadence of the idle rich and the emptiness of modern religion.... This is neither an easy nor unpleasant book to read. More a series of connected vignettes than a novel, its haunting lyricism frames a tale of greed, evil and, finally, the promise of redemption."

689 Allen, Bruce. "Fiction." *Library Journal* 99 (1 November 1974): 2873.

   A mixed review of *The House of the Solitary Maggot.* Allen writes, "This novel is hard to read, but worth the effort. Beneath its naggingly flat prose, and awkward repetitions, Purdy's midwestern family tragedy is a powerful mythical exemplum of the country's fall from perfection into divisiveness."

690 "Fiction." *Publishers' Weekly* 206 (5 August 1974): 51-52.

   A positive review of *The House of the Solitary Maggot* which notes, "an essential part of James Purdy's considerable talent is his ability to create a crazy-quilt work, fill it with bizarre characters and make it all seem as normal as apple-pie. Almost." And, "not for everyone by any means, but admirers will follow this Pied Piper willingly through his odd fancies that mix laughter with uneasiness."

691 French, Warren. "Review." *Great Lakes Review* 1 (winter 1975): 88-93.

   A positive review of *The House of the Solitary Maggot.* French writes "One can only be awed by a book that succeeds where so many other attempts have failed in incorporating our most urgent present neuroses of alienation and rootlessness into a somber reinvigoration of the supposedly spent spirit of the epic—an effort nourished by an outraged vision of the loss of the community rooted in the soil in the increasingly urbanized and mechanized Midwest."

692 Ingoldby, Grace. "American Blues. "*New Statesman* 111 (17 January 1986): 32.

   A review of three new novels including *The House of the Solitary Maggot.* A positive review in which Ingoldby writes that the novel is "A thoroughly original and enjoyable read set in a landscape where characters and place are perfectly matched."

693 Keates, Jonathan. "Small-Town Gothic." *The Observer* (London), 18 January 1986, p. 48.

A review of four new novels including *The House of the Solitary Maggot*. Keates does not believe that this novel is as good as Purdy's earlier books and writes that this novel "discloses ... a rigidity of pose reminiscent of those lava-hardened figures caught in the act of fleeing from Pompeii." Review includes a photograph of Purdy.

694 "Language and Literature: English and American." *Choice* 11 (February 1975): 1780.

A short, negative review of *The House of the Solitary Maggot* which states: "For those readers, the novel's black humor and heavy Jungian symbolism will suffice; for many others, the weakness of the characters and the thinness of the plot will weigh too heavily."

695 Malin, Irving. "New Fiction." *New Republic* 171 (26 October 1974): 31-32.

A positive review of *The House of the Solitary Maggot*, which Malin describes as a "mythical and disturbing novel, where motives are mixed, where love is bloody, and where maggots dwell in family constructions."

696 Phillips, James A. "Book Review." *Best Sellers* 34 (15 December 1974): 424-425.

A review of *The House of the Solitary Maggot*. The reviewer stresses plot and character and concludes, "Not for the squeamish or faint of heart is this book about an atavistic family that always does the wrong thing, over and over."

697 "Review." *Kirkus Reviews* 42 (1 August 1974): 832.

A negative review of *The House of the Solitary Maggot*. The reviewer notes, "The novel is written in a stilted language that appropriately matches its (sublime?) gothic ridiculousness."

698     Bailey, Paul. "Loss of Faith." *London Magazine* 12
        (February/March 1973): 157-160.

> A review article of six contemporary novels including
> Purdy's *I Am Elijah Thrush*, Moore's *Catholics* and
> Braine's *The Queen of a Distant Country*. Bailey gives
> *Elijah Thrush* a very negative review: "I hated it
> because it's the type of book that gives camp a bad
> name: its strident insistence on the bizarre is no
> substance for the real, right thing."

699     Boyd, Robert. "A Fantasy Out at Elbows." *The Nation*
        214 (15 May 1972): 635-636.

> A negative review of *I Am Elijah Thrush*, which notes
> the novel "is doubly disappointing for us, first because
> it seems to imply a return by Purdy to the spirit of
> 'Sermon,' and second, because—taken purely as
> fantasy—it lacks incentiveness and originality which
> brought his earlier work such well-deserved acclaim."

700     "Briefly Noted: Fiction." *New Yorker* 48 (27 May 1972):
        114-115.

> A short, mixed review of *I Am Elijah Thrush* which
> notes, "The book has its bad moments when it relies
> on stupid or obscene behavior to create its effects, but
> at other moments the effects are dazzling."

701     Cuddon, J. A. "Review." *Books and Bookmen* 18 (March
        1973): 79.

> A review of three novels including, *I Am Elijah Thrush*,
> which receives a favorable write-up. Cuddon writes,
> "This is a stylish novel in which the manner is very
> well suited to subject matter, and the comic tone is
> judged to a nicety. In general, it is Firbankish, an
> exuberantly gay exercise in the bizarre, a series of
> elegant acrobatics and graceful gestures which have
> about them a certain iridescence like the shimmer of
> peacock feathers."

702      Davies, Russell. "Whizz Dads: New Fiction." *The Observer* (London), 22 October 1972. p. 35.

>A review of three novels including a very negative review of *I Am Elijah Thrush*. Davies ends his review with: "it was a new experience, though—like being pelted with warm meringues."

703      "Fiction." *Booklist* 68 (15 July 1972): 974.

>Review of *I Am Elijah Thrush* which states "The bizarre, absorbing tale is a dramatic departure in intent and tone from *The Nephew* and previous Purdy fiction."

704      "Fiction." *Publishers' Weekly* 201 (6 March 1972): 57.

>A positive review of *I Am Elijah Thrush* which states: "The newest by the author of *Malcolm* and many other novels, is a bizarre tale, a rather savage if often ambiguous satire of American life." And, "A short novel, it demands close attention, but for the few who relish the outer reaches of imagination as explored by a skillful writer, it's well worth the effort."

705      "Golden Suction." *Times Literary Supplement* (3 November 1972): 1305.

>A review of *I Am Elijah Thrush* which ends: "So perhaps, after all, this *Thrush* is not only a *Satyricon* but an American parable. Set in a fairy tale city of New York, this dark exotic jewel, as if fathered by Cocteau on F. Scott Fitzgerald, seems like the pianist with dark circles in his moon-pale face and a geranium in his buttonhole, flashing looks of malevolent hatred at the audience 'when he was not playing Cécile Chaminade or Eric Coates.' "

706      Graver, Lawrence. "Three Novels and a Novella." *New York Times Book Review* (2 July 1972): 6-7.

>A review of Purdy's *I Am Elijah Thrush*, Fine's *Their Family* and Tracy's *The Quiet End of Evening*. The negative review of *I Am Elijah Thrush* ends by asking, "If, however, this befuddled black man and his

fraudulent friends are supposed to be subjects of satire, one wonders why Purdy thought their zany antics are worth such extended ridicule."

707     Hunter, Jim. "Success." *The Listener* 88 (19 October 1972): 513.

A review of four novels including Purdy's *I Am Elijah Thrush* and Raphael's *April, June and November*. A very negative review which notes, *"Elijah Thrush* is a muddle-headed and rather obscene novel."

708     Mano, Keith D. "Meanings and Mannerisms." *National Review* 24 (1 September 1972): 961.

A review of three novels including Purdy's *I Am Elijah Thrush*, William's *Captain Blackman* and Sharp's *The Innocents*. A very negative review of *I Am Elijah Thrush*. The reviewer dislikes all of Purdy's writing. He writes, "His novels are saprophytic; they feed on the manifestoes of nineteenth and twentieth century symbolist authors—either consciously or unconsciously."

709     Meehan, Karen. "SR Reviews." *Saturday Review* 55 (10 June 1972): 68-69.

A negative review of *I Am Elijah Thrush*. Meehan writes, "Admittedly, he (Purdy) writes beautifully (or do I mean preciously?); however, his bizarre metaphors leave this reviewer cold."

710     "Notes on Current Books." *Virginia Quarterly Review* 48 (autumn 1972): 120.

A short positive review of *I Am Elijah Thrush* which states "Fantasy and allegory are inextricably mixed in Mr. Purdy's latest experiment in the field of fiction, written with characteristic audacity and cunning as high comedy."

711     O'Connell, Shaun. "American Fiction, 1972: The Void in the Mirror." *Massachusetts Review* 14 (winter 1973): 190-207.

An essay review of forty new novels which lists Purdy's *I Am Elijah Thrush.*

712 "Review - Paperbacks." *Book World* (*Washington Post*) (13 May 1973): 13.

A short, negative review of *I Am Elijah Thrush.*

713 "Review." *Kirkus Reviews* 40 (1 March 1972): 279.

A negative review of *I Am Elijah Thrush.* The reviewer writes, "It's hard to say whether James Purdy's campy style is more of an intoxicant or an irritant, whether it's to be taken seriously with all that droll, fussy, exotica; or whether it can be taken as comedy since it is also quite feral."

714 Waugh, Auberon. "Faecal Felicities." *Spectator* 229 (21 October 1972): 626-627.

A review of Purdy's *I Am Elijah Thrush* and Tournier's *The Evil King.* The review is very negative. Writing about *Elijah Thrush,* Waugh states, "Mr. Purdy's new novel is a classic case of an author's aim being higher than his reach.... Fantasy-writing, if it is to be read, must obey exactly the same laws of dramatic suspense and surprise as ordinary writing; and surprise can only be achieved by the creation of an alternative logic. Mr. Purdy's book has no such system; none of the events or characters carries conviction; there is no dramatic suspense, nor even the faintest curiosity about what happens next. It is a mess, and should be read by all aspiring novelists as a terrible example."

715 Wimble, Barton L. "Fiction." *Library Journal* 97 (15 May 1972): 1827.

A short review of *I Am Elijah Thrush.* The reviewer "found the luxuriance of the prose to be some of Purdy's best writing, though the novel is short and not equal to some of his earlier works in terms of depth of characterization and plot."

716      Adams, Phoebe-Lou. "Review." *Atlantic Monthly* 237 (March 1976): 108.

> A very short, to-the-point review of *In a Shallow Grave*. Adams notes that "Mr. Purdy writes well and the opening of his novel ... catches interest constantly. Then the tale fogs off into dim fantasy."

717      Charyn, Jerome. "In a Shallow Grave." *New York Times Book Review* (8 February 1976): 2-3.

> A very positive review of *In a Shallow Grave*. "*In a Shallow Grave* is a funny, sad and touching book." Charyn labels the novel a "modern Book of Revelation, filled with prophecies, visions, and demonic landscapes." He also writes: "The very awkwardness of his lines, that deliberate scratching of the reader's ear, is Purdy's greatest strength. It allows him to mix evil and naiveté without spilling over with melodrama and tedious morality plays.... Purdy's brittle language is a sadness that is heartbreaking, the horror of isolated beings who manage to collide for a moment, do a funny dance and go their separate way."

718      Davis, Hope Hale. "A Quest for Love." *New Leader* 59 (24 May 1976): 14-15.

> A positive review of *In a Shallow Grave*. In the review Davis refers favorably to Purdy's earlier work including *The Nephew*, *Cabot Wright Begins*, *Malcolm* and *Jeremy's Version*. Ms. Davis asks, "Can books that deal with 'nightmare subjects'—which Purdy's admittedly do—affirm the value of life? They may well be the only ones that truly can."

719      "Fiction." *Booklist* 72 (1 April 1976): 1090.

> A positive review of *In a Shallow Grave* which states "The power and tenacity of human affection are splendidly revealed in Purdy's brief tale of a disfigured soldier who returns from the battlefield to rebuild his body and his spirit ... a remarkable and touching study of love and redemption."

720     "Fiction." *Publishers' Weekly* 208 (8 December 1975):
        43.

> A very positive review of *In a Shallow Grave* which
> notes, "Despite the increasing length of his career, and
> its often impressive moments (*Malcolm*, and *The
> Nephew*), Purdy remains just a bit apart from what we
> think of as a successful novelist. In a sense, he's
> almost too good." And, "The result is strange,
> haunting and allegorical, a novel that engages as it
> entertains, draws the reader as it draws something out
> of him. In other words, a very impressive book."

721     "Fiction: Briefly Noted." *New Yorker* 52 (12 April 1976):
        142.

> A negative review of Purdy's *In a Shallow Grave*,
> which labels the novel "a mawkish black fantasy."

722     Firestone, Bruce M. "Fiction." *Library Journal* 100 (15
        December 1975): 2344.

> A review of *In a Shallow Grave*. Firestone writes,
> "Rather than concern himself with a credible plot,
> Purdy seems to focus instead on the bonds that tie his
> characters, and on the metaphor of his living (and
> slowly healing) corpse. But the bonds themselves are
> ambiguous and constantly shifting, and the metaphor
> grows old long before the character does."

723     Foote, Bud. "Purdy's Soft Nightmare Delivers the Real
        Goods." *National Observer* 15 (28 February 1976): 21.

> A very positive review of *In a Shallow Grave*. Foote
> writes, "It is a softly nightmarish book, full of gently
> crazy people; and the matter-of-fact tone in which
> Garnet narrates it is what makes it work. Purdy
> obviously loves his characters, and so, before it is over,
> do we; and the strength of the book is in the skill with
> which it affirms love and life."

724     Horton, Jim. "Book Review." *Best Sellers* 36 (May 1976):
        40.

A negative review of *In a Shallow Grave*. Horton writes, "In this novel, the reader is repulsed, too, by the author's intent, which ascends into the mystical, religious and perverse all at once."

725    Miller, Nolan. "Recent Fiction." *Antioch Review* 34 (summer 1976): 506.

A short, very positive review of *In a Shallow Grave*. Miller writes, "Spellbinder that Purdy is, he has seldom been as powerful as in this short, spoken work. For once the jacket blurb is correct: the story is 'nothing less than the story of the resurrection of human love and feeling from the very depths.' "

726    "New and Noteworthy." *New York Times Book Review* (18 September 1977): 59.

A brief mention of the paperback edition of *In a Shallow Grave*.

727    "New and Noteworthy." *New York Times Book Review* (1 July 1984): 28.

Short reviews of 11 titles of which Purdy's *In a Shallow Grave* is noted with a positive quote from Jerome Charyn's 1975 review. Issued in paperback.

728    Olderman, Raymond M. "American Fiction 1974-1976: The People Who Fell to Earth." *Contemporary Literature* 19 (autumn 1978): 497-527.

A general review of fiction published during the three-year period. The article mentions Purdy as one of the established writers who published in this period and lists Purdy's *In a Shallow Grave* under the "Selected Reading List: American Fiction 1974-1976."

729    Pieiller, Evelyne. "Un Habitat de l' Enfer." *La Quinzaine Letteraire* 299 (15 April 1979): 10-11.

A review in French of Purdy's *In a Shallow Grave*.

730    "Review." *Kirkus Reviews* 43 (1 December 1975): 1349.

A positive review of *In a Shallow Grave*. The reviewer states: "Purdy is such a calculatedly outlandish writer you have to put this novella aside from time to time to catch your breath and readjust your sights.... Reading Purdy involves a surrender to the peculiar pleasures of his language—a melange of loose wristed, magnolia-scented gothicisms, straight dialect and various metaphoric decorations hung on a strictly directed narrative. It's this distinctive style which makes him more than a regionalist or a contemporary curiosity."

731    Sage, Lorna. "Longing and Loathing." *The Observer* (London), 2 April 1978, p. 25.

A review of three new novels including a mixed review of *In a Shallow Grave*. Sage notes, "James Purdy seems almost overburdened with charm these days, but he's rescued from camp or sentimentality by his extraordinary power with images and cadences."

## In the Hollow of His Hand

732    Espey, John. "Review." *Los Angeles Times*, 5 October 1986, Book Review Section, p. 8.

A positive review of *In the Hollow of His Hand*, which notes, "In his new novel, James Purdy stands once again on his Midwestern home ground in the 20's, writing in his personal blend of surface realism, hilarious burlesque and flashes of divine magic to explore two of his obsessive themes: the blood forces of generations and the mutual needs of a father and a son.... That Purdy's view of American life—loveless, hypocritical, money-grubbing—has undergone little change over the years seems obvious. The particular attraction of *In the Hollow of His Hand* lies in the transformation of possible tragedy into comedy and the suggestion that something beyond either may—just may—be realized; for in scene after scene, hallucinating or real, Purdy's characters either strip themselves or are stripped to their essential nakedness and truth."

733     Masters, Hilary. "American Odysseys & Oddities: The Dark Landscape in James Purdy's Fiction." *Washington Post*, 16 December 1986, p. C9.

>A mixed review of *In the Hollow of His Hand*. Masters writes that the new novel "has established his reputation as an authentic original, a permanent truant, to use his own description of a character in the American school of contemporary literature." The review states, "If James Purdy writes out of anger toward those institutions that have orphaned the American spirit, with anger toward those material vulgarities that smother the free soul, he does offer as an artist a kind of redemption with *In the Hollow of His Hand*, one that gives up a prayer, if not a solution, and who is to say which is the more effective? Meanwhile, those of us who cannot share his anger should, at least, give some thought by reading him."

734     Rosenheim, Andrew. "Figuring Out the Father." *Times Literary Supplement* 25 (19 February 1988): 186.

>A negative review of *In the Hollow of His Hand* and *The Candles of Your Eyes*. Concerning *In the Hollow of His Hand*, Rosenheim writes "this is quirky, perverse, its voice alternately deadpan Midwestern and camp arch and Mandarin." About *The Candles of Your Eyes*, Rosenheim writes, "His stories show the least attractive side of the black humour so modish in the 1960's, and if, like that movement, Purdy's work has moved out of fashion, he makes no concessions to regain his readers."

735     Schmieder, Rob. "Fiction." *Library Journal* 111 (1 September 1986): 216.

>A short review of *In the Hollow of His Hand*. Schmieder notes, "Purdy's characters inhabit an extravagant world in which lakes 'savagely churn' and a dying man's lips are 'curtains of blood.'" The reviewer highly recommends the novel.

736     Smith, Lee. "Kidnapped by Everyone." *New York Times Book Review* (19 October 1986): 15.

A positive review of *In the Hollow of His Hand*. Smith writes, "For three decades James Purdy has been spinning his tales of foundlings lost in a grotesque and absurd world. *In the Hollow of His Hand* is a good introduction to his work for anyone unfamiliar with this author's considerable output, which includes twelve other novels, four collections of poetry and four collections of stories and plays. Mr. Purdy's latest novel is typical of the whole in its vision of a violent, meaningless world in which only bizarre, obsessive love is possible; where the emblematic characters behave in nonrational ways; where the author's black humor often fails to alleviate the final bleakness of his world view. Mr. Purdy writes again and again about the search for—and the impossibility of finding—an identity. But *In the Hollow of His Hand* is in some ways a departure for him. Not quite so dark, finally, the book's ending offers a resolution; not quite so violent, this novel's plot lacks the gratuitous bloodletting sometimes seen in his earlier novels. And the absence of a writer-character (a Purdy trademark) makes this book more real, less self-consciously a fiction."

737    Steinberg, Sybil S. "Fiction." *Publishers' Weekly* 230 (25 July 1986): 172.

A negative review of *In the Hollow of His Hand* which states, "Unfortunately Chad's adventures read haltingly as though they'd been composed sentence by sentence with long periods of time in between, a quality that seriously diminishes the tale's narrative drive, as well as the reader's enjoyment."

## *Jeremy's Version*

738    "Bookmarks." *Prairie Schooner* 46 (spring 1972): 91.

A short, positive review of *Jeremy's Version* which ends with the novel having "a feeling of destiny that is both personal and communal, a sense of place and a sense of history—it's almost Faulknerian. And there aren't many writers who can be almost Faulknerian."

739     Boston, Richard. "Clash of Symbols." *Observer Review* (6
        June 1971): 29.

        A review of three current novels which includes
        *Jeremy's Version*. Boston writes a positive review and
        notes: "*Jeremy's Version* is too complex for all its
        themes to be listed here. Amongst other things the
        novel is fiction about fiction, and an essay in illusion
        and reality. But what gives the book its power, and
        makes reading it such a disturbing experience, is the
        intensity with which Purdy investigates the minds of
        the Fergus family as they tear themselves and one
        another apart."

740     Cuddon, J. A. "Fiction." *Books and Bookmen* 16 (July
        1971): 37-38.

        A review of five new works published in England
        including Purdy's *Jeremy's Version*. Purdy's novel
        receives a very positive review and Cuddon writes:
        "James Purdy is a stunning storyteller. The
        development of character, the inter-linking of episode,
        the analysis of motive, the evocation of the
        environment, are all accomplished with great skill. The
        atmosphere of doom, of impending tragedy, is sustained
        without strain and offset by a good deal of comedy. It
        is a solid, well-made, professional novel and a fine
        foundation for its successors."

741     Davenport, Guy. "Jeremy's Version." *New York Times
        Book Review* (15 November 1970): 4, 61.

        A positive review of *Jeremy's Version*. Davenport
        notes: "The novel is, therefore, a complex story which
        is the echo of the one we are reading ... character is a
        role written for us by our families; only in loneliness
        and desperation do we dare leave the stage. Mr.
        Purdy's astute design in this novel allows us only a
        few jolting glimpses of his characters out of their roles,
        but we feel that these views are the real ones."

742     "Fiction." *Publishers' Weekly* 198 (27 July 1970): 67.

        A positive and short review of Purdy's *Jeremy's
        Version* which notes, "here the author of *Malcolm* and

other books has drawn some devastating yet often sympathetic portraits of fully realized characters entangled in an emotional morass of their own making."

743    Haworth, David. "Kid Stuff." *New Statesman* 8 (11 June 1971): 814-815.

A review of five new novels of fiction including *Jeremy's Version*. Haworth gives a mixed review and writes, "James Purdy extends himself in his latest book with a saga of almost classic proportions concerning the rivalry and hatred between two family dynasties, as recounted years later." Also, the book is "a sharp, accurate and brooding portrait of elegant savagery which vibrates the imagination. Too long, though."

744    "Keeping It in the Family." *Times Literary Supplement* (4 June 1971): 637.

A mixed review of *Jeremy's Version* which notes, "this book, like much of Purdy, is saturated in theatricality. The whole thing is a 'tall' story and often appears too far-stretched. Matt, who 'tells' the story, has been an actor, an ambition shared by at least three of the leading characters in the novel itself. Scenery is always described flatly, like a backcloth, most meetings are old-fashioned 'dramatic,' the characters make a deliberate entrance or exit or both, and the people themselves live in a welter of operatic flood, tears and sweat."

745    "Language and Literature: English and American." *Choice* 8 (March 1971): 69.

A short review of *Jeremy's Version* which states: "But the central theme, the problem which dominates not only the relationships of the various members of the Fergus family to each other but the relationship of Jeremy to the story of the Fergus family is that curious mixture of repulsion and nostalgia for the innocence of the past. Highly recommended."

746 Lindroth, James R. "Book Reviews." *America* 124 (27 February 1971): 211.

> A very positive review of *Jeremy's Version*. Lindroth writes that "Purdy succeeds in evoking the appalling emotional difficulties involved in raising a family in a small town. Financial pressures, sibling rivalries, Oedipal conflicts to dissipate the illusion of a Utopian existence in rural America.... What makes the Purdy novel particularly interesting is the ambition of its scope and technique. Depth of characterization is insured by multiple points of view which make the narration complex, sophisticated and flexible." Lindroth ends: "As one of the most talented novelists of the sixties, Purdy, with this novel, promises to become one of the most significant voices of the seventies."

747 Mahan, Derek. "No Freedom." *The Listener* 85 (10 June 1971): 759.

> A positive review of *Jeremy's Version*, which notes that "the novel is opaque: the opacity is deliberate." The reviewer makes favorable comparisons of the novel to Faulkner's *Requiem for a Nun* and to Hawthorne, noting, "This fireside tale, never straying far from the idiom of small-town gossip, is a history of the American psyche in a direct line of descent from Hawthorne."

748 Moody, Minnie Hite. "Purdy's Third Title Attains Major Status." *Columbus Dispatch*, 8 November 1970, p. 16.

> A positive review of *Jeremy's Version*, Purdy's sixth (not third) novel. Moody writes that James Purdy is "one of the most distinguished writers today in America. His work grows—and grows on you.... Surprises, suspense, nuances, grace of vision and manner, makes James Purdy's prose a delight rich and rare."

749 Murray, Michele. "Prose and Cons: Succinct Looks at New Books." *National Observer* 9 (30 November 1970): 25.

A very negative review of *Jeremy's Version*. The reviewer notes, "All the Purdy characteristics are present here—the unsparingly cynical view of humanity, the mechanisms, the pointlessly complicated structure."

750 "Notes on Current Books." *Virginia Quarterly Review* 47 (spring 1971): lvi.

A short negative review of *Jeremy's Version* which notes, "Until other versions of these tangled lives are presented, or until the author ventures upon further explication, no satisfactory conclusions are possible at this early stage."

751 "Reservations - Fiction." *Antioch Review* 34 (fall/winter 1970/71): 458.

A short review of *Jeremy's Version* which notes, "His [Purdy's] theme remains familiar—the fate of the innocent, exploited and defiled in our lost Eden."

752 "Review." *Kirkus Reviews* 38 (1 August 1970): 825.

A negative review of *Jeremy's Version*. The reviewer concludes, "In spite of Purdy's tidy skills in dialogue and witty overviews, this story of desire under the poison sumac is overly oblique."

753 Scott, Michael Maxwell. "Recent Fiction." *Daily Telegraph*, 10 June 1971. p. 9.

Five reviews of new novels including Purdy's *Jeremy's Version*. Scott ends his short, positive review by declaring: "Outwardly, as I say, this is a period piece, but Mr. Purdy uses the fustian, the stock attitudes, to create not just a set of figures, but believable people."

754 Shrapnel, Norman. "Plain and Fancy." *The Guardian*, 3 June 1971, p. 15.

A review of six new books including Purdy's *Jeremy's Version*. The brief review is negative. Shrapnel writes, "If you go for fictional baroque, *Jeremy's Version* is a ripe example."

755    Symonds, Julian. "The Other Island." *Sunday Times*
(London), 8 June 1971. p. 32.

A review of six new novels including Purdy's *Jeremy's
Version*. A positive review which begins: "In *Jeremy's
Version*, James Purdy has abandoned, temporarily at
least, his stance as America's most extreme Gothic
Romantic, to write a family saga that might have been
sired by William Faulkner out of Mrs. Henry Wood....
Mr. Purdy's admirers will eagerly await the next
volume."

756    Williams, David. "Fiction." *The Times* (London), 3 June
1971, p. 12.

A mixed review of *Jeremy's Version* which concludes,
"So all things considered, we must suspend judgment
and wait to see what Mr. Purdy is going to do next. So
far he has created a very strange America indeed, filled
with hot-dog stands and hand-operated gasoline
stations, and close by, standing up dark and
threatening, dark towers to which Childe Roland might
have come."

757    Wimble, Barton L. "The Beginning of Purdy's Cycle of
Two Families." *Library Journal* 95 (1 October 1970):
3306.

A positive book review of *Jeremy's Version*. Wimble
begins his review: "This is quite obviously the first
part of a large cycle, conceived so much as part of the
whole that it stops abruptly and leaves one reaching for
the next volume.... Purdy is one of the great technicians
now writing in America, and his outrageous
flamboyance and melodrama are so well handled that
they only seem irksome on retrospection."

758    Wolff, Geoffrey. "Stung Ventricles." *Newsweek* 76 (12
October 1970): 122-123.

A very negative review of *Jeremy's Version*. The
reviewer criticizes Purdy's use of language, which he
refers to as "the turgid music of this soap opera."
Contains a photograph of Purdy.

759    Balliet, Whitney. "Underseas with Purdy and Humes." *New Yorker* 35 (19 December 1959): 138.

        Book review of *Malcolm* and *Men Die* by H. L. Humes. The review of *Malcolm* is unfavorable, in which the writer asks, "Is the book an exercise in surrealism for surrealism's sake?  Or is it an easy parody of all surrealism, fantasy and myth?"

760    Binding, Paul. "In a State of Waiting." *Times Literary Supplement* (7 April 1995): 25.

        An important review of the latest (1994) English paperback edition of *Malcolm*. The review, which is very positive and analytical, also discusses Purdy's *63: Dream Palace* and *The Nephew*. Binding writes "What impresses most about these three books is how distinctive and original Purdy's vision and art were from the outset; each also represents a different strand of the writer's complex imagination, which in time became interwoven." Binding continues his analysis of Purdy's writing: "Purdy is a creative genius who at his finest—in *Eustace Chisholm and the Works*, *Narrow Rooms*, and *Mourners Below*—has given literature in English some of the most impressive visionary novels of the past half-century. And without these excursions into the 'camp,' which were later integrated into full and imaginatively resonant portrayals of homosexual predicaments, Purdy would not be Purdy."

761    Bradbury, Malcolm. "Four Reviews." *London Magazine* 7 (July 1960): 81-82.

        A review of Purdy's *Malcolm*, Windham's *The Hero Continues*, Martin's *A Matter of Time* and Humana's *Looking In, Looking Out*. Bradbury gives *Malcolm* a mixed review: "There is nothing in *Malcolm*, his best book so far, to show him to be anything but a most delightful but surely not yet major talent." "The book is deliberately stylized and set out of period; but while its theme certainly concerns the lack of direction of man today, the decor is of the twenties, of a gilded era; and one experiences charm rather than recognition."

762     Bryden, Ronald. "Nineteen Sixty-Four." *The Spectator* 204 (29 April 1960): 633-634.

A review of four different novels, including *Malcolm*, which receives a short, negative review.

763     Carlile, Clancy. "It Took Less Than 20 Years for Malcolm to Mature." *San Francisco Chronicle*, 18 October 1959, p. 29.

A mixed review of *Malcolm* which ends: "But if *Malcolm* is a failure, it is a splendid failure, for all that. Purdy has a fluid and beautifully controlled style, an intent that cannot be impugned, and a light-heartedness about solemn matters which makes him, as they say in the reviews, a writer to be reckoned with."

764     Cook, Donald. "By the World Possessed." *New Republic* 141 (9 November 1959): 26-27.

A positive review of *Malcolm* which states: "There is a great deal of depravity and perversity in *Malcolm* and the remarkable thing about the book is the author's ability to touch upon these things with gentleness and wit, and thereby to provide new illuminations.... This book pulls together many of the themes of Purdy's shorter works, and prunes out some merely indulgent morbidities which sometimes mar them."

765     Curley, Thomas F. "The Sleep-Waker." *Commonweal* 71 (16 October 1959): 80.

A mixed review of *Malcolm*. Curley writes, "The more I read of Mr. Purdy the less I understand. That he has a strong talent, even a genius, is at once so assured technically and so 'crazy' in its intuition that I wonder if he will ever come to grips with the familiar, the vulgar, the everyday." Curley briefly compares Purdy to Poe when he notes, "What strikes me as odd is that sensation of moving in, or watching, a dream, but a dream that is controlled by a conscious and ever vigilant dream master, Mr. Purdy himself. It was Poe who used the term 'sleep-waker,' and though at first encounter they are worlds apart there is somewhat of the mathematician of dreams in Purdy as there is in Poe."

766  Dorman, David. "Fiction." *Library Journal* 84 (15 October 1959): 3153.

A short, negative review of *Malcolm* which states, "The story is disjointed and rambling, the symbolism ranging from the obvious to the obscure and the writing frequently immature."

767  "Fiction." *Kirkus Service* 27 (1 August 1959): 562.

A negative review of *Malcolm*. The reviewer writes, "a fantasia which is almost a freakshow is handled with contrasts of deliberate naiveté and sophistication—and if there's a message, it's easy to miss."

768  Finn, James. "Critics' Choices for Christmas." *Commonweal* 71 (4 December 1959): 293.

Finn's choice is *Malcolm* and he writes that the novel is "a wild and witty, zany and controlled story that deals with an adolescent loose among the oddities of our culture. This novel, which seems to derive its force from a contained hysteria, is an original among today's many copies."

769  Hicks, Granville. "Literary Horizons: Purdy, Humes, Ellis." *Saturday Review* 42 (26 September 1959):15.

A mixed review of *Malcolm* in which Hicks refers to the novel as "a fantasy, whose grotesqueness is terrible rather than amusing.... Purdy's disciplined style is enough to entitle him to respect, and his grotesque characters are brilliantly conceived. What he is up to, however, is not clear at all."

770  "The Innocent Zany." *Times Literary Supplement* (6 May 1960): 285.

A review of three current novels includes Purdy's *Malcolm*. The reviewer writes, "Read as simple bizarrerie this extravaganza is entirely satisfactory in entertainment value. Mr. Purdy's prose is skillful, disciplined, and visually apt; the fertility of his original imagination produces a series of lazzi which bring to mind the comic absurdities of the circus ring and bear just the right amount of resemblance to the commonplace to distinguish the scene from the never-never land of pantomime. Some of the more sinister and sardonic incidents recall the world of Harold Pinter's plays."

771    Johnson, George. "New & Noteworthy." *New York Times Book Review* (20 December 1987): 28.

Notes that Purdy's *Malcolm* and *The Nephew* have been reprinted by Weidenfeld and Nicolson.

772    Keown, Eric. "New Novels." *Punch* 238 (18 May 1960): 704.

A review of four novels including Purdy's *Malcolm*. Keown writes, "Mr. Purdy's comic portraits are marvelous. To combine artificiality and farce as he does is a rare feat, but he is a really imaginative writer, and though he may be too agile for the general taste, I think him a great discovery."

773    Lewis, R.W.B. "Baffling, Perverse, Demonic, Original." *New York Herald Tribune Book Review* (11 October 1959): 5.

A very positive review of *Malcolm*. Lewis writes that this first novel confirms his "earlier impression that James Purdy is a writer of exceptional talent, who must be acknowledged in the company, say of Saul Bellow and Ralph Ellison—with whom, in all his uniqueness, Mr. Purdy has much in common." And "Mr. Purdy possesses a demonic originality, but it is an originality chiefly of angle of perspective and selection of detail. The themes he sounds are the great ones. Malcolm himself is a familiar American fictional hero. Like Melville's *Billy Budd*, he is a helplessly god-like young man. He is passive, beguiling and nearly mindless; the object of a constant and furious yearning; at once an inspiration and a disaster for his new acquaintances." And Lewis concludes, "There is, then, something large and comprehensive in this hectic little book. But it is something seen from below the water-surface, the layers of habit and reason. What Mr. Purdy has seen with his disturbingly unfamiliar eyes is a crucial portion of the truth about ourselves, and he has recorded it with uncommon and inimitable fidelity." Contains a photograph of Purdy.

774     Lezard, Nicholas. "Paperback Round-Up." *The Guardian*, 21 March 1985, sec. T, p. 12.

A brief, positive review of the reprint edition of *Malcolm*. Lezard believes "Purdy is an unfairly neglected writer."

775     McLaughlin, Richard. "Malcolm." *Springfield Republican* (22 November 1959): 5.

A short, negative review of *Malcolm*, in which McLaughlin writes "It is fashionable today to write outre novels, with implausible situations and not much rhyme or reason to plot or characters. James Purdy's *Malcolm* is tailored to this pattern. This bizarre tale is about the 'short long life' of fifteen-year old Malcolm. Sort of a cross between creations of Ronald Firbank and Djuna Barnes, with a dash of Truman Capote's feyness thrown in."

776     Miller, Nolan. "Of the Many, a Few: A Fiction Summary." *Antioch Review* 20 (summer 1960): 248-256.

An essay which reviews over a dozen different, current publications and provides a short review of *Malcolm*.

777     "New Fiction." *Times* (London), 28 April 1960, p. 17.

A review of six new novels including *Malcolm*. A positive review which states: "*Malcolm* is a novel of some distinction. Mr. Purdy writes like an angel, with accuracy, wit, and freshness (not a cliché of feeling or expression occurs), but a fallen angel, versed in the sinful ways of man."

778     "New in Paperback." *Book World* (*Washington Post*) (30 November 1980) : 12.

A brief note on the publication of the Penguin edition of *Malcolm*, which notes, "Purdy's first novel remains unequaled in his own oeuvre, no doubt to his regret."

779     "Paperbacks: New and Noteworthy." *New York Times Book Review* (23 November 1980): 51.

A short note on the publication of the Penguin edition of *Malcolm* with the Edward Albee foreword.

780     Peden, William. "Pilgrimage to Destruction." *New York Times Book Review* (27 September 1959): 5, 30.

A positive review of *Malcolm* in which Peden notes, "Writing a novel like *Malcolm,* combining as it does the methods and elements of traditional story-telling, allegory, the *roman à clef*, and the parody, is like attempting to walk a tightrope while juggling a handful of billiard balls and balancing a typewriter. If he slips occasionally, Mr. Purdy always regains his balance. Ribald and poignant by turns, he has written a compelling allegory, fascinating, disgusting and disturbing, full of humor but devoid of merriment, crackling with mordant commentary on the bestiality which surrounds us, permeated with the cold melancholy accompanying the presence of evil."

781     Powys, John Cowper. "On Malcolm." *Powys Notes: A Publication of the Powys Society of North America* 4 (spring 1988): 1-2.

A very positive review of *Malcolm*, which Powys wrote for the original publishers on July 12, 1959. However, this essay never appeared until 1988. Powys ends his essay by writing: "The tale floats and rocks like a boat on that mysterious river of which none of us really know either the beginning or the end, the river of human life upon earth."

782    Raksin, Alex. "Now in Paperback." *Los Angeles Times*, 11
       October 1987, Book Review Section, p. 14.

       A review of the new paperback edition of *Malcolm*,
       published by Weidenfeld & Nicolson. Raksin notes,
       "By implying that Malcolm is too innocent for this
       world, Purdy thus leaves others with a somewhat sour
       feeling about the human community that was,
       heretofore, heartachingly portrayed." He ends his
       review: "Still, most of his novel is well-crafted, an
       entertaining, picaresque journey through fluctuating
       emotions in the lives of ordinary people."

783    Richardson, Maurice. "New Novels." *New Statesman* 59
       (7 May 1960): 688.

       A review of four novels including Purdy's *Malcolm*. A
       negative review in which the reviewer notes: "My own
       conviction is that the farce, fantasy, and realism do not
       really quite blend, and that often entertaining, it is too
       often just a bit too silly to be a really good book."

784    Shrapnel, Norman. "A New Round in the Old Struggle?"
       *The Guardian*, 6 May 1960, p. 8.

       A short, positive review in which Shrapnel writes,
       "*Malcolm* is a very good novel ... a comic fantasy, and
       you must add that it is also wise and sad."

785    Wright, Andrew. "Frivolousness Is Weakness of New
       Novel by Purdy." *Ohioana* 2 (winter 1959): 150-151.

       A negative review of *Malcolm*. The review notes, "It
       is a gallery of grotesques—but they are grotesque in
       relation to nothing. This may, indeed, be what the book
       is about: nothing. It is not enough."

## *Mourners Below*

786    Bell, David. "Fiction Briefs." *Saturday Review* 8 (June
       1981): 55-56.

       A negative review of *Mourners Below* which ends:
       "Pretentious utterances, clichés, and non-sequiturs

turn his ill-conceived and awkwardly executed gallery of bellowing mourners into an unintentional comedy."

787    Charyn, Jerome. "Unloved and Angry." *New York Times Book Review* (26 July 1981): 8.

A positive review of *Mourners Below*. Charyn notes: "The story is deceptively simple. It's a kind of battlefield where the living play dead, and the dead begin to warp those 'mourners below.' Most of the novel exists in that last hour 'between very late and very early.' This has always been the strength of Mr. Purdy's writing. He cuts below the skin and doesn't become involved with the sociology of any particular time or place. He uses locale to isolate hysteria and deal with that terrible anger of being unloved. The rhythms of his prose have nothing to do with mimicry, or the rendering of American speech. He has never sought to be a caricaturist, to parody the best or the worst of our lives. That slight awkwardness of Mr. Purdy's corrosive style, the deadpan electricity his characters speak with is the crazy jumping sound of the heart's own music. James Purdy is one of the very best writers we have. He exists in some strange limbo between adoration and neglect. Perhaps this is because Mr. Purdy doesn't play the peacock in his books or strut around with his talents. You have to peek under the feathers to catch the wildness of his prose."

788    Clark, Tom. "A United Family of the Dead and the Survivors." *Los Angeles Times*, 10 July 1981, pt. 5, p. 18.

A very positive review of *Mourners Below*. Clark believes Duane Bledsoe, the main character is "one of the most interesting character-creations in recent fiction." Clark writes, "James Purdy taps deep rivers, disturbing undercurrents, in a prose that's poetic in the best senses—a metaphorical structure that compresses and illumines reality without copying it."

789    Cohen, Debra Rae. "Review." *Village Voice* 29 (22 July 1981): 37.

A very positive review of *Mourners Below*. The reviewer begins: "James Purdy has the unmistakable voice and gently antiquated phrasing of a radio announcer. His stilted, lilting colloquialism infects each of his characters with a common tempo flatness of tone and gives his narration the rickety preciousness of a porch swing. The voice fits the timeless midwest of Purdy's best stories—and of his new novel, *Mourners Below*." Review contains a photograph of Purdy.

790    DeVries, Jan. "Nothing of Value at Center." *Philadelphia Evening Bulletin*, 5 July 1981.

A very negative review of *Mourners Below*. DeVries writes: "I am disturbed that 300 pages of (small town American) life are offered with such an absence of feeling and that the young man with whom we are concerned is, despite the gamut he's forced through, utterly unfleshed."

791    "Fiction." *Publishers' Weekly* 219 (17 April 1981): 50.

A very positive review of *Mourners Below*, which states, "Purdy fans will welcome with open arms the author's latest contribution, a powerful story of a Midwestern family and town." And, "Purdy's talent shines through in his highly polished characterizations, the intricate set of interrelationships, and deeply foreboding insight."

792    Hall, Joan Joffe. "Writing in a Language That Exists Nowhere Else." *Houston Post*, 19 July 1981.

A very negative review of *Mourners Below*. Hall writes, "But Purdy's writing is so bad that it keeps getting in the way of the enjoyment the story has to offer and obscures the characters' motivations."

793    Hochswender, Woody. "Living in the Shadow of the Legendary Departed." *Los Angeles Herald Examiner*, 20 November 1991.

A negative review of *Mourners Below* which states, "to be different you have to be good. Very, very good. Purdy isn't."

794    Hooper, William Bradley. "Adult Fiction." *Booklist* 77 (May 1981): 1187.

> A short, negative review of *Mourners Below* which ends: "The primary problem though, is that his realism and fantasy are like oil and water, making the novel a jarring juxtaposition of sentimentality and sensationalism."

795    "In a Wiped Out Village." *Financial Times* (26 May 1984): 12.

> A review of five novels including Purdy's *Mourners Below*. A positive review which notes, "He [Purdy] uses a lot of dialogue and his dialogue is amazingly good, so reading him is rather like sitting in on a play, an intensely dramatic experience in the true sense. On the other hand, his tone is quiet and reserved, and for long stretches little seems to happen, the action advances in a jerky talk and disconcertingly abrupt events, at once funny and moving; the whole atmosphere unlike anyone else's."

796    Jordis, Christine. "Par Ordre des Trepasses." *La Quinzaine Litteraire* (March 1984): 8.

> *Mourners Below* translated into French by Claire Malroux. Review of *Les Inconsoles*.

797    Klein, Julia M. "Brief Reviews." *New Republic* 185 (18 July 1981): 39.

> A positive review of *Mourners Below*, in which Klein writes, "*Mourners Below* recapitulates many of Purdy's concerns with small-town families in crises, the explosiveness of contained emotion, the marriage between the dead and the living." Purdy is "creating a world where the supernatural merges with the real, he illuminates a reality whose core, if not its contours, matches our own."

798    Krist, Gary. "Review." *American Book Review* 4 (May - June 1982): 11.

A very positive review of *Mourners Below* which notes, "The book remains elusive, and this fact, while certainly inconvenient for the critic, is perhaps the novel's greatest strength.... While Purdy's language resembles the flat prose of an Ann Beattie or a Raymond Carver carried to its extreme, it is imbued with an archaic formality quite unlike anything else in contemporary fiction. It is the language of no world I am familiar with outside of Purdy's novels. James Purdy is, in short, an unusual and remarkable writer. He may even be an important one, and *Mourners Below*, one of his best novels, will do nothing to hurt his reputation. If we are ever to appreciate the true value of his body of work, however, it is imperative that we stop viewing him as either embarrassing cult idol or neglected genius, and begin seeing him for what he is— a compassionate storyteller and an original stylist of the very first order."

799    "Paperbacks:  New & Noteworthy." *New York Times Book Review* (18 July 1982): 27.

A positive brief review of Purdy's *Mourners Below* in paperback.

800    Polk, David. "James Purdy: Laughing at Our Weakness." *Louisville Courier-Journal*, 6 September 1981.

A very positive review of *Mourners Below*. Polk writes that this novel is perhaps Purdy's best. He says, "Purdy is a tough-minded moralist with a wonderfully dark sense of humor, and, though set in a small Midwestern town, this is a sophisticated comedy written after facing the most there is to know about us."

801    Portis, Rowe. "Fiction." *Library Journal*  106 (15 May 1981): 1100.

A very brief review of *Mourners Below* which notes, "What Purdy is aiming at in all this is never resolved very clearly."

802    "Review."  *Kirkus Reviews* 49 (15 April 1981): 530.

A mixed review of *Mourners Below*. The reviewer notes that "Purdy is nothing if not a one-of-a-kind writer, and one probably shouldn't be surprised as he lurches here from soap-opera into Gothic complications and ghost-story ... half divertisement, half balderdash, then—another curious book by an always curious writer."

803    Treadwell, T. O. "The Dead More Alive Than the Living." *Times Literary Supplement* (31 August 1984): 977.

A negative review of *Mourners Below*. Treadwell writes, "The meaning of *Mourners Below* lies on the symbolic, even allegorical level—where spiritual desolation is suggested by houses with too many rooms, and sweat and saliva become the water of life." The review concludes, "He is, of course, quite entitled to demand that his readers work to get below the arid surface of the novel, but the rewards for making the effort are meagre."

804    Walsten, David M. "Novel No. 10 for Purdy; It's Another Dud." *Chicago Sun-Times*, 7 June 1981.

A negative review of *Mourners Below*. Walsten writes, "Storytelling has never been Purdy's forte—or indeed, his interest. The rules of cause and effect, which we have a right to expect in novels as much as anywhere, simply are not invoked."

805    Wood, Steve. "Review." *Tulsa World*, 6 September 1981.

A positive review of *Mourners Below*. Wood writes, "The story seems simple enough on the surface, but is in fact rather disturbing. Purdy's small, quiet American town is a disguise for solitary passions."

## Narrow Rooms

806    Bianco, David. "Book Review." *Best Sellers* 38 (June 1978): 71.

A positive review of *Narrow Rooms* which notes: "The
story is filled with moments of violence and passion. It
is easy to become involved with the characters and
share their hopeless frustrations, even as their twisted
logic and odd behavior keep them distanced from us.
No irrelevant details  intrude into Purdy's concise
narrative as it moves to its chilling, grotesque climax."

807     Bresnick, Paul. "Love in the Zone." *New York Arts
        Journal*  9 (April/May 1978): 15-16.

A strong, positive review of *Narrow Rooms* as well as
a perceptive view of Purdy's writing in total. Bresnick
begins his lengthy review with a quote from Leslie
Fiedler: "There can be no terror without the hope for
love and love's defeat." He writes, "Virtually
everything James Purdy has written ... can be read as
variations on this theme.  For Purdy, Christ's message
was the last great event—the critical idea—in the
history of human consciousness: 'love one another as I
have loved you.'  But Purdy is also a Calvinist (by way
of Presbyterianism); he's a firm believer in man's fallen
state.... When you put Christ and Calvin together, you
wind up with the conflict at the heart of Purdy's vision:
Christ held out the hope for love; man continually
assures love's defeat; hence, terror.  So Purdy's books
are love/horror stories.  In a significant sense, they are
typically American tales of love and death (to borrow
another of Fiedler's formulations).  They are chronicles
of thwarted, aborted, twisted, hopeless, failed love.
Purdy examines aspects of eros that we'd rather not
acknowledge: the part of love that is hate; love as a
struggle for supremacy; love as constantly shifting
pattern of submission and dominance; lovemaking as an
act of revenge, or as ritualized murder; loving as
obsessive behavior—the uncontrolled urge to possess,
to sublime, to consume another; love a cannibalism.
Purdy's subject is the suffering, blundering, cruelty of
love—a cruelty arising from its very helplessness.  And
here, is the recognition of the innocent, helpless springs
of love, is Purdy's surprising affective sweetness."
Concerning *Narrow Rooms* Bresnick writes, "In fact,

186

one might go so far as to say that *Narrow Rooms* is the
most thorough, honest, human treatment of homosexual
love by a writer of serious fiction in America, period.
Purdy must be praised for having the courage to
examine a hitherto ignored area of human experience in
a serious novel—for illuminating these passions in a
'bright book of life.' If only for this, Purdy's novel
deserves to be recognized as groundbreaking—
revolutionary, even. For there are certainly other
reasons to praise this book. For one thing, Purdy has a
remarkably accurate ear for American speech
patterns—for the cadences and special flavors of the
vernacular."

808    Everson, Stephen. "Shorter Reviews." *New Statesman*
       110 (30 August 1985): 27.

       A very positive review of *Narrow Rooms*. Everson
       notes that the novel is "extraordinary ... a compelling
       and harrowing book. Purdy relentlessly creates a world
       in which passion is a force of nature."

809    Fender, Stephen. "Parodying Porn." *Times Literary
       Supplement* (14 March 1980): 296.

       A negative review of *Narrow Rooms*. Fender ends: "I
       can only express the hope that Purdy has not decided
       to write only for the coterie of gays and thesis writers
       who have read all of his earlier work and that of his
       more intelligent critics, and that in the future he will
       again find it philosophically honorable to spare a little of
       his wit and vigour for ordinary readers."

810    "Fiction." *Booklist* 74 (1 May 1978): 1413.

       A negative review of *Narrow Rooms* which states,
       "Purdy's convincing Southern Gothic mannerisms
       seem overpowered by a series of increasingly
       grotesque incidents and encounters; the culminating
       horror of the final scene, with its implication of
       redemption through love-death, receives fragile
       justification from the sensationalized sequence of
       events that leads upon it."

811     "Fiction." *Publishers' Weekly* 213 (6 February 1978): 90.

> A negative review of *Narrow Rooms*, which ends: "Many readers will find this Southern Gothic tedious, poorly written and painful to read."

812     "Fiction." *West Coast Review of Books* 4 (May 1978): 32.

> A mixed review of *Narrow Rooms*. The reviewer notes that the novel "is a difficult book to review. Difficult, because it gives evidence of the author's abilities both as a craftsman and as a storyteller, without his offering a totally satisfactory novel."

813     Mauries, Patrick. "Le Tres-Etroit: James Purdy's *Narrow Rooms*, *In a Shallow Grave* and *Je Suis Vivant dan ma Tombe*." *Critique: Revue Generale des Publications Francaises et Etrangenes* 35 (November 1979): 964-971.

> A review in French of Narrow Rooms and In a Shallow Grave.

814     Mitchell, Roger. "Fiction." *Library Journal* 103 (15 March 1978): 684.

> A very positive review of *Narrow Rooms*. Mitchell writes "Purdy understands, much as Faulkner did, how the whole of a person's life can be shaped by rejection through people and events that, at best, are extraordinary and, at worst, are merely theatrical."

815     Naughton, John. "Tales of Pain." *The Listener* 103 (6 March 1980): 318-319.

> A review of four novels including Purdy's *Narrow Rooms*, Aldiss's *Life in the West*, Bailey's *Old Soldiers* and Laquer's *The Missing Years*. Naughton gives *Narrow Rooms* a very positive review as he writes, "*Narrow Rooms* is a sparce tale of extraordinary power which describes the vicious, incomprehensible and inexplicable tensions built up around four young homosexual men in a remote part of West Virginia."

816    Pollitt, Katha. "Ovid and the Boys." *New York Times Book Review* (23 April 1978): 10-11, 46.

A very negative review of Purdy's *Narrow Rooms* and David Malouf's *An Imaginary Life*. Pollitt feels that the novel is "well below the level of Mr. Purdy's great work."

817    "Recommended Novels of the Quarter." *Antioch Review* 36 (summer 1978): 388.

Five novels are recommended including Purdy's *Narrow Rooms*. The reviewer calls the novel "a spellbinder, as expected, from the master of the modern tale.... Purdy's ear for flat American speech is forever memorable."

## The Nephew

818    Arnold, James W. "Review." *Ave Maria* 93 (March 1961): 26.

A very positive review of *The Nephew*. Arnold writes, "Readers of Mr. Purdy's are never quite sure whether this superb technician (his characterizations are always fresh, perceptive dialogue could easily be a model for creative writing classes) is playing it for laughs or tragedy.... Mr. Purdy has the gift of seeing both the humor and dignity of the human condition and communicating it with clarity and perception. His message here is that all men are really strangers to each other, and that human love, imitating divine love, should be willing to overlook abundant faults."

819    Baro, Gene. "A Second Novel and a Change of Pace." *New York Herald Tribune Book Review* (6 November 1960): 8.

A mixed review of *The Nephew*. Baro begins the review: "Where *Malcolm* was imaginative, vivacious and even somewhat florid, *The Nephew* is constrained, solemn and monochrome. It affirms a number of Mr. Purdy's considerable abilities and is important in

theme, but it strikes one, in effect, as lesser work."
Baro concludes: "I should say that *The Nephew* is
admirable in the cogency of its vision, but lacking in
force. Nevertheless, it is a rewarding book for the
number of its fine touches; it could only have been
written by a novelist of great gifts." Contains a
photograph of Purdy by Fabian Bachrach.

820  Charles, Gerda. "New Novels." *New Statesman* 61 (24
March 1961): 484.

A review of four new novels published in England
including Purdy's *The Nephew*. A mixed review: "*The
Nephew* is a pliant, supple, echoing little piece
encompassing within a simple framework ..." and
concludes: "To my perhaps crude ear he seems to pipe
away, giving a very accurate, very distinguished little
performance on a very tiny flute. I admire; but he does
not gage my attention."

821  Davenport, John. "A Masterpiece From America." *The
Observer* (London), 19 March 1961.

A review of five works including *Colour of Darkness*
and *The Nephew*. Davenport considers *The Nephew*
"a modest masterpiece [and] Purdy's best book to
date." About *Colour of Darkness* he writes, "At a first
glance these pieces have a surface glitter that suggests
Truman Capote, but the virtuosity is misleading. There
are no clichés, but there is no posturing; the intensity of
the style is designed to achieve naturalness. And even
when Mr. Purdy is diving deep into the waters of
perversity he never drowns in them."

822  Deasy, Philip C. "Review." *Critic* 19 (December
1960/January 1961): 68.

A very negative review of *The Nephew*. Deasy writes,
"*The Nephew* certainly gives no evidence of genius,
and as far as writing talent goes, all it reveals is that
Mr. Purdy is capable of putting together a potboiler only
slightly above slick magazine quality."

823    Didion, Joan. "The Edge of the Precipice." *National Review* 9 (19 November 1960): 315-316.

    A positive review of *The Nephew*. Ms. Didion writes that the novel "is a sure, spellbinding, chillingly good little novel, an uncanny triumph of matter over mind. Like Mr. Purdy's far more surrealist *63: Dream Palace*, *The Nephew* compels by the sheer brilliance of its telling—but you had best draw your chair up to the edge of the precipice, because there's no widowered apothecary in sight."

824    Dolbier, Maurice. "Daily Book Review: The Nephew." *New York Herald Tribune*, 8 October 1960, p. 9.

    A positive review of *The Nephew*. After a detailed plot and character summary Dolbier writes, "There is an odd and compelling kind of resonance in the telling of the story—the colloquial phrases used by the characters seem to stir old echoes in the reader's mind, reverberatory as the striking of the courthouse clock. There is a sadder significance in the number of things that are said and that remain unheard—time and again there are lines like 'her voice was not loud enough to reach through his deafness.' Mr. Purdy's own voice is becoming stronger and clearer with each book." Contains a photograph of Purdy.

825    "Fiction." *Booklist* 57 (15 October 1960): 117-118.

    A short review of *The Nephew* which calls it "a well written story that portrays characters, emotions and place with depth and precision. For discriminating readers."

826    "Fiction." *Kirkus Service* 28 (1 August 1960): 646.

    A positive review of *The Nephew*. The reviewer writes, "In its low-keyed way, this is a true, rather sad picture of old age, and a rather surprising book after *Malcolm* in which the young and talented writer was far less accessible."

827    Gold, Herbert. "Dame Edith Was Right." *New Republic* 143 (3 October 1960): 17.

A positive review of Purdy's *The Nephew* in which Gold compares Purdy to Kafka: "Purdy, like Kafka, tells dreams which turn out to be stories and at the same time retain their fretful, oppressive dream quality." Also, Gold notes, "like Nabokov in *Lolita*, Purdy is pervaded by a hopeless, witty, intelligent nostalgia."

828    Harnack, Curtis. "An Allegorical Comedy of Odd Folks at Home." *Chicago Sunday Tribune Magazine of Books* (9 October 1960): 6.

A very positive review of *The Nephew*. Mr. Harnack writes, "The prose throughout the novel is scrupulous, provocative; it has the surface appearance of a calm, realistic style, but isn't. This whole allegory-fantasy is in no sense recognizably realistic, yet one is constantly struck by the perceptions that are relevant to our real-unreal times."

829    Harrison, Keith. "Journey Without Maps." *The Spectator* 212 (21 February 1965): 258.

A review of *Colour of Darkness*, *Malcolm* and *The Nephew*. Of the three titles, Harrison finds *The Nephew* to be his favorite and *Malcolm* his least favorite. Overall, Harrison writes, "Mr. James Purdy is a writer *sui generis*. The exact flavour of his style is hard to describe, he is wry, farcical at times, and some of his characterizations are close to fantasy. But always he is concerned with the truth of his subject, deeply committed to the area of reality that he chooses to explore."

830    Hassan, Ihab. "After the Grotesque." *Shenandoah* 13 (spring 1962): 62-65.

A review of four American novels by O'Connor, Hawkes, Purdy and Malamud. Hassan compares Purdy's *The Nephew* to Sherwood Anderson's writing. He ends his review with, "There is less studied eccentricity, and at the same time more inertness, more diffuseness, in his novel than in earlier works of Purdy; yet it is a book about the inwardness and perversity of that truth which has sometimes gone by the name of innocence in America."

831    Houlihan, Thomas F. "Fiction." *Library Journal* 85 (15 September 1960): 3104.

A favorable review of *The Nephew* which states "Mr. Purdy can be proud of this fine, second novel. For all collections."

832    Hughes, Riley. "Novels." *Catholic World* 192 (February 1961): 310-311.

A positive review of Purdy's *The Nephew*. The reviewer writes, "What is most telling about the book and what makes it most worth reading is the quiet realism about the states of mind of the two old people, Alma and Boyd."

833    Keown, Eric. "New Novels." *Punch* 240 (29 March 1961): 517-518.

A review of four novels including Purdy's *The Nephew*. A positive review in which Keown writes, "*The Nephew* is not so uproariously funny as *Malcolm*, but its deceptive simplicity masks a rare degree of wisdom."

834    Lewis, R.W.B. "Our Jaws Are Sagging After Our Bout With Existence." *New York Times Book Review* (9 October 1960): 5.

A very positive review of *The Nephew*. Lewis notes, "The movement of the story is from detachment to reality, from vulgarity to beauty, from a faint, ominous timelessness and placelessness to a 'here' and a settled 'now.' "

835    McLaughlin, Richard. "*The Nephew* by James Purdy." *Springfield Republican*, 30 October 1960, sec. D, p. 4.

A very positive review of *The Nephew* in which McLaughlin writes, "It is indeed a pleasant surprise to find that James Purdy can produce a compelling and compassionate picture of everyday life within the framework of his present novel.... The fact that he does not have to fall back on the bizarre subject matter or experimental technique so evident in his previous books, and can wring from commonplace such genuine pathos and anguish—and terrible truths—makes one wonder if he isn't after all, among the more gifted of the new crop of U.S. novelists. In fact, it is so very different that one is almost tempted to think that he must have a soberer twin."

836    Miller, Nolan. "Three of the Best." *Antioch Review* 21 (spring 1961): 118-128.

A review of Purdy's *The Nephew*, Updike's *Rabbit Run*, and Spencer's *The Light in the Piazza*. Miller writes, "With James Purdy, I am delighted to say, whether in any of his powerful and distinctive short stories or in *Malcolm*, and, finally, with *The Nephew*, the target, if not always in plain view, comes into view in the most astonishingly revelatory way." Miller notes that Purdy's work has been warmly appreciated by a small group of readers, and has had little popularity.

837    "New Fiction." *Times* (London), 23 March 1961, p. 17.

A review of six novels including *The Nephew* and the reissue of *Colour of Darkness*. A negative review of the collection of short stories, *Colour of Darkness*, and a positive review of *The Nephew* is given. The reviewer writes, "*The Nephew* is a vast improvement on the short stories." And, "Mr. Purdy slides into the heart of his characters with a deceptive simplicity which tends in the short stories to be blotted out by the sheer nastiness of his subjects."

838    "Notes on Current Books." *Virginia Quarterly Review* 37 (winter 1961): 7.

A short, positive review of *The Nephew* which states, "Mr. Purdy now gives us an incredibly well articulated story of life in a small town with warmly human beings whose apparently simple lives turn out to be upon examination infinitely complex.... He has quite definitely written a superior book and one consonant with our best literary traditions."

839      "Ohio Nights." *Time* 76 (17 October 1960): 110-111.

A positive review of *The Nephew*. The reviewer writes, "In his previous books, *Color of Darkness* and *Malcolm*, Ohio-born James Purdy, 37, dealt with nightmare subjects in a complex, brooding style that often baffled readers. This time, in the manner of a futurist painter determined to allow doubters, he can be a master of realistic drawing if he chooses. Purdy uses a simple, controlled and explicit prose to achieve his eerie effects. Whether he is being opaque or clear, novelist Purdy peoples his books with troubling and troubled human beings, proves himself a writer of considerable power and impressive originality." Contains a photograph of Purdy.

840      "Paperbacks: Fiction." *Publishers' Weekly* 191 (24 April 1967): 96.

A positive review of the Noonday edition of *The Nephew* which includes an introduction by R. W. B. Lewis. The reviewer quotes Lewis who claims this is a very original work and was unjustly criticized when first published.

841      Peden, William. "Mystery of the Missing Kin." *Saturday Review* 43 (26 November 1960): 22.

A very positive review of *The Nephew*. Peden writes, "There are no false moves, no wrong turns in *The Nephew*. From humor to pathos, from farce to caricature or to straight narrative, Mr. Purdy is in constant control of his material. His vision is as sharp and clean as a hound's tooth, his narrative method is swift, unencumbered, and uncluttered. If any doubts exist concerning Mr. Purdy's unique abilities, this slender, unpretentious, thoroughly admirable novel should dispel them. There may have been a more impressive American novel published in 1960, if so, I have not heard about it."

842     Peterson, Clarence. "Paperbacks." *Chicago Tribune Books Today* (11 June 1967): 6.

A brief listing of the new Noonday edition of *The Nephew* with an introduction by R. W. Lewis.

843     Phillipson, John S. "Book Review." *Best Sellers* 20 (1 November 1960): 295.

A very negative review of *The Nephew*. The reviewer writes that the novel "is slow-moving, talky and digressive."

844     Pickrel, Paul. "Bark in America." *Harper's Magazine* 221 (November 1960): 120.

A negative review of *The Nephew*. Pickrel writes, "The subject is developed very amateurishly, the characterization is not incisive and most of the characters bear only the slightest resemblance to the kinds of people who actually live in small, Middle Western towns."

845     "Recommended New Titles - Fiction." *New York Times Book Review* (12 August 1973): 16.

A positive notice about *The Nephew*.

846     "Review - Paperbacks." *Book World* (*Washington Post*) (26 August 1973): 13.

A short, positive review of *The Nephew*.

847     Rubin, Louis D., Jr. "Six Novels and S. Levin." *Sewanee Review* 70 (summer 1962): 504-514.

A review of six current novels including Purdy's *The Nephew*. Rubin gives the novel a negative review and writes, "The novel is precisely wrought, clearly written; nothing is left to chance, and everything is in its proper place. Yet having said that, what else is one to say? The quiet desperation of the characters is too muted to be important. Rainbow Center's problems are by implication the world's, but the whole thing is keyed so low that there is no incentive to explore the implications."

848    Saal, Rollene W. "Pick of the Paperbacks." *Saturday Review* 50 (26 August 1967): 34.

    A brief mention of the Noonday edition of *The Nephew*. Notes that "Purdy's novels are peopled with the oddest company."

849    Seymour-Smith, Martin. "Novels." *Encounter* 27 (August 1961): 81-84.

    A review of seven novels including Purdy's *The Nephew*, Nabokov's *Laughter in the Dark* and Middleton's *A Serious Woman*. Seymour-Smith writes, "*The Nephew* is a sad, subtle, tender, and frighteningly competent novel. I have only one reservation about it, and that is sometimes Mr. Purdy writes as though he were a robot, invented by Professor Trilling for the purpose of demonstrating how the Jamesian novel has been transformed by Freud."

850    Singer, Burns. "New Novels." *The Listener* 65 (23 March 1961): 541.

    A review of four novels including Purdy's *The Nephew*, English's *Four Voices*, Colette's *Break of Day*, and Hanley's *The Journey Homeward*. A positive review of *The Nephew*, which notes that "The book is full of surprises, the kind which are a major sign of a major writer ... there is only one thing to do with Mr. Purdy. Read him."

851    Southern, Terry. "New Trends and Old Hats." *The Nation* 191 (19 November 1960): 380-381.

    A review essay of seven current novels including Purdy's *The Nephew*. A mixed review in which Southern writes, "Mr. Purdy, like Mr. Barth, has a highly developed and often deceptive sense of the absurd; his work continues to show an intense fidelity to his own particular perception of things, and whether or not this assumes a too highly personal form for most tastes, it is none the less upon this kind of alliance that any strength of American writing depends."

852    Tornquist, Elizabeth. "The New Parochialism."
       *Commentary* 31 (May 1961): 449-452.

> A review of Purdy's *The Nephew* and Morris'
> *Ceremony in Lone Tree*. A mixed review of *The
> Nephew* in which Tornquist notes, "What is most solid
> in the book is his vision of these ordinary people as a
> grotesque; the characters are not conscious of it, for it
> is not a part of their experience, which is flat and
> conventional. The result is that the novelist's
> viewpoint becomes very obvious while the characters
> remain as flat as their experience."

853    Tucker, Martin. "All Ambivalent." *Commonweal* 73 (21
       October 1960): 99.

> A negative review of *The Nephew*. Tucker points out,
> "Where Purdy fails this time is in employing only
> sincerity and an extraordinary writing style in which
> every sentence seems the result of centuries of
> meditation. People also are needed for a novel. The
> plain fact is that the central character, Aunt Alma, is
> just not very interesting in the manner Purdy presents
> her.... Also, what Purdy lacks is a conclusion, a Molly
> Bloom episode, some way gathering up the shells
> picked up on the trip.... In *The Nephew*, he tries for
> compassion and high seriousness with such
> earnestness that he verges on sentimentality one
> moment and on vagueness the next."

## *On Glory's Course*

854    Brunsdale, Mitzi M. "Finding Almost Every Permutation
       of Passion." *Houston Post*, 8 April 1984.

> A very positive review of *On Glory's Course* which
> ends: "Purdy is one of those writers, like Chaucer, who
> has chosen to convey his view of the world by means of
> the comic, rather than the tragic, mode. His work rings
> unquenchably true because of it."

855    Deveson, Richard. "Book Review." *New Statesman* 109
       (1 February 1985): 32.

A review of three novels including *On Glory's Course*. Deveson gives the Purdy novel a negative review and concludes, "There's no accounting for awful taste."

856 "Fiction." *Publishers' Weekly* 224 (2 December 1983): 81.

  A positive review of *On Glory's Course*. The reviewer writes, "Purdy ... is a master of a comic art as distinctive as that of P. G. Wodehouse but deeper toned." The review ends: "The whole story is an amusing and outrageous potpourri of subtly linked human relationships—and maybe not so far removed from reality as all that."

857 Galloway, Stephen. "*On Glory's Course* Takes a Stab at Satirizing Smalltown, U.S.A." *Los Angeles Herald Examiner*, 26 March 1984.

  A very negative review of *On Glory's Course*. Galloway writes, "The problem is, the humor is strained. It is very difficult to care for these people or believe in their reality—not just because of plot convolutions and the characters' eccentricities, but also because Purdy's language is flat and the dialogue is, at best, unconvincing."

858 Kaveney, Roz. "Body-searches." *Times Literary Supplement* (8 March 1985): 286.

  A mixed review of *On Glory's Course*. Kaveney writes, "In spite of its bitchy airs and tawdry graces, the novel is partly redeemed by the way Purdy keeps the reader turning pages but you cannot beat a moralist and a sniggeress."

859 Klein, Julia M. "A Chronicle of Lust and Decay in Small-town America." *Philadelphia Inquirer*, 19 February 1984.

  A review of *On Glory's Course* which deals with the plot more than it criticizes the work. Klein writes, "The ambivalence he provokes is not unrelated to his own apparent ambivalence about matters of spirit and flesh. While deploring repression, Purdy depicts passion and love alike as elusive and degrading."

860    Lodge, Sally. "Paperback: Fiction Reprints." *Publishers'*
       *Weekly* 227 (4 January 1985): 68.

       A short note on *On Glory's Course* which states,
       "Purdy is a master of comic art, as distinctive as that of
       P. G. Wodehouse but deeper toned."

861    "New & Noteworthy." *New York Times Book Review*
       (17 March 1985): 44.

       A brief review of the new paperback edition of *On
       Glory's Course*. Robert J. Seidman's 1984 review of
       this novel is quoted.

862    Parrinder, Patrick. "Father, Son and Sewing Machine."
       *London Review of Books* 7 (21 February 1985): 22-23.

       A review of three new novels including Purdy's *On
       Glory's Course*. Parrinder gives the novel a mixed
       review. He writes, "The novel proceeds in brief,
       dramatised scenes, and before long the tempo of
       bizarre revelations becomes so heady that it seems
       likely to overwhelm the deadpan narrative. And on and
       on it goes, in an immensely skillful stylised melodrama,
       a tornado of small-town gossip."

863    Pendleton, Dennis. "Fiction." *Library Journal* 109 (1
       February 1984): 192.

       A positive review of *On Glory's Course* which states:
       "This is a novel of beautifully realized small town life,
       gossip, and aspirations. The mannered way of
       speaking seems fresh and new. There's not much plot
       here, but this is a world uniquely Purdy's and
       altogether engrossing."

864    Sallis, James. "Underneath a Placid Pretense, the
       Turbulence of Quiet Desperation." *Texas Morning News*,
       1 April 1984.

       A positive review of *On Glory's Course* in which the
       reviewer writes, "We are clearly once again in Purdy
       country, small-town intrigue and wry comedy only a
       veneer over the continual reality of private despair."

865    Schulte, Jean. "Small-Town Life Not Pretty in New
       Novel." *Columbus Dispatch*, 13 May 1984, sec. G, p. 8.

       A positive review of *On Glory's Course*. The review
       provides a detailed account of the plot and characters in
       the novel. Schulte notes that "the real strength of the
       novel lies in Purdy's unnerving portrayal of the subtle
       ways these characters draw comfort from one another,
       then use each others' idiosyncracies as grist for the
       rumor mill." Includes a photograph of Purdy.

866    Seidman, Robert J. "War Between Mothers and Sons."
       *New York Times Book Review* (26 February 1984): 25.

       A negative review of *On Glory's Course*. Seidman
       writes, "In attempting to catch the verbal rhythms of
       the 30's, Mr. Purdy has employed an idiom so
       ponderous that with the single exception of the rough-
       hewn Val Dougherty, all of his characters have trouble
       speaking their lines.... The failure of the novel's style
       makes *On Glory's Course* seem long-winded and self-
       conscious. Mr. Purdy has written—and probably will
       write—better novels."

867    Stewart, Rosemarie. "Review." *San Diego Magazine* 36
       (May 1984): 114.

       A positive review of *On Glory's Course*. Stewart
       writes, "James Purdy's latest novel has a style not
       unlike a particularly hilarious Benny Hill show. His
       characters have a richly absurd quality that gives
       literary zest to this humor that pokes fun at various
       sexual and social peccadilloes not entirely unknown
       beyond the confines of Fonthill and the printed page."

868    Von Blon, Joanne. "The Search for James Purdy."
       *Minneapolis Tribune*, 25 March 1984.

       A review of *On Glory's Course* and of Purdy's recent
       visit to the Walker Art Center, where he read from *On
       Glory's Course*. Of special importance are the following
       two quotes about Purdy: "These realities under the
       skin, the truths we had about ourselves that come out
       in times of emotional crisis, are, Purdy told his
       audience, the things that interest him." And, "He

writes, he told us, out of his unconscious. Things just
come to him without a great deal of planning beyond the
initial idea."

869    Walsten, David M. "Purdy Returns to Old Form." *Chicago
Sun-Times*, 3 June 1984, p. 32.

A positive review of *On Glory's Course*. Walsten
writes, "Now, after a falling off of some years from his
masterful early stories, Purdy is back in control with his
comic novel *On Glory's Course*, in which he treats us to
life of half a century ago in Fonthill, a town in what
would seem to be Ohio, where Purdy spent his own
childhood." Comparing Purdy to Sherwood Anderson,
Walsten notes, "Where Anderson saw only the dark
side of destiny, however, Purdy discovers endless
comedic opportunities." Contains a photograph of
Purdy.

## Out With the Stars

870    Baker, Phil. "Paperbacks." *The Sunday Times* (London),
4 July 1993, sec. Books, p. 14.

A negative review of *Out With the Stars*. The reviewer
ends by noting "Purdy's writing is as glittering and
artificial as the opera itself, and the story is resolved
with such a triumphant happy ending that he seems to
be waving his good fairy's work over it."

871    "Book Review - Out With the Stars." *Publishers' Weekly*
240 (5 July 1993): 61.

A positive review of *Out With the Stars* which notes,
"Purdy's trademark blood on high camp, bizarre
characters, outrageous satire and piercing realism
animates this offbeat romp.... While Purdy satirizes
avant-garde artiness and America's obsession with
celebrities, he displays affectionate sympathy for his
comic characters."

872    Coe, Jonathan. "Book Review." *London Review of Books*
14 (23 July 1992): 22-23.

A review of three current novels by Americans published in England and includes Purdy's *Out With the Stars*. Coe gives the novel a mixed review and refers to Purdy as "a well-established maverick who can still find room in his fiction for the truly bizarre and unpredictable." And Coe notes that "The dialogue is superbly fruity, and the book reaches a pitch of high camp."

873    Dieckmann, Katherine. "Viva Diva." *Village Voice Literary Supplement* 39 (8 March 1994): SS18.

A review of six contemporary works, including Purdy's *Out With the Stars*, which received a mixed review. Dieckmann's review notes, "The queen still creaks in James Purdy's compulsively cheesy novel ... in short, *Out With the Stars* is pure camp, if there even is such a thing anymore, or ever was."

874    Dyer, Richard. "Purdy Recreates a Gay, Surreal Old Time." *Boston Globe*, 11 February 1994, p. A22.

A mixed review of *Out With the Stars*. Dyer writes that: "This new novel isn't exactly a *roman à clef*, although aspects of the principal characters resemble aspects of such immediately recognizable figures as the composer Virgil Thomson, the novelists/photographer Carl Van Vechten and his wife, the silent movie siren Fania (nee Fanny) Marinoff. Another figure suggests an amalgam of Ned Rorem and the young James Purdy, hatched in Ohio and freshly arrived in New York, where as a racy young novelist (*Malcolm*) he was once unforgettably photographed by Van Vechten." Dyer also notes that Purdy writes with "an extraordinary, airy and effortless elegance of style." And, "an attraction of *Out With the Stars* is that it is such a gay book in both the ancient and modern senses of the word—deft, amusing, full of laughter, sunlit and dark, and suffused with a gay sensibility. There is almost no explicit sexual detail, yet the book is far sexier than the lewdest efforts of younger writers because it takes so much entirely for granted."

875     Granovetter, Shirley. "A Simple Shepherd." *Jerusalem Post*, 11 June 1993.

 A very negative review of *Out With the Stars* which states "If you want to leave the real world for two hours, read James Purdy's latest novel, *Out With the Stars*. But you will find neither purpose nor meaning in it. The stars are creature geniuses in the world of serious music and theater.... The writing is prosaic and the tale insignificant."

876     Hensher, Philip. "Drama in Dressing Gowns." *The Guardian*, 30 July 1992, p. 27.

 A negative review of *Out With the Stars* which notes, "The latest of James Purdy's excursions into camp American Gothic is concerned with the preparation and performance of an opera on the life of a novelist and photographer. Half of the characters are geniuses; the other half are widows. And they all have utterly silly names." The review ends: "Purdy is an intriguing and in many ways a good writer. But I think he's fallen into the trap of a lot of writers who have a cult rather than a readership. With not much public to surprise, why bother being surprising? It's much easier just to be extravagant."

877     Kahn, Lisa. "A Shelf of Fiction." *Jerusalem Post*, 18 February 1994, p. 27.

 A review of three current novels including Purdy's *Out With the Stars*. A positive review which states, "Purdy's total control is evident in every line, polished to perfection, kitsch beyond kitsch.... This highly stylized novelist is not for everyone but those who venture will surely gain."

878     Kanga, Firdaus. "From the High Ceiling." *Times Literary Supplement* (26 June 1992): 21.

 A mixed review of *Out With the Stars*. Kanga writes, "Purdy has certainly never been funnier, his writing never more self-assured. And yet, his book comes to us as one without meaning—even the blasphemy he has been building through his career, of Jesus Christ as

a lover of boys, fails to excite. He has made his
characters into playthings without fitting them into a
grand construct, so that, with the exception of
Petrovna, they look to us as small as cars from an
airplane."

879     Kenney, Brian. "Fiction." *Library Journal* 118 (1 October
        1993): 128.

        A very positive review of *Out With the Stars*, which
        describes the novel as a "dazzling gothic comedy [by]
        one of our greatest writers.... Purdy has never been
        funnier."

880     Knudsen, James. "English: Fiction." *World Literature
        Today* 68 (summer 1994): 571.

        A mixed review of *Out With the Stars*. Knudsen notes
        that the "novel is occasionally funny ... and touching in
        its presentation of Val's relationship with Luigi. It can
        be rough going for any reader who demands subtle
        characterization."

881     MacAdam, Barbara. "A Bizarre but Profound Tale of
        Creativity." *Newsday* 11 (9 December 1993): 76.

        A very positive review of Purdy's work and his
        fifteenth novel, *Out With the Stars*. MacAdam writes,
        "Purdy's style is straightforward American vernacular,
        and seductive in the great storytelling tradition. His
        apocalyptic tales and images border on the mythic,
        while what he writes about is difficult, remote,
        unbelievable, and sometimes even unendurable. But
        the impact is direct and profound." Though most of
        Purdy's characters are gay, homosexuality is not his
        subject. Rather, creativity of all kinds is what Purdy is
        considering and seems to be the aim of his use of
        sexuality here. In *Out With the Stars*, unlike many of
        his other books, graphic sex is at a minimum, while
        love, insecurity, and the nature of human bonds are at
        play.... The book is also a graceful, Gothic tale about
        aging, reconciliation and reasoned resignation."

882    Malin, Irving. "Book Review." *Review of Contemporary Fiction* 14 (summer 1994): 208-209.

A very positive review of *Out With the Stars*. Malin begins his review, "Although Purdy is one of our best writers—*Malcolm*, *The Nephew*, and *I Am Elijah Thrush* are, perhaps, his masterpieces—he has never received the critical attention he deserves.... His odd conjunctions of pity, satire, and the grotesque are surely miraculous because they confuse our simple responses." Malin further writes, "I am pleased to finds that his latest novel—published in his seventieth year—is among his best. Although he offers us a cruel and comic mediation on the meaning of fame, he is also concerned with the relationship of art to spiritual longing." Finally, the review notes, "Purdy has always been attacked as a camp writer. He is, ironically, a religious artist who recognizes that his words—perhaps all art—will never be enough to save him."

883    Moore, Caroline. "The Lord of the Ringlets." *The Spectator* 268 (20 June 1992): 36.

A mixed review of *Out With the Stars*, which notes, "Add a generous lashing (possibly the right word here) of camp religiosity, and it all adds up to a highly-coloured, utterly believable and enjoyable book, which I hesitate to recommend to you."

884    Steinberg, Sybil S. "Fiction." *Publishers' Weekly* 240 (5 July 1993): 61.

A review of *Out With the Stars* in which Steinberg writes, "Purdy's trademark blend of high camp, bizarre characters, outrageous satire and piercing realism animates this off-beat romp."

885    Weir, John. "Everything Was Purpler Then." *New York Times Book Review* (16 January 1994): 24.

A negative review of *Out With the Stars* in which the reviewer says, "You have to have a taste for this kind of writing. And I'm afraid I found it generic ... in the end, Mr. Purdy demonstrates that high camp is just another masculine ploy, a means to remain unaffected by loss."

## 63: Dream Palace: Eleven Stories and a Novella

886    Hampshire, Stuart. "Four Reviews." *Twentieth Century*
       172  (summer 1963): 134.

       A short but very positive note on Purdy's *63: Dream
       Palace* which states, "It seemed to me immensely
       powerful and original, however strange and narrow;
       particularly the title story, which has the concentration
       of a masterpiece."

887    Hopkinson, Tom. "The Life of the Damned." *The Observer*
       (London), 30 June 1957, p.12.

       A negative review of *63: Dream Palace*. Hopkinson
       writes that the novel "is a scorched, aborted
       masterpiece. It has no form, or rather the author
       forgets the form with which he started—as he dives
       deeper into darkness and disintegration." The review
       ends: "Mr. John Cowper Powys is unduly pessimistic
       when he calls this narrow, demonic talent, 'the best
       kind of original genius of our day.' " This review was
       followed by Mr. Powys' rebuttal in the July 14, 1957
       issue of *The Observer*.

888    Macdonald, Dwight. "Fictioneers." *Encounter* 9
       (September 1957): 76-79.

       A review of eleven new novels, including Purdy's *63:
       Dream Palace*, which received a negative review.
       Macdonald writes "But Mr. Purdy is unable to break
       out of his private world, which is to say he is not
       talented, the ability to communicate to others one's
       own world being one mark of talent."

889    McLaren-Ross J. "Review." *Punch*  233 (28 August
       1957): 250.

       A very negative review of *63: Dream Palace*.
       McLaren-Ross writes that "the novella is hysterically

novelettish, overcharged, and clumsily written; its opening sentence ... seems to indicate an almost total lack of feeling for words."

890 Michie, James. "Book Reviews." *London Magazine* 4 (October 1957): 64-67.

> A review of four current works including *63: Dream Palace*. Michie has a mixed reaction to the book: *63: Dream Palace*, he writes, "Wanders off the track, falls into mannerisms, at times seems to sleepwalk, but its good qualities almost get it home: its tremendous sense of outrage, its compassion for both innocence and evil, its simplicity in presenting primitive emotion without embarrassment." Concerning the short stories in this collection, Michie states, "The best are extraordinarily powerful, more concentrated than the novella, lit by a harder, less stagy light, and observed as if through the unblinking eye of a tiger or a child."

891 "New Fiction." *Times* (London), 4 July 1957, p. 13.

> A review of five new novels including *63: Dream Palace*. A short mixed review which states, "The short stories lack substance but the novella shows true creative power. There is nothing negative about it. Cruelty and tenderness mean more to Mr. Purdy than they do to most writers."

892 Powys, John Cowper. "Desperate City." *The Observer* (London), 14 July 1957, p. 11.

> Letter to *The Observer* responding to a June 30, 1957 review by Tom Hopkinson of James Purdy's *63: Dream Palace*. Mr. Powys takes Mr. Hopkinson to task for his misreading of Purdy's novel. Mr. Powys begins his letter: "I have been reading with astonishment and indignation" and ends: "Do you, or don't you, try to dig down to the heart of life upon the Planet Earth along with Homer and Shakespeare and Milton and Dante, as James Purdy struggles to do?" The letter is followed by a response from Mr. Hopkinson to Powys' letter in which he states, "I am quite content to stand" [by the review].

893     "Under the Skin." *Times Literary Supplement* (19 July 1957): 437.

> A very positive review of *63: Dream Palace*, which states, "This very considerable novelist and short story writer is in the very highest rank of contemporary American writers.... The straight undeceivable but compassionate insight into the individual, as into the innocent heart is extraordinary.... Mr. Purdy is a superb writer, using all the fires of the heart and the crystallizing powers of the brain."

## *63: Dream Palace: Selected Stories 1956-1987*

894     Kaganoff, Penny. "Paperbacks: Fiction Originals." *Publishers' Weekly* 238 (18 October 1991): 57.

> A review of *63: Dream Palace: Selected Stories 1956-1987*. Kaganoff notes that "this volume affords readers a new opportunity to evaluate this rare stylist."

895     McCann, Richard. "Lives of Quiet Desperation." *Book World (Washington Post)* (12 January 1992): 3.

> A positive review of *63: Dream Palace: Selected Stories 1956-1987*, published by Black Sparrow Press. McCann ends his long review by noting that this collection "constructs a strange but hugely impressive ediface—something at once grotesque and beautiful, as strangely shaped and as ultimately sacred as Gandhi's modern but gargoyle-laden cathedral."

896     Moss, Roger. "Mouthfuls of Malice." *The Independent* (5 March 1992): 25.

> A positive review of *63: Dream Palace: Selected Stories 1956-1987*. Moss writes, "the worst of James Purdy's stories are little more than reticent melodrama." And, "the best of the stories (which is most of them) are more like black farce." Moss notes: "What saves these stories from being just another addition to the great American freak-show is Purdy's scrupulous attention to language. To his own, of

course; but also to the inarticulate idiom of his characters." And, "The stories are particularly acute in their attention to what is lazily called 'body language' but which is shown here instead to be the things that bodies do to distract people from the anxiety or embarrassment occasioned by what they say. Purdy's most distinctive territory is the mouth itself, as a place of pre-articulate noises and sensations ('mumbling and making other silly sounds, filling with saliva, as though it was only her mouth now which had the seat of her emotions') occupying a grey area between the body and the spoken word."

897    Wilhelm, Albert E. "Fiction." *Library Journal* 116 (1 November 1991): 134.

Review of *63: Dream Palace: Selected Stories 1956-1987*. A positive review which states, "With a few exceptions these stories are well crafted, but so many pieces with similar characters and themes may produce an emotional overload."

## Miscellaneous Reviews

898    Aletti, Vince. "Fogged In." *Village Voice* 37 (14 April 1992): 109-110.

A negative review of Purdy's first American production of his first full-length play, *The Rivalry of Dolls*. Aletti notes, "Purdy's women are voracious, willfully fierce; men are no match for them." However, "The drama, instead of building, seeps relentlessly away. We're left with a few hot flashes of passion, some stretches of dazzlingly bizarre dialogue, and like Amelia, a lot of fog." The play was produced at the Theater for the New City, New York, NY, from March 26-April 19, 1992 and directed by John Uecker.

899    Brustein, Robert. "Albee's Allegory of Innocence." *New Republic* 154 (29 January 1966): 34, 36.

A negative review of Albee's play *Malcolm* which was adapted from Purdy's novel. Of special interest is the note that "Albee's declared intention was to attract readers to Purdy's writings, but he seems to have precisely the opposite effect."

900    Canby, Vincent. "Review/Film; Recluse Woos Widow in In a Shallow Grave." *New York Times* (6 May 1988): C21.

A mixed review of the movie version of Purdy's *In a Shallow Grave*. Canby writes that "it is nicely acted, handsome looking and impenetrable."

901    Carmen, John. "Love Triangle Has a Sad Edge." *San Francisco Chronicle*, 21 February 1990, p. E1.

A review of the American Playhouse adaptation of Purdy's *In a Shallow Grave*, which was aired on television.

902    Clements, Andrew. "Dream Palace: Munich Biennale." *Financial Times*, 15 May 1990, sec. 11, p. 21.

A review of the 2nd Munich Biennale at which Hans-Jurgen Von Bose's adaptation of Purdy's *63: Dream Palace* was performed as an opera. Clements writes, "It is a brave attempt to come to terms with Purdy's teeming, eloquent novel, however, from which the composer has distilled a taut, and thoroughly operatic libretto."

903    Crisp, Quentin. "The Discreet Charm of Mr. James Purdy." *The European Gay Review* 3 (1988): 18-23.

Mr. Crisp writes about hearing James Purdy read one of his "fabulous stories" and an interview he had with Purdy. He discusses Purdy's writing with emphasis on *In a Shallow Grave* and *The Candles of Your Eyes*. He mentions that Mr. Purdy should not be classified as a gay writer. Mr. Crisp notes, "I imagine that Mr. Purdy's work will appeal most strongly to an older readership—to people who wish there was some beauty or some humour in the world rather than to the young whose only desire is to live in a state of perpetual sexual arousal or social outrage. But whoever reads his books must surely marvel at his compassion for—nay, his identification with—the victims of fate." Includes a photograph of James Purdy by Robert Giard.

904    Feingold, Michael. "Half Nelson." *Village Voice* 35 (27 February 1990): 87-88.

A review of Richard Nelson's play, *Some Americans Abroad* and Purdy's two one-act plays, *Til the Eagle Hollers*, directed by John Uecker and presented by Theater for the New City, New York, NY. A positive review in which Feingold finds Purdy's writing "a steady parade of phrases that tickle the ear and reverberate off the heart." He especially liked the Myrna DuArte sets and Sheila Dabney's acting. Played February 8-25, 1990.

905    ——. "Waking Dreams." *Village Voice* 34 (4 April 1989): 81-82.

A review of a play, *Sleeping Dogs*, by Neal Bell and two one-act plays, *Heatstroke* and *Souvenirs*, by Purdy under the general title *Sun of the Sleepless*. Purdy's plays were directed by John Uecker and presented by Theater for the New City, 162 First Avenue, New York, NY. Feingold compares the two playwrights' dreamlike language. "Only in Purdy's case it's spun out by an old master whose simplicity of approach makes the dream seem as casual and riveting as an accident on the street.... Violence and the more sordid reaches of the erotic are Purdy's stock and trade but he sees both as stemming from love gone awry, hence the delicacy that makes the dialogue lilt and his action progress with the implacable slow grace of a minuet." High praise is given to actress Sheila Dabney. Played March 23-April 9, 1989.

906    Flanagan, Sylvia P. "Movies to See." *Jet* 74 (12 June 1988): 61.

A brief mention that the movie *In a Shallow Grave*, based on Purdy's novel of the same name, is worth seeing. This reference is included only to indicate the wide range of journals in which Purdy's work is reviewed. *Jet* is "Black America's leading news magazine."

907    Kaufman, Bill. "A Former Soldier's Self-Imposed Isolation." *Newsday*, 6 May 1988, sec. Weekend, p. 7.

A positive review of the movie version of Purdy's *In a Shallow Grave*. Kaufman writes: "The well-crafted movie exudes a pervasive sense of barrenness and Montrose's despair is palpable."

908    "Literature." *Booklist* 75 (15 December 1978): 656.

*True* was recently performed in New York. A short, positive review of *Two Plays*, which ends: "Purdy overcomes vulgar sensationalism with a sense of tenderness."

909    Loynd, Ray. "TV Reviews; A Compelling Love Triangle on American Playhouse." *Los Angeles Times*, 21 February 1990, p. F10.

A positive review of the television production on American Playhouse of *In a Shallow Grave*.

910    Malanowski, Jamie. "Previews: Michael Biehn and James Purdy." *Interview* 18 (April 1988): 21.

A review of the movie *In a Shallow Grave* based on Purdy's novel of the same name. Malanowski interviews the writer and director Kenneth Bowser, Michael Biehn, the actor who plays Garnet Montrose and James Purdy. All are pleased with the film. Purdy declares, "I liked the film very much.... I think Ken understands my work quite well ... the film is a real achievement." Article contains a large photograph of James Purdy and Michael Biehn by Andrew Brucker.

911    McCarten, John. "Innocent Astray." *New Yorker* 41 (22 January 1966): 74.

A very negative review of Albee's play based on Purdy's novel *Malcolm*.

912    Morris, Robert K. "Outspoken." *The Nation* 208 (9 June 1969): 737-738.

A mixed review of the four-record Spoken Arts recording of *63: Dream Palace*. Morris notes, "The new release of James Purdy's reading (complete) of his novella, *63: Dream Palace*, while preserving the voice of a significant contemporary and a solid slice of his writing as well, falls somewhat below the ideal one might have envisioned for doing a work of this sort. Not so far below as to cool one's ardor for the ambitious and noble project, but just enough to provoke the question whether, at times, the word is not more forceful or memorable as written, rather than as spoken." Morris finds the recording much too long and "Purdy's voice, in general, not exciting."

913    Oliver, Edith. "Off Broadway." *New Yorker* 39 (12 October 1963): 91-92.

A review of an Off Broadway production based on Purdy's *Color of Darkness*. The play was produced as a "series of old-fashioned sentimental vignettes, most of which started out as short stories by James Purdy. The production at Wright Stage is, if not avant, at least moyenne garde, with scrims that pull back and forth, masks, choruses of conversing voices, gloomy string music behind the poignant bits, and lone players, many of them sobbing or quietly in tears, picked out by spotlights on a darkened multi-level stage, but the general effect, unfortunately, is more precious than stylish." Also noted, "The actors, under William Francisco's direction, mostly do pretty well, considering. Of the five plays presented, four were adapted by Ellen Violett; Mr. Purdy himself did the fifth."

914    Pettitt, Stephen. "With British Help." *Times* (London), 2 June 1990, p. 39.

A review of Hans Jurgen von Bose's opera, *63: Dream Palace*, based on the work by James Purdy. Performed in Munich.

915     "Reservations—Fiction." *Antioch Review* 30 (spring 1970):129-130.

> Review of the recording of Purdy's reading his short stories "Eventide and Other Stories" on the Spoken Arts Label. The reviewer writes, "Purdy reads in a tense monotone with overtones of disturbing detachment. It is a voice, like the words spoken, that makes uncompromising havoc with the reader-listener's emotions."

916     "Review." *Cinema Movie Reviews* (31 December 1988).

> A short, negative review of the film *In a Shallow Grave* based on Purdy's novel.

917     "Review." *Time* 87 (21 January 1966): 50.

> A very negative review of Albee's adaptation of Purdy's novel, *Malcolm*. The reviewer writes that: "He (Albee) finds all his vintage wines in another man's cellar. The trouble is that these wine bottles are now empty, and the wind whistles over them all evening in a low, monotonous, deadly moan."

918     Rothstein, Edward. "Concert: Clarion Chorus." *New York Times*, 7 February 1982, p. 65.

> A positive review of Richard Hundley's "The Sea Is Swimming Tonight," which is based on James Purdy's poems.

919     "Speech, Theatre and Dance." *Choice* 3 (September 1966): 534.

> A review of Albee's adaptation of Purdy's *Malcolm* in which the play receives an unfavorable review. However, Purdy's novel, *Malcolm*, is noted as "a clever and well written novel which portrays innocence being contaminated by existence. Purdy's use of irony, humor and improbable situations is fresh and expansive."

920     Thomas, Kevin. "Movie Review; Shallow Grave, A Fable of Love." *Los Angeles Times*, 6 May 1988, sec. 6, p. 6.

A review of the movie *In a Shallow Grave* based on Purdy's novel.

921    ——. "Reviews of AFI Festival Movies." *Los Angeles Times*, 23 April 1981, Calendar, p. 5.

A positive review of the movie adaptation of Purdy's *In a Shallow Grave*. Thomas notes that "The result is a sensitive but languid mood piece."

922    Turnbaugh, Douglas. "A Buried Wonder." *Advocate* (24 May 1988): 67-69.

A negative review of the film *In a Shallow Grave* based on Purdy's novel. Turnbaugh writes, "Purdy is still the best kept secret of literate America. But this film will help keep him so. His name should be removed from this travesty. It is a deliberate distortion and, therefore, is best described as a fraud."

923    Von Rhein, John. "Revision of Tchaikovsky's 'Other' Piano Concerto Imperfect but Welcome." *Chicago Tribune* (7 July 1986): sec. Tempo, p. 3.

A brief review of Joseph Fennimore's one-act opera, *Eventide*, which is based on the short story by Purdy. The reviewer notes that the chamber opera is impressive "as a moving and evocative American mood piece, its vocal declamation and instrumental writing shaped by a knowing hand. Its lyric essence was beautifully projected by the Chelsea [Chamber Ensemble] under Tim Rolek's direction."

924    Wortis, Irving. "Theatre." *Library Journal* 91 (1 June 1966): 2868.

A short review of Edward Albee's *Malcolm*, adapted from Purdy's novel. "It is dull from start to finish."

925    Yohalem, John. "Review." *American Theatre* 6 (April 1989): 8.

A positive review of Purdy's double bill of one-acts, *Heatstroke* and *Souvenirs* under the title *Sun of the Sleepless*. Yohalem notes that "Purdy is better known as a dramatist in Australia, Canada and Europe, where his *Children is All* has been widely seen and admired." Yohalem quotes Purdy as saying, "I think in all my plays, despite the so-called violence, there's always a resolution to the conflict, even if there isn't a happy ending." The play ran through April 9.

# D.  Dissertations and Theses

926    Boulware, Mark M. *The Fragmented Self: The Novels of James Purdy Considered in the Light of Modern Psychology.* M.A. thesis, Midwestern University (Wichita Falls, Texas), 1974.

A master's thesis which examines the work of Sigmund Freud, Carl Jung and Ronald Laing who "draw a picture of a man divided against himself to greater and lesser extents.  This self-division contributes to man's alienation from his fellows and from the world in which he lives."  Boulware demonstrates that James Purdy has adapted "the idea of the divided self" with a careful analyses of the individual characters in *Malcolm, The Nephew, Jeremy's Version* and *I Am Elijah Thrush*.  The thesis concludes: "We may live in a demented, fragmented society, but a door had been opened which offers us a way out.  There exists such a thing as love and Purdy's works illustrate that 'love can cure, love can heal, love can bind a flowing wound.'  Our realization of love's true existence and power can easily be our justification and, hopefully, our salvation."

927    Cramer, Carmen Kay. *The New Democratic Protagonist: American Novels and Women Main Characters, 1960-1966.* Ph.D. dissertation, Texas Christian University, 1980.

This study examines twelve novels published between the years 1960 and 1966 which all have a woman as the main character.  The novels studied were:  James Purdy's *The Nephew*; Joan Didion's *Run River*; H. D.'s (Hilda Doolittle's) *Bid Me to Live*; Shirley Jackson's *We Have Always Lived in the Castle*; Harper Lee's *To Kill a Mockingbird*; Larry McMurtry's

*Leaving Cheyenne*; Anais Nin's *Seduction of the Minotaur*; Joyce Carol Oates's *With Shuddering Fall*; Sylvia Plath's *The Bell Jar*; Thomas Pyncheon's *The Crying of Lot 49*; J. D. Salinger's *Franny and Zooey* and Wallace Stegner's *A Shooting Star*. Cramer analyzes *The Nephew* in depth and details the development of Alma Mason, the major character in the novel. Cramer writes that "James Purdy creates one of the most pitiable and most unusual characters in that she does not achieve actual adulthood until she is past the age of retirement."

928  Fiske, C. Louis. *Purdy's World View as Expressed in His Early Work* M.A. thesis, California State University, Sacramento, 1976.

A master's thesis which examines Purdy's earlier works: *Color of Darkness*, *Children is All*, *Malcolm* and *The Nephew*. The thesis analyzes Purdy's "settings and style, his uses of language and his characters, to explain his world view." Fiske places his emphasis on the individual characters in each short story or novel. Fiske writes, "In Purdy's world the raw material— youth, is torn apart without creating anything good, or is simply allowed to dissolve without notice. The young do not progress, the old only stagnate; the result is an even more unpleasant society in which the next generation must attempt to exist. Purdy's characters have no hope, no future; the only directions in which they can move are backward and down."

929  Gregg, Louise Caffey. *James Purdy: Not of Time, But Timeless*. M.A. thesis, Midwestern State University (Wichita Falls, Texas), 1976.

A master's thesis devoted to critical study of *63: Dream Palace, Malcolm* and the short stories: "Sermon," "Daddy Wolf," "Some of These Days," "Why Can't They Tell You Why?," "Eventide," "Man and Wife," "A Good Woman," "Sound of Talking," and "Summer Tidings." Gregg analyzes Purdy's conscious and unconscious motives for creativity as they are revealed in subject, style, theme and form.

Gregg summarizes Purdy's efforts, and states, "I believe I have proved that Purdy is not a case of the man meeting the moment—capitalizing on the American existentialist movement but a timeless artist whose business it is to reveal the soul, the universal soul, of men." The dedication reads "For James Purdy, who gave me identity."

930    Hughes, Charles Willis. *Three Modern American Novels as Idea and Experience*. M.A. thesis, Texas Technological College, 1968.

A master's thesis which studies "the role of ideas and experience in modern American fiction as embodied in three novels: *Malcolm* by James Purdy, *Miss Lonelyhearts* by Nathaniel West, and *The Adventures of Augie March* by Saul Bellow." Hughes classifies *Malcolm* and *Miss Lonelyhearts* as idea-ground novels, and *Augie March* as a novel of experience. From his study of *Malcolm*, Hughes finds the novel "puzzling and frustrating ... dull ... static."

931    Kennard, Jean Elizabeth. *Towards a Novel of the Absurd: A Study of the Relationship Between the Concept of the Absurd As Defined in the Works of Sartre and Camus and Ideas and Form in the Fiction of John Barth, Samuel Beckett, Nigel Dennis, Joseph Heller, and James Purdy*. Ph.D. dissertation, University of California, Berkeley, 1968.

A study in which Kennard defines "what is meant by the word 'absurd' when it is applied to" the five contemporary novelists, Barth, Beckett, Dennis, Heller and Purdy, by comparing their ideas to those of Sartre and Camus and by tracing the connection between their ideas and their techniques." The novelists were also compared to one another to see whether their similarities in themes and techniques sufficiently outweigh their differences to justify considering them as novelists of the absurd or whether this label is more misleading than accurate. In chapter four, "James Purdy: Absurdity as Dream," Kennard analyzes in detail Purdy's novels, *Malcolm, The Nephew, 63:*

*Dream Palace* and *Cabot Wright Begins*. In summary, Kennard writes, "It seems clear from the views that he expresses that Purdy is deliberately attacking preconceptions about the novel as a form and this would explain the way in which he ends each of his novels. Within the final chapter of each book Purdy gives an account of what happens to each of his characters after the novel finishes. He gives the appearance of tying up all the loose ends in complete contradiction to the idea of non-progression in human life which he expresses everywhere.... This is a parody, of course, of the conventional ending of a realistic novel, which comes to a conclusion and assumes that life can be as neatly patterned as fiction."

932   Kich, Martin. *Everyone Goes Around Acting Crazy: A Study of Recent American Hard-Core Naturalists*. Ph.D. dissertation, Lehigh University, 1989.

Examines the works of Nathaniel West, Erskine Caldwell, John O'Hara, Hubert Selby, Jr., Harry Crews, Jerzy Kozinski, Barbara Sheen and James Purdy. These writers, who represent the hard-core naturalism movement in literature, have been "ignored unfairly, criticized for a lack of thoughtfulness ... and for seeing us humanly rather than humanistically." Chapter four is entitled "Mutilation by Sexual Preference in the Inner City: Hubert Selby, Jr's *Last Exit to Brooklyn* and James Purdy's *Eustace Chisholm and the Works*." Kich does an excellent job of analyzing "how the equally negative stereotype of the urban underclass serves as much the same sort of baseline for understanding Selby's and Purdy's homosexuals, whores, and tenement marriages." Kich discusses in detail the authors' style, characters and situations in each novel. The dissertation contains a very comprehensive bibliography of the hard-core naturalists.

933   Lovely, Bernie. *The Quest for Identity As Found in James Purdy's First Five Novels: Malcolm, Eustace Chisholm and the Works, Jeremy's Version, The Nephew, and Cabot*

*Wright Begins.* M.A. thesis, Morehead State University, 1972.

> A master's thesis which analyzes the major characters in each of Purdy's five novels. The common thread runnning through each novel is that "all of the main characters are in a quest for identity." Lovely writes, "The characters in Purdy's novels had either to seek for an identity, whether they wanted to or not, or have an identity sought for them. They had no choice of refusing identity; their only choice lay in the degree they would seek or be sought, in the performance of the quest." The bibliography is brief.

934  Lucchetti, Marjorie Lange. *Fabulation and Realism in James Purdy's Novels: A Response to the Problem of Form.* Ph.D. dissertation, University of Chicago, 1974.

> A study of Purdy's seven novels to date [1974]. Lucchetti writes with insight and positive appreciation of Purdy's creative writing. Lucchetti succeeds in her stated premise: "To demonstrate the effect the author's [Purdy's] choice of technique has in each novel and to indicate the step each word seems to represent in his view of the aesthetic problem of form which the modern writer faces." Though each chapter is devoted to one novel, Lucchetti does a superb job of comparing, contrasting and interrelating each novel. The seven works studied and their related titles are: Two Alternate Worlds—*63:Dream Palace*; A Fabulous Tale—*Malcolm*; A Realistic Microcosm—*The Nephew*; The Rhetoric of Exaggeration—*Cabot Wright Begins*; The Poisoned Cup of Love—*Eustace Chisholm and the Works*; A Delicate Balance—*Jeremy's Version*; A Puzzling Fable—*I Am Elijah Thrush.*

935  Mertz, Robert Joseph. *Culture As Cataclysm: Disaster and Mass Values in Selected Contemporary American Fiction.* Ph.D. dissertation, University of Minnesota, 1974.

> A study which intends "to explore one aspect of the imagination of disaster; namely, the interrelationship between mass society theories, mass culture criticism, and selected works of fiction written primarily since

1957." The works of fiction include those of Frederick Pohl, Ray Bradbury, Taylor Caldwell, Pat Frank, Walter Van Tilburg Clark, Kurt Vonnegut, William Burroughs, Ralph Ellison, Charles Wright, and James Baldwin. Chapter six, entitled "Horatio Alger Meets the Beast," deals with Nathaniel West, Alan Harrington, Richard Brautigan and James Purdy. Purdy's *Malcolm* and *Cabot Wright Begins* are discussed.

936    Miller, George Eric. *The Novels of James Purdy: An Assessment*. M.A. thesis, Pennsylvania State University, 1966.

Miller has written an excellent study of Purdy's first three novels, *Malcolm*, *The Nephew*, and *Cabot Wright Begins*. Each novel is analyzed in detail by plot and individual characters. Miller refers to all the important critical studies of the novels. Miller is successful in his treatment of each novel, "both as a distinct literary creation, and as a successful examination of Purdy's unique vision of our time and condition." Of special importance in this study is the early biographical information Miller has uncovered. Since biographical information on Purdy is limited and often inconsistent, Mr. Miller's research provides some of the best data available. Miller states, "Contrary to all printed accounts, James Otis Purdy was born on July 17, 1916, in Bowling Green, Ohio (not 1923 as most sources indicate)."

937    Moore, Iyllis Hutchin. *James Purdy: The Early Novels*. M.A. thesis, University of Wyoming, 1986.

A well written, insightful thesis which carefully analyzes Purdy's *Color of Darkness*, *Malcolm*, *The Nephew*, *Cabot Wright Begins*, *Eustace Chisholm and the Works*, *Jeremy's Version*, and *I Am Elijah Thrush*. Moore uses 'the orphan model' which runs through each of these works to help one appreciate Purdy's writing. *Eustace Chisholm* receives the longest scrutiny with emphasis on its "significant sexual and parental relationships." Also, throughout the thesis

Moore describes Purdy's brilliant use of language and his ability to communicate. The bibliography contains fifty-four essential references.

938    Perry, Joan Ellen. *Visions of Reality: Values and Perspectives in the Prose of Carlos Castaneda, Robert M. Pirsig, Ursula K. Le Guin, James Purdy, Cyrus Colter and Sylvia Plath*. Ph.D. dissertation, University of Wisconsin, 1976.

A study which uses the premise that Castaneda, Pirsig, LeGuin, Purdy, Colter and Plath "are unified by the concern shown in their prose work for values, and the effects of values on perspectives." Purdy, Colter and Plath are grouped together because they "attempt to display for the reader the negative effects which do occur to both the individual and the society through lack of awareness of the degree to which values influence perspective." Perry notes, "The work of James Purdy describes the implementation of the values of a rigid psychic structure by American society. Both marriage and money in American society, according to Purdy's vision, are directed toward producing fear of the unknown. The values of each promulgate an emphasis on genital sexuality and societal role at the necessary expense of love and identity." The works used to illustrate her premise are *63: Dream Palace*, *I Am Elijah Thrush*, *Eustace Chisholm and the Works*, *Malcolm*, *The Nephew*, and *Cabot Wright Begins*. The bibliography contains 24 major critical references.

939    Rice, Joseph Allen. *Flash of Darkness: Black Humor in the Contemporary American Novel*. Ph.D. dissertation, Florida State University, 1967.

A study which analyzes two dozen "Black Humor" novels including Purdy's *Malcolm*, *The Nephew* and *Cabot Wright Begins*. Rice notes that "Black Humor is valid in its portrayal of 20th century man, valid in its themes, valid in its relationship to the world we find ourselves living in ... the study is divided into three large sections: examination of the individual depicted in Black Humor literature; examination of the forces of his environment; examination of the technique with which the Black Humorist depicts individual and environment." To illustrate his premise the author quotes frequently and freely. Other authors analyzed are Baker, Barth, Donleavy, Friedman, Hawkes, Heller, Kesey, Percy, Pynchon, Southern, Stern, and Vonnegut.

940 Rosen, Gerald. *James Purdy's World of Black Humor*. Ph.D. dissertation, University of Pennsylvania, 1969.

A study which maps the world of black humor in order to locate, in Purdy's fiction, the causes for its emergence. Rosen provides a detailed description of each character in each short story and novel as they relate to Purdy's view of life. Rosen notes that "James Purdy sees modern urban America as a world of Black Humor in which all cultural restriction and standards are insistently violated and cultural energies have been depleted until instant gratification of all desires has become the central goal of the people and distraction has become the central desire alongside of this modern hell ... there exist remnants of the older, traditional American culture, in the small towns of Modern America. These small towns once dominated American culture in the past ... but they can no longer avoid the new urban world of Black Humor to which they are tied by industrialism and modern communications." Rosen carefully analyzes Purdy's *63: Dream Palace*, *Malcolm*, *The Nephew*, *Children is All*, *Cabot Wright Begins*, and *Eustace Chisholm and the Works*. Contains an extensive bibliography.

941 Singh, Yashoda Nandan. *The City as Metaphor in Selected Novels of James Purdy and Saul Bellow*. Ph.D. dissertation, Loyola University of Chicago, 1979.

A study of the "urban visions of Purdy and Bellows by examining their fictional techniques, including style." Singh found that Purdy "evokes or creates a hellish vision of life in the modern city, that his fictional city is a metaphor for the evil reality he sees in contemporary life." Singh also suggests that Purdy "is a satirist who castigates the world but at the same time points toward those positive human values that would help to alleviate the misery of our lives such as compassion, friendship, loyalty, courage, and the open expression of feelings." The five city novels with a locale in either Chicago or New York or both are *63: Dream Palace*, *Malcolm*, *Cabot Wright Begins*, *Eustace Chisholm and the Works*, and *I Am Elijah Thrush*. Singh summarizes his study of Purdy by writing, "All [critics] agree that the vision he presents of modern man and his civilization is horrible to contemplate, since it is totally nihilistic. Purdy achieves his effect by calculated, rigorous selectivity in his portrayal of cityscape by the use of surrealistic settings and events, and by giving his characters a highly specialized speech. Inasmuch as the city focalizes the predicaments of modern man, the apocalyptic vision of the city that emerges from his works becomes that of the whole country."

942    Skeen, Anita. *The Importance of Age in the Short Stories of James Purdy*. M.A. thesis, Bowling Green State University, 1970.

A master's thesis which analyzes each story in Purdy's two collections of short stories, *Color of Darkness* and *Children is All*. Skeen concludes her thesis: "James Purdy's stories have given us the human being in his incompleteness. His characters are never happy nor have they been certain of love. They can find no sense of personal fulfillment nor can they understand their own hearts and minds. And, most important, they have not been able to convey their deepest feelings and desires to other individuals. These characters have lived their lives in isolation, mental and physical, and the richest form of communication they have experienced is a kind of mutual tolerance for and indifference toward one another."

943    Sloan, Gary G. *The Fiction of James Purdy: Theme and Meaning*. Ph.D. dissertation, Texas Tech University, 1973.

A study which investigates the theme and meaning in Purdy's short stories and novels. Sloan writes with great understanding and appreciation of Purdy's work. Sloan notes that "While certain elements of Purdy's fictions are ... incontestably unique, at the same time he tends to repeat some of the same effects throughout his work.... The most notable instance of such repetition concerns the recurrence of two particular character types ... namely, that of the young man who is either an orphan or of uncertain parentage, and that of the imperious madame, strong-willed and fiercely independent, a truly imposing personage." Sloan discusses Purdy as a writer of black humor. Sloan divides and discusses Purdy's work in two major categories. The first is "Rural Settings" in which *The Nephew*, *Jeremy's Version*, "Sound of Talking," "Man and Wife," "Cutting Edge," "Eventide," "Night and Day," "A Good Woman," "Everything Under the Sun," "Plan Now to Attend" and "Sermon" are analyzed in depth. The same treatment of Purdy's work categorized as "Urban Settings" is provided for *63: Dream Palace*, *Malcolm*, *Cabot Wright Begins*, *Eustace Chisholm and the Works* and *I Am Elijah Thrush*.

944    Smith, Marcus Ayers Joseph, Jr. *The Art and Influence of Nathaniel West*. Ph.D. dissertation, University of Wisconsin, 1994.

In this study, Smith discusses eleven contemporary authors whose works have been influenced by West. Numerous articles have been written about Purdy's work which compares Purdy to West. However, Smith wrote to Purdy and printed Purdy's rejection (dated March 12, 1993) of this idea. Purdy wrote, "I have never read West at all until I got so tired of hearing how I was like him that I finally read some of him after I had written *Malcolm* and *Color of Darkness*. Nathaniel West was Jewish and was from a large city and this fact is reflected in his style and his idiom. I do not really have anything in common with him, except our subject matter is sometimes the same. A critic named de Mott said my story 'Daddy Wolf' was based on West. These critics can't read, obviously they have no ear.... If you want more information, I will be glad to write to you, but I don't think this will be of any help. Critics make me sick, as they are always looking for influences, as though a writer just copies from other writers."

# E. Miscellaneous Works

945     Albee, Edward. "Foreword." In *The Nephew* by James
        Purdy. Middlesex, England: Penguin Books, 1980.

       Albee notes that Purdy is "a truly original storyteller."
        Albee lists four things about Purdy's work that appeal
        to him: "Its wit, its eroticism, its quirky, pungent prose,
        and its compassion."

946     "Book Notes." *New York Times*, 28 December 1988, p.
        C24.

       A note about New American Library's success in
        publishing books by gay writers including anthologies
        of gay fiction that includes works by James Purdy.

947     Daiches, David. "Preface." In *Malcolm* by James Purdy.
        New York: Farrar, Straus and Cudahy, 1959.

       Daiches writes, "The opening sentence won me over at
        once. It has the beautifully matter-of-fact clarity of a
        fairy tale (complete with the reference to gold), the
        stark realism of the documentary, and the provocative
        deadpan of the satire." And concludes, "It is a very
        funny book, and whatever else the careful reader will
        find in it, he will find the delight of the truly original
        comedy." Reprinted in *Antioch Review* 22 (spring
        1962): 122-130.

948     Gardner, John. "Moral Fiction." *Saturday Review* 5 (1
        April 1978): 29-33.

       Article adapted from his book *On Moral Fiction*. On
        page 32, he lists as important artists: John Barth,
        Thomas Pynchon, Joyce Carol Oates, Robert Coover,
        Donald Barthelme, James Purdy, William Geddes, John
        Hawkes, Katherine Anne Porter, Gay Davenport, John
        Cheever, Bernard Malamud, J. D. Salinger, Eudora
        Welty, and John Updike.

949 Henry, William A., III. "A Man for Parallel Seasons:
Director Adrian Hall Juggles Theaters in Providence and
Dallas." *Time* (17 March 1986): 86.

A report of Hall's problems with the Trinity board
which was caused in part by Hall's production and
adaptation of Purdy's *Eustace Chisholm and the Works*.

950 Knudsen, James. *Conversations with Edward Albee*.
Jackson, Mississippi: University Press of Mississippi,
1988.

A collection of twenty-seven interviews with Edward
Albee which "focus on Albee's diverse
accomplishments and interests, scaling the high points
of his life in the theatre and also documenting some of
the low ones." In four of the interviews Albee is asked
about his adaptation of Purdy's novel, *Malcolm*. In the
1966 interview with William Flanagan, Albee says, "I
don't feel intimidated by the unanimously bad press
that *Malcolm* got.... I haven't changed my feeling about
*Malcolm*. I liked doing the adaptation of Purdy's
book."

951 Lewis, R.W.B. "Foreword." In *The Nephew* by James
Purdy. New York: Noonday Press, 1967.

A positive introduction in which Lewis considers *The
Nephew* "highly original."

952 Luckenbill, Dan. *Sylvester & Orphanos: Catalog of an
Exhibit, October - December 1990*. Los Angeles:
Department of Special Collections, University Research
Library, University of California, 1990.

A catalog which highlights the limited editions
published by Ralph Sylvester and Stathis Orphanos.
Of the twenty-five publications included are works by
Isherwood, Oates, Vidal, Styron, Greene, Cheever,
Williams, Bowles, Updike, and Purdy's *Scrap of Paper
and The Berry-Picker*.

953 Medley, Stanley. *Some Postwar American Writers*.
Sveriges Radio, 1962.

A collection of fourteen radio talks, broadcast in
Sweden, about "American writers who emerged after
World War II (and who) are enmeshed in the
traditional problems of their craft. Each writer, from his
own vantage point, presents a personal and intimate
account of life around him. He does not attempt to give
an over-all view of his area nor of his time." Purdy,
O'Connor, Capote, Bradbury, Baldwin, Lowell,
Kerouac, Stafford, Vidal, Updike, Bellow, Rexroth, Grau
and Styron are included. Each program includes a brief
biography and a selection from the author's work. A
portion from *Malcolm* is used. Each chapter includes a
photograph. Photograph of Purdy by John R. Freeman.

954     "New and Noteworthy." *New York Times Book Review*
        (19 January 1986): 32.

        Brief note on the paperback edition of *Cabot Wright
        Begins*.

955     "Notable Books of the Year." *New York Times Book
        Review* (6 December 1981): 14.

        Purdy's 11th novel, *Mourners Below*, is listed as one of
        the notable books.

956     Schneider, Steve. "Steve Schneider Frequently Reports on
        Developments in Cable." *New York Times*, 29 September
        1985, p. 28.

        A note that Purdy's *Sleep Tight* will be shown on cable
        television.

957     Sitwell, Dame Edith. "Introduction." In *Color of
        Darkness* by James Purdy. Philadelphia, Pennsylvania:
        Lippincott Press, 1961.

        Purdy's earliest supporter, Dame Sitwell, writes a
        strong, positive introduction and review of *Color of
        Darkness*. "This very considerable novelist and short
        story writer is in the very highest rank of contemporary
        American writers." Ms. Sitwell describes *63: Dream
        Palace*, "Man and Wife" and "Sound of Talking" as
        "masterpieces." She notes that "Purdy is at his
        greatest in tragedy, but he can also be, and often is,

        230

riotously funny, as in 'Plan Now to Attend.' This is brilliant comedy." Ms. Sitwell ends her essay by writing: "Mr. Purdy's work has great variety, and all the varieties are alive. He is a superb writer, using all the fires of the heart and the crystallizing powers of the brain."

958    Tanner, Tony. "Introduction." In *Color of Darkness & Malcolm*. New York: Doubleday, 1974.

A new paperback edition which combines *Color* and *Malcolm* for the first time. The introduction by Tony Tanner is an excellent essay on the meaning of Purdy's writing. Tanner relates Purdy to Chekov and compares *The Cherry Orchard* to *Malcolm*. Tanner notes that "Purdy's vision is certainly autumnal rather than vernal, though to limit a writer of such extended and nuanced awareness to any one season would be a mistake. He is as much a poet of bewildered youth as he is an elegist of emotionally depleted age, as aware of the problems of the state of contemporary language as he is of the sad and often ruinous dislocation in the modern family. And he takes us to a place where, at one time or another, we all have to go."

959    Turnbaugh, Douglas. "Fighting for His Words." *Advocate* (9 October 1982): 82.

Writer and poet James Purdy is profiled. Purdy has successfully published poetry and novels in Europe but cannot find a publisher in United States. Purdy calls America's literary establishment "The Fat Brigade."

960    Woodhouse, Reed. "James Purdy's Escape from the Wasteland." *Harvard Gay & Lesbian Review* 1 (summer 1994): 24-26.

A very supportive essay decrying the absence of Purdy's acknowledgment as "not only one of our best [gay] novelists, but something more: an indispensable one." Woodhouse articulates "many reasons Purdy has never found a wide audience." The first reason "is that [his] fiction fits into none of the usual categories. He is that very odd thing, a prophetic or vatic writer."

A second reason for Purdy's neglect "is his liking for odd subjects, his love for unlovable people." A third factor is Purdy's "indifference to what passes for 'realism' in most contemporary fiction. One sees this most easily in his dialogue, which at first strikes one as awkward, even wrong." A fourth obstacle is Purdy's "gay characters, for example, are not recognizable as such.... They are not looking for love, sex, friendship, or revolution." Purdy's "profoundly, upsetting vision of love. Love to Purdy's characters comes as an invading force to be resisted tooth and nail.... He is not then, writing to normalize homosexuality, or indeed any sexuality, but to unnormalize the reader; to break us out of the prison of conventional thought and feeling." Woodhouse ends his excellent article on Purdy by concluding: "In Purdy homosexuality is not, to be sure, a political cause nor even a sexual identity. It is something both larger and smaller. It is a symbol of one's fate; a fate which leads Purdy's characters to a life of heroic unresignation to the world. That is why, despite Purdy's deliberate, provocative unfashionableness, his disdain for any kind of label, gay or straight, he belongs to my pantheon of gay writers. And belongs, further, among the benefactors of the liberated post-Stonewall world on which he has so steadfastly turned his back."

961        ——. "James Purdy (Re)visited." *Harvard Gay & Lesbian Review* 2 (spring 1995): 16-17.

Woodhouse writes about his visit with Purdy in his "handsome corner studio apartment in Brooklyn Heights." Woodhouse notes, "Enthusiastic praise of his works he takes as his mere due; he does not conceal his hunger for applause or his deserving of it. He is perfectly capable of resenting the success of others.... His conversation is a warrior's ostentation of wounds; books that have dropped out of print, vindictive reviewers, poverty." Woodhouse quotes Purdy as saying, "Telling what you don't want to tell" and notes that this statement "is what separates Purdy from other contemporary novelists, gay or straight. For him, the difficulty of writing is not purely technical or stylistic—the art of juggling perspectives or foreshadowing a plot—but rather the habit of attention to what resists attention." Woodhouse's statement that Purdy was "raised in the semi-Appalachia of Southern Ohio" is not factual. Purdy was born in northern Ohio near Fremont.

962    "Young Writers - James Purdy, Harold Brodkey." *Harper's Bazaar* 91 (April 1958): 178.

Brief biographical information on Purdy with a photograph by Richard Avedon.


# F. Bibliographies and Entries in Reference Works

## 1. Selected Bibliographies

963    Bush, George E. "James Purdy." *Bulletin of Bibliography* 28 (January-March 1971): 5-6.

The first extensive checklist of Purdy's individual works and criticisms about them. Covers the years 1956 to 1970 and includes both primary and secondary sources.

964    *First Printings of American Authors: Contributions Toward Descriptive Checklist*. Detroit, Michigan: Gale Research Company, 1977.

A five-volume reference work which provides information on about 415 authors and first printings of their works. In volume 2, Purdy's sixteen titles are listed and five titles are illustrated with their title pages.

965    Ladd, Jay "James Purdy: A Bibliographical Checklist." *American Book Collector*, new series 2 (September - October 1981): 53-60.

A bibliographical checklist of Purdy's first American and English editions. Contains descriptive information on each edition.

966    Lepper, Gary M. *A Bibliographical Introduction to Seventy-five Modern American Authors*. Berkeley, California: Serendipity Books, 1976.

Provides a checklist describing Purdy's first printings of his primary works. Fifteen individual publications by Purdy are listed.

## 2. Reference Works

967    Adelman, Irving and Rita Dworkin. *The Contemporary Novel: A Checklist of Critical Literature on the British and North American Novel since 1945*. Metuchen, New Jersey: Scarecrow Press, 1972.

An alphabetical list by author providing references under a "General" heading and then under each title of the novel. Under Purdy, seven entries are listed under "General," three for *Cabot Wright Begins*, five for *Eustace Chisholm and the Works*, twelve for *Malcolm*, and nine for *The Nephew*.

968    *Almanac of Famous People*. 5th edition. Detroit, Michigan: Gale Research, 1994.

A comprehensive two-volume reference guide to more than 27,000 famous and infamous newsmakers from Biblical times to the present. James Purdy is listed, and the entry provides twenty-nine references to additional information.

969    *Author's and Writer's Who's Who*. 6th edition. London: Burke's Peerage Limited, 1971.

Contains a short entry on James Purdy, listing his publications, recreations and address.

970    Baskin, Ellen and Mandy Hicken, compilers. *Enser's Filmed Books and Plays ... 1928-1991*. Brookfield, Vermont: Ashgate Publishing, 1993.

A list of over 6000 books and plays worldwide from which films have been made. Arranged by film title with author index. Purdy's *In a Shallow Grave*, 1988 production, with Director Kenneth Bowser at Skouras Studio is listed.

971    Bloom, Harold, editor. *Twentieth-Century American Literature*. New York: Chelsea House, 1985.

*Twentieth-Century American Literature* is an eight-volume set and is part of the thirty-seven volume, "Chelsea House Library of Literary Criticism," which is designed to present a concise portrait of the critical heritage of every crucial British and American author. Each entry presents the most representative essay and review along with a brief biography, and a list of additional readings. Volume eight contains a list of Purdy's writings from 1956-1987 and an early photograph of Purdy. Under Purdy in volume six are excerpts from David Daiches' "A Preface to James Purdy's *Malcolm*," R. W. B. Lewis' "Our Jaws Are Sagging After Our Bout with Existence," Winfield T. Scott's "The Zephyrs of Death," Susan Sontag's "Laughter in the Dark," Nelson Algren's "It's a Gay and Dreary Life," Julia M. Klein's review of *Mourners Below*, and Gerald Weales' "No Face and No Exit: The Fiction of James Purdy and J. P. Donleavy."

972    Breed, Paul F. and  Florence M. Sniderman, editors. *Dramatic Criticism Index: A Bibliography of Commentaries on Playwrights from Ibsen to the Avant-garde*. Detroit, Michigan: Gale Research Company 1972.

Under Edward Albee and his adaptation of *Malcolm* five references are provided.

973    Bryfonski, Dedria, editor. *Contemporary Authors Autobiography Service*. Detroit, Michigan: Gale Research Company, 1984.

This seventeen-volume set provides autobiographical information on contemporary writers of interest to current readers. Volume one is devoted to creative writers and includes a brief autobiographical essay by Purdy in "which he takes on the critics who have not properly recognized the particular genius he brings to American letters." (pp. 299-305.) Purdy's essay contains a photograph of the Ohio home Purdy lived in with his parents and grandmother for the first six years of his life. The house stands near the St. Joseph's River, above the Ohio-Indiana border. Also contains an early (1946) photograph of Purdy. The essay also contains two letters from Edith Sitwell, and Purdy describes their effect on him. The bibliography includes his novels, plays, the poetry and sound recordings.

974    Buchanan-Brown, J., editor. *Cassell's Encyclopedia of World Literature*. Revised and Enlarged edition in three volumes. New York: William Morrow, 1973.

Volume three contains a short entry on James Purdy which notes, "His fiction shows a subtle blend of violence with a delicate wit which belies the grotesqueness of his subject matter." Also lists his writings as of 1970.

975    Bufkin, E. C. *The Twentieth Century Novel in English: A Checklist*. 2nd edition. Athens, Georgia: University of Georgia Press, 1984.

A reference book which contains a list of Purdy's novels from *Malcolm* (1959) through *Mourners Below* (1981). The book is of little value because the information is readily available in many other sources.

976    Burke, William Jeremiah and Will D. Howe. *American Authors and Books: 1640 to the Present Day*. 3rd revised edition by Irving Weiss and Anne Weiss. New York: Crown Publishing, 1972.

A basic, alphabetical listing of important American authors including birth and death dates, titles and publication dates of important works.

977      *Contemporary Literary Criticism*. Detroit, Michigan: Gale Research Company, 1973–.

> A basic reference source. Each entry contains excerpts from criticism of the works of current novelists, poets, playwrights, short story writers, scriptwriters and other creative writers. Entries "provide readers with critical commentary and general information on more than 2,000 authors now living or who died after December 31, 1959 ... and excerpts from interviews, feature articles, and other published writings that offer insight into the author's works." Purdy is in volumes two, ten, twenty-eight and fifty-two.

978      Curley, Dorothy, editor. *Modern American Literature: A Library of Literary Criticism*. New York: Frederick Ungar Publishing, 1976.

> The first three volumes of the fourth edition (1969) did not include Purdy. However, the volume four supplement, issued in 1976, does include him and has excerpts from twenty-one important "evaluative comments" ranging from R. W. B. Lewis, Edith Sitwell to Bettina Schwarzschild and Tony Tanner.

979      *A Directory of American Poets and FictionWriters* (1993-1994 edition). New York: Poets and Writers, 1994.

> James Purdy is listed with his Brooklyn address and telephone number and information on his latest publications, *Out With the Stars* and *63: Dream Palace: Selected Stories, 1956-1987*.

980      Ehrlich, Eugene and Gorton Carruth, editors. *The Oxford Illustrated Literary Guide to the United States*. New York: Oxford University Press, 1982.

> An unusual guide that provides "information about the homes and work places of more than fifteen hundred literary figures from Colonial times to the present." Under the section on Chicago, James Purdy is mentioned as having been a student at the University of Chicago in 1945 and 1946 and that he set his novel *Eustace Chisholm and the Works* in Chicago during the Depression years.

981     *Encyclopedia of World Literature in the 20th Century.*
        Revised edition.  New York: Frederick Ungar, 1984.

> Based on the earlier edition by Wolfgang Bernard
> Fleischman.  Volume one lists Purdy's *Cabot Wright
> Begins* as a work of distinction in the surrealistic and
> fabulistic modes.  Under the topic of Black Humor,
> Purdy is mentioned.  Volume three contains a
> biographical sketch of Purdy.  It notes Purdy was born
> July 14, 1923 near Fremont, Ohio, was a child of
> divorced parents, graduated from high school in
> Chicago; attended the University of Chicago and the
> University of Puebla in Mexico; taught English in a
> private boys' school in Havana, Cuba; in 1953, after
> graduate study, traveled abroad and, for four years,
> was on the faculty at Lawrence College in Wisconsin;
> "He has since devoted himself to writing full time."
> Four volumes and index.

982     Ferrara, Miranda H. and  George W. Schmidt, editors.
        *The Writers Directory* (1994-1996).  Detroit: St. James
        Press, 1994.

> Provides brief, basic information on James Purdy,
> including a list of his published work.

983     Fogel, J. F., editor.  *Pourquoi Ecrivez-vous?*  Paris,
        France: Le Livre de Poche, 1985.

> This is a French "Who's Who" of current writers.
> Purdy is listed in the United States section.

984     Frank, Frederick S.  *Guide to the Gothic:  An Annotated
        Bibliography of Criticism.*  Metuchen, New Jersey:
        Scarecrow Press, 1984.

> A specialized bibliography covering the entire field of
> Gothic literature worldwide.  There are two references
> to Purdy:  Malin's *New American Gothic* and
> Baldanza's *Northern Gothic.*

985     Franklin, Benjamin, V.  *Dictionary of American Literary
        Characters.*  New York: Facts on File, 1990.

A reference book devoted to describing "the major characters in significant American novels—in addition to those in some uncelebrated novels." The fifteen characters in Purdy's novel, *Malcolm*, are identified. The book is arranged alphabetically by name of author.

986     Furtado, Ken and Nancy Hellner. *Gay and Lesbian American Plays: An Annotated Bibliography*. Metuchen, N. J.: Scarecrow Press, 1993.

An alphabetical listing by author providing: title of each play, publication information, type of play, plot synopsis or description; number of acts, male and female characters, doubling, interiors and/or exteriors; production information and how to obtain a copy. Under Purdy are listed *The Berry-Picker*, *Clearing in the Forest*, *A Day After the Fair*, *How I Became a Shadow*, *What Is It, Zach?* Curtis Brown Ltd. is listed as Purdy's play agent.

987     Geller, Evelyn. "WLB Biography: James Purdy." *Wilson Library Bulletin* 38 (March 1964): 572, 574.

A brief biographical sketch which notes he was born July 14, 1923, the son of William and Vera (Civick) Purdy; studied at the University of Chicago, the University of Puebla, Mexico and the University of Madrid; faculty member at Lawrence College 1949-1953; published *63: Dream Palace*, *Malcolm*, *The Nephew*, *Children is All*, and *Cabot Wright Begins*. Also reprinted in *World Authors, 1950-1970*.

988     Gerstenberger, Donna and George Hendrick. *The American Novel: A Checklist of Twentieth Century Criticism on Novels Written Since 1789. Volume Two: Criticism Written 1960-1968*. Chicago: Swallow Press, 1970.

A basic reference work arranged alphabetically by author. Under "Purdy" are fourteen references.

989     Goring, Rosemary, editor. *Larousse Dictionary of Writers*. New York: Larousse, 1994.

A basic reference work which contains over 6,000 concise and informative entries of the most significant or prominent international creative writers. James Otis Purdy is listed as an "American satirical novelist and short-story writer, much concerned with socially and sexually marginal characters or groups."

990     Hart, James. *The Oxford Companion to American Literature*. New York: Oxford University Press, 1983.

A standard reference handbook of American literature. The Purdy entry is brief and emphasizes his major writings.

991     Helbing, Terry, editor. *Gay Theatre Alliance Directory of Gay Plays*. New York: J. H. Press, 1980.

An alphabetical list by title of plays "with major gay characters and/or predominant gay themes." Descriptions include: information on type of play, number of acts, number of male and female characters, number of interior and exterior settings, plot synopsis, location and date of first production. Plays listed by Purdy include: *Adeline*, *The Berry-Picker*, *Clearing in the Forest*, *A Day After the Fair*, *How I Became a Shadow*, *Malcolm*, *Scrap of Paper*, *True*, *What is it Zach?*, *Wonderful Happy Days*.

992     Helterman, Jeffrey and Richard Layman, editors. *American Novelists Since World War II*. Detroit: Gale Research Company, 1978.
(Dictionary of Literary Biography, Volume 2.)

The essay on Purdy, written by Warren French and Donald Pease, contains brief biographical information along with detailed information and summaries of Purdy's writing. Also contains a list of Purdy's published books and a list of twenty-six most important references to Purdy's writings. Notes that Schwarzschild's *The Not-Right House* was the first book devoted to Purdy and that Tanner's essay "Frame Without Pictures" is "the most valuable assessment so far of his works." Contains a photograph and an example of Purdy's signature.

993    *International Authors and Writers Who's Who.* 14th
       edition. Cambridge, England: International Biographical
       Centre, 1995.

       A basic reference source "to prominent living writers in
       all of the major genres, fiction, non-fiction, poetry, and
       drama. Entrants are primarily those who write in
       English and who have had their books published in the
       UK or the USA." Purdy's major works are cited.
       Includes information on his awards and honors and a
       list of journals in which he has published. Also
       includes the name of his current agent.

994    *The International Who's Who* (1994-1995 edition.).
       London, England: Europa Publications Limited, 1994.

       Standard reference work on the world's most famous
       and influential men and women. James Purdy is listed
       with brief, basic information.

995    Ivask, Ivar and Gero von Wilpert, editors. *World
       Literature Since 1945: Critical Surveys of the
       Contemporary Literature of Europe and the Americas.*
       New York: Frederick Ungar, 1973.

       This volume offers "a balanced survey of developments
       in the individual literatures of the western world since
       the end of World War II, and gives some idea of the
       supernational correlations in Western literature as a
       whole." The chapter on American Literature, written
       by Ihab Hassan, contains a section on James Purdy
       under the heading "Prominent Novelists." Hassan
       writes that "Violence and nostalgia, those twin forces
       of American literature, have converged in the work of
       James Purdy (born 1923). He has evolved an original
       style, deceptively simple, which vaguely recalls Kafka
       as well as Purdy's fellow Ohioan, Sherwood Anderson.
       Purdy's humor—black, surreal—has disguised the
       world of violated innocence."

996    Jones, Howard Mumford and Richard M. Ludwig, editors.
       *Guide to American Literature and Its Backgrounds Since
       1890.* 4th revised and enlarged edition. Cambridge,
       Harvard University Press, 1972.

A basic bibliography by subject to the best books on and of American literature. Purdy's *Cabot Wright Begins*, *Color of Darkness* and *The Nephew* are listed.

997  Keller, Dean H. *Index to Plays in Periodicals*. Revised and expanded edition. Metuchen, N. J.: Scarecrow Press, 1979.

An index to 267 periodicals which contain plays. Arranged alphabetically by author. Under Purdy are *Children is All* in *Mademoiselle* (1962), *Wedding Finger* in *New Directions in Prose and Poetry* (1974). The 1990 supplement volume (1977-1987) lists *True* in *New Directions in Prose and Poetry* (1976). Missing is *A Day After the Fair* in the *Texas Arts Journal* (1977).

998  Kiell, Norman, editor. *Psychoanalysis, Psychology, and Literature: A Bibliography*. 2nd edition. Metuchen, New Jersey: Scarecrow Press, 1982.

A bibliography containing 19,674 entries of "psychological writing about literature." There are seven entries for James Purdy.

999  Kirkpatrick, D. L., editor. *Reference Guide to American Literature*. Chicago: St. James Press, 1987.

A basic reference work which provides a brief autobiography, a complete list of the writer's published books, and a selected list of bibliographic and critical studies on each writer. The Purdy entry is written by Lois Gordon.

1000  Libman, Valentina Abramova. *Amerikanskaia Literature v Russkish Perevodakh i Kritike: Bibliografiia 1776-1975*. Moscow, Russia: Nauka, 1977.

A Russian bibliography of American literature. Contains seven entries for Purdy including three book reviews, two studies and two short stories.

1001  Libman, Valentina Abramova., complier. *Russian Studies of American Literature: A Bibliography*. Chapel Hill, North Carolina: University of North Carolina Press, 1969.

Translated by Robert V. Allen. Edited by Clarence Gohdes.

A basic bibliography covering a period of 150 years prior to 1964 of Russian writings on American Literature. Contains one reference to Purdy's *Color of Darkness*: I. Levidova's Trudnye sud' [Difficult Destinies] in "Literaturnia Gazeta," December 5, 1959.

1002   Loney, Glenn Meredith. *20th Century Theatre*. New York: Facts of File, 1983.

A two-volume chronology of the theatre in America, Britain and Canada. For each year the important premieres, revivals/repertories, births, deaths and debuts and theaters/productions are noted. In volume two under January 11, 1966, the opening of *Malcolm*, the play adapted by Edward Albee, is noted. "Despite his best efforts and director Alan Schneider's talents, it fails to come into focus. There are only seven performances."

1003   Ludwig, Richard M. and Clifford A. Nault, editors. *Annuals of American Literature, 1602-1983*. New York: Oxford University Press, 1986.

A reference book, arranged chronologically, listing the main literary output for each year. Purdy's major writings are listed, starting with *Color of Darkness*, 1957 through *Mourners Below*, 1981.

1004   McPheron, William and Jocelyn Sheppard. *The Bibliography of Contemporary American Fiction, 1945-1988: An Annotated Checklist*. Westport, Connecticut: Meckler, 1989.

A checklist of fifty-three individual books listing multiple authors and 560 entries for individual authors. Three studies for Purdy are cited and the Bush and Ladd bibliographies are noted.

1005   *Merriam-Webster's Encyclopedia of Literature*. Springfield, Massachusetts: Merriam-Webster, 1995.

A reference book covering world literature. The brief entry (p. 915) on James Purdy mentions eleven of his writings. Notes Purdy's "works present a vision of human alienation, indifference and cruelty."

1006 Murphy, Bruce, editor. *Benet's Reader's Encyclopedia.* 4th edition. New York: HarperCollins, 1996.

A basic reference book on world literature. Contains a brief entry on James Purdy, emphasizing his literary output, ending with *63: Dream Palace: Selected Stories 1956-87*, published in 1991.

1007 Natoli, Joseph and Frederik L. Rusch, compilers. *Psychocriticism: An Annotated Bibliography.* Westport, Connecticut: Greenwood Press, 1984.

A bibliography which "covers the literature and psychology relationships as presented in secondary works (critical and scholarly) from 1969-1982." Under Purdy are listed two entries by Frank Baldanza.

1008 Nelson, Emmanuel S., editor. *Contemporary Gay American Novelists: A Bio-Bibliographical Critical Sourcebook.* Westport, Connecticut: Greenwood Press, 1993.

A collection of fifty-seven pieces on contemporary gay American novelists. For each study sections on "Biography," "Major Works and Themes," "Critical Reception," "Major Works by," and "Selected Studies" are included. The entry on Purdy is written by James Morrison. Under the section "Major Works and Themes," Morrison devotes a majority of his writing to *Eustace Chisholm and the Works* because he feels that this novel "remains Purdy's most consolidated work, bringing together as it does the major strains of Purdy's fiction." Under the section "Critical Reception," Morrison discusses the writings of Schwarzschild, Chupack, Adams and Tanner as the major critical studies of Purdy's work. The biography of Purdy is brief and contains two major mistakes: Purdy was born in 1923 (not 1927) in northwest (not southern) Ohio.

1009    Nemanic, Gerald, editor  *A Bibliographical Guide to Midwestern Literature*. Iowa City, Iowa: University of Iowa Press, 1981.

A basic reference book which provides bibliographic references to the study of midwestern literature and culture. Besides topical bibliographies, basic bibliographical data on 120 major midwestern authors is given for materials published to 1976. Under James Purdy his major works are listed followed by a checklist of twenty-seven important secondary sources. This bibliography was compiled by George E. Bush.

1010    Parker, Peter, editor. *A Reader's Guide to the Twentieth-Century Novel*. New York: Oxford University Press, 1995.

A literary reference guide to over 850 English-language titles by 427 authors. Thirty-eight contributors chose books they admired. The volume "provides a rather broader historical survey than is usual in literary encyclopedias." The arrangement is chronological from 1900 through 1993. Within each year the arrangement is alphabetical by author. "Each entry provides a brief resume of the plot as well as some background information and critical analysis which may add to the reader's understanding or enjoyment of the novel described." Occasionally the resumes contain quotations from the work cited. James Purdy's *In a Shallow Grave* (1975) is included. There is a section of "Author Biographies" which contains brief information. There is a "Titles of Books Listed by Year," an index by author and title and by title only. The book was first published in Great Britain as *The Reader's Companion to the Twentieth-Century Novel in 1994*.

1011    ——. *A Reader's Guide to Twentieth-Century Writers*. New York: Oxford University Press, 1996.

A companion volume to *A Reader's Guide to the Twentieth Century Novel*. This guide contains biographical accounts and details of some 1,000 writers in the English language. The arrangement is alphabetical, divided into these categories: "Fiction," "Poetry," "Non-Fiction," "Edited," "Translations for

Children," "Collections" and "Biography." The entry
for Purdy notes that he "was born in the country near
Ohio [*sic*], the son of a businessman and lawyer of
Huguenot farming stock. His mother was a descendant
of James Otis, a signatory of the American Declaration
of Independence. After studying at the University of
Ohio [*sic*], Purdy did postgraduate work at the
University of Puebla, Mexico, and in Madrid."

1012    Perkins, George, Barbara Perkins and Phillip Leininger,
        editors. *Benet's Reader's Encyclopedia of American
        Literature*. New York: HarperCollins, 1991.

        A new edition of a basic comprehensive reference work
        on American Literature from the period of European
        exploration to 1990. Provides basic information on
        Purdy's major writings.

1013    Perkins, George and Barbara Perkins, editors.
        *Contemporary American Literature*. New York: Random
        House, 1988.

        A history of American Literature from 1945, covering
        novelists, poets and playwrights. James Purdy is noted
        in the section "American Literature in the 1960's and
        After," and under "Edward Albee." The editors write,
        "James Purdy has won a small, passionate following
        for his bitter and savage comedies portraying subjects
        like homosexuality and rape."

1014    Pownall, David E. *Articles on Twentieth Century
        Literature: An Annotated Bibliography 1954 to 1970*. New
        York: Kraus-Thomson Organization, 1973-1980.

        A large seven-volume reference set. Volume five
        includes nineteen references to Purdy's works.

1015    Richardson, Kenneth, editor. *Twentieth Century Writing:
        A Reader's Guide to Contemporary Literature*. London:
        Newnes Books, 1969.

        A basic reference book which includes a brief paragraph
        on Purdy which compares his writing to the early work
        of Truman Capote, and *Eustace Chisholm and the
        Works* to the novels of Faulkner.

1016    Rogal, Samuel J. *A Chronological Outline of American Literature*. New York: Greenwood Press, 1987. (Bibliographies and Indexes in American Literature, Number 8.)

> A reference source which provides information by year for the birth and death dates of major literary figures and the publication dates of their principal works. Also noted by year are events related to literature in the United States. For Purdy, sixteen entries are made from 1923, the year of his birth, through 1981 and publication of his novel *Mourners Below*.

1017    Rood, Karen Lane, editor. *American Literary Almanac From 1608 to Present*. New York: Facts on File, 1988.

> A basic reference book which presents an original compendium of facts and anecdotes about literary life in the United States. Of special importance about Purdy is the fact that he attended the University of Chicago in 1941 and 1946.

1018    Room, Adrian. *Literally Entitled: A Dictionary of the Origins of the Titles of Over 1300 Major Literary Works*. Jefferson, North Carolina: McFarland, 1996.

> A unique reference book which list alphabetically by title over 1300 works of literature in the English language. The majority are American fiction titles from the 19th and 20th centuries. Purdy's *In a Shallow Grave* is listed with the annotation, "The American writer's novel has as its theme the redemption of suffering through love, a theme that is developed through the experiences of a 26-year-old Vietnam veteran Garnet Montrose. The 'shallow grave' of the title is the pile of corpses under which Montrose had lain for several days, before being rescued and returned to his native Virginia. This comes to represent the shallow psychological grave of his past, from which he must now also be rescued."

1019    Rosa, Alfred F. and Paula A. Eschholz. *Contemporary Fiction in America and England, 1950-1970: A Guide to*

*Information Sources*. Detroit, Michigan: Gale Research Company, 1976.

> A basic bibliography of novels and short stories by important literary figures. Under Purdy are listed five novels, seven collections of short stories and eighteen critical sources.

1020    Sacher, Susan. "New Creative Writers: 28 Novelists Whose First Work Appears This Season." *Library Journal* 82 (1 October 1957): 2435-2440.

> A brief biographical sketch of James Purdy upon the publication of *63: Dream Palace* (New Directions, 1957). Notes that Purdy: studied in American schools; attended the University of Puebla, Mexico, and the University of Chicago; was born in Ohio, now lives in Allentown, Pa.; and has had short stories published in *Mademoiselle, Black Mountain Review, Evergreen Review* and *New Yorker*.

1021    Sader, Marion, editor. *Comprehensive Index to English-Language Little Magazines 1890-1970*. Millwood, New York: Kraus-Thomson Organization, 1976.

> An eight-volume index to one hundred important periodicals of which fifty-nine are partly or totally American little magazines. Volume six contains 31 references to works by and about Purdy.

1022    ——, series editor. *The Reader's Adviser*. 14th edition. New Providence, New Jersey: R. R. Bowker, 1994.

> The latest edition of a basic and popular reference source begun in 1921 by Bessie Graham. The present edition consists of six volumes. Volume one, *The Best in Reference Works, British Literature and American Literature* is edited by David Scott Kastan and Emory Elliott. The Purdy entry (pp. 1033-1034) provides brief biographical information and short descriptions of some of his novels. The bibliography lists only nine titles and one critical study of Purdy, Bettina Schwarzschild's *The Not-Right House*. The entry on Purdy concludes, "Purdy remains a writer with a distinctive voice that not everyone hears too clearly, but he has found an

audience, mainly academic critics who are willing to respond to the challenge of novels and stories that seem to cry out for analysis and interpretation."

1023 Salzman, Jack and Pamela Wilkinson, editors. *Major Characters in American Fiction.* New York: Henry Holt, 1994.

A major reference work which provides detailed biographical information on nearly 1,600 characters appearing in American fiction between 1970 and 1991. Information is arranged alphabetically by major character. Malcolm (*Malcolm*), Alma Mason (*The Nephew*), Elvira Summerland (*Jeremy's Version*) and Cabot Wright (*Cabot Wright Begins*) are described. Also includes lists of authors and titles, and a list of characters' alternate names.

1024 Seidel, Alison P. *Literary Criticism and Authors' Biographies: An Annotated Index.* Metuchen, New Jersey: Scarecrow Press, 1978.

An index of 195 books which provide references to individual authors. Under Purdy are noted three references: Moore's *Contemporary Novelists*; Peden's *The American Short Story*, and Hill's *Writer's Choice*.

1025 Seymour-Smith, Martin, editor. *Funk & Wagnalls Guide to Modern Literature.* New York: Funk and Wagnalls, 1973.

Notes that American critics are mostly hostile to James Purdy. "One can see why: his homosexual Gothic is unmitigated and his control of it is doubtful, and, in any case, inelegant. But he has unquestionable power." Mentions Carl Van Vechten as one of Purdy's early supporters. Discusses *63: Dream Palace*, *Color of Darkness*, *Malcolm*, *The Nephew*, *Cabot Wright* and *Eustace Chisholm*. The article under Albee noted his play adaptation of *Malcolm*.

1026 ———. *Novels and Novelists: A Guide to the World of Fiction.* New York: St. Martin's Press, 1980.

A reference work which provides brief biographical information about 1,300 writers of fiction. A brief notation is made to James Purdy and contains an early photograph (p. 202). Lists only *Malcolm, The Nephew* and *I Am Elijah Thrush*. The author thinks Purdy's earlier work is superior to his later work.

1027    Somer, John L. and Barbara Eck Cooper. *American and British Literature, 1945-1975: An Annotated Bibliography of Contemporary Scholarship*. Lawrence, Kansas: The Regents Press of Kansas, 1980.

A basic annotated bibliography divided into: General Studies, Drama, Fiction and Prose, Poetry and Critical Theory. Under Purdy are nineteen citations.

1028    Straumann, Heinrich. *American Literature in the Twentieth Century*. 3rd rev. edition. New York: Harper and Row, 1965.

A brief history of current literature by a Professor of English Literature, University of Zurich. Purdy is listed along with Capote, Goyen, Hersey and Morris as "writers with similar aims and techniques."

1029    Stringer, Jenny, editor. *The Oxford Companion to Twentieth-Century Literature in English*. New York: Oxford University Press, 1996.

A basic reference book which includes entries on literary movements, periodicals, and over 400 individual works and some 2,400 authors. Purdy is listed along with the usual biographical information and a brief discussion of some of his novels.

1030    Summers, Claude J., editor. *The Gay and Lesbian Literary Heritage: A Reader's Companion to the Writers and Their Works, From Antiquity to the Present*. New York: Henry Holt, 1995.

A useful reference source of over 350 essays in the field of gay literature. This comprehensive survey "Provides overviews of the gay and lesbian presence in a variety of literatures and historical periods, in-depth critical essays on major gay and lesbian writers in world literature and briefer treatments of other topics." The essay on James Purdy is written by Stephen Guy-

Bray (pp. 576-577). Guy-Bray writes "Purdy's style is one of his most distinctive qualities. Like Mark Twain and Sinclair Lewis, Purdy attempts to reproduce everyday American speech both in his dialogue and his narration. This flatness and simplicity of style form an effective background for his stories of obsession." Guy-Bray decries the fact that Purdy has not received any popular fame and ends his essay by noting "He has, however, always been highly regarded by other writers and has had a great influence on such younger gay writers as Dennis Cooper and Paul Russell." The bibliography lists six of the most important references to Purdy. In other sections, Purdy's *Malcolm*, *The Nephew*, *Cabot Wright Begins*, and *Eustace Chisholm and the Works* are discussed.

1031    Szilassy, Zoltan. *American Theatre of the 1960's.* Carbondale, Illinois: Southern Illinois University Press, 1986.

Mentions Albee's adaptation of Purdy's *Malcolm* in a chapter devoted to Edward Albee's work.

1032    *20th Century American Literature: A Soviet View.* Moscow: Progress Publishers, 1976.

A collection of essays on classic and contemporary American literature held at the first All-Union Conference on American studies in Moscow, January, 1975. Alexander Mulyarchik writes that "The main feature of this outlook is the rejection of bourgeois civilization, but not in the name of a more perfect social structure." An important supplement to this study is a checklist of some 250 American writers whose work has been translated in the USSR from 1960 to 1974. Under Purdy are three references: two translations into Russian (1969, 1973) and one into Lithuanian (1970). Translated from the Russian by Ronald Vroon.

1033    *Twentieth-Century Library Criticism.* Detroit, Michigan: Gale Research, 1978–.

An important ongoing reference work of over fifty volumes. Covers more than 500 authors and over

25,000 titles with excerpts of basic critical reviews.
Volume 54 has a section on "American Black Humor
Fiction" on pages 1-85. There are numerous
references to Purdy's works.

1034 Vinson, James, editor. *20th-Century American Literature*.
New York: St. Martin's Press, 1980.

Volume 13 of *Great Writers Student Library*.
Introduction by Warren French. A basic reference book
which provides a biography, a complete list of
publications, a selected list of published bibliographies
and critical studies on writers. The Purdy entry is by
Lois Gordon.

1035 ——. *Contemporary Novelists*. 3rd edition. New York:
St. Martin's Press, 1982.

This is a third edition of an important reference work
which includes five hundred and sixty-four individual
author entries of contemporary writers of the English
language. Each entry consists of a biography, a full
bibliography, a comment by the writer about his or her
works and a signed, critical essay on the writer's
works. The statement by Purdy is a lengthy one for
him and he says "I prefer not to give a biography since
my biography is in my work, and I do not wish to
communicate with anybody but individuals, for whom
my work was written in the first place. I began writing
completely in the dark, and so continue." The critical
essay written by Irving Malin briefly annotates Purdy's
major writing as of 1981.

1036 Vrana, Stan A. *Interviews and Conversations With 20th-
Century Authors Writing in English*. Metuchen, New
Jersey: Scarecrow Press, 1990.

A comprehensive index to over 5,600 interviews with
nearly 2,500 authors. Over 350 periodicals and
newspapers and more than 200 books and reference
books were searched to compile this index. In addition
to the list of sources used, the book includes an index
of interviewers and editors. Under Purdy five
references were found.

1037 Wakeman, John, editor. *World Authors, 1950-1970. A Companion Volume to Twentieth Century Authors*. New York: H. W. Wilson, 1975.

> An excellent introduction to Purdy and his writings. First section contains an autobiography in which Purdy notes the help he received from Osborn Andreas, Edith Sitwell and Carl Van Vechten. The second section contains description of Purdy's work, *Color of Darkness, Malcolm, The Nephew, Cabot Wright Begins, Eustace Chisholm and the Works, Jeremy's Version*, and *I Am Elijah Thrush* with quotes from critics. The third section lists Purdy's principal writings and articles about his work.

1038 Walker, Warren S., compiler. *Twentieth-Century Short Story Explication: Interpretations 1950-1975 of Short Fiction Since 1800*. 3rd edition. Hamden, Connecticut: Shoe String Press, 1977.

> Twenty-three references to short stories by Purdy are listed as follows: Supplement 1, (1980), eight; Supplement 2, (1984), one; Supplement 3, (1987), one; Supplement 4, (1989), six; Supplement 5, (1991), eight.

1039 Weaver, Bruce L. *Novel Openers: First Sentences of 11,000 Fictional Works, Topically Arranged with Subject, Keyword, Author and Title Indexing*. New York: McFarland, 1995.

> A reference source which includes eleven references to works by Purdy under the following headings: "Clergymen," "Death," "Driving," "Environment," "Likes and Dislikes," "Love," "Sitting," "Streets and Roads," "Suspicion" and "Theater."

1040 Weiner, Alan R. and Spencer Means. *Literary Criticism Index*. 2nd. edition. Metuchen, New Jersey: Scarecrow Press, 1994.

> A reference book which indexes bibliographies and checklists to sources of criticism of specific works of literature. Arranged by author. Under Purdy are 90 entries to short stories and novels.

1041 Weixlmann, Joe. *American Short Fiction Criticism and Scholarship, 1959-1977: A Checklist*. Chicago: Swallow Press, 1982.

A basic bibliography of more than 500 authors listing references to their individual work, general studies, bibliographies and interviews. Under Purdy are listed 4 references to *Color of Darkness*, 12 to *63: Dream Palace*, 3 to "Why Can't They Tell You Why?," 11 under "General Studies," 4 to "Daddy Wolf," 3 to "Eventide," and one each to "Cutting Edge," "Don't Call Me by My Right Name," "Encore," "Everything Under the Sun," "Goodnight, Sweetheart," "Home by Dark," "The Lesson," "Mr. Evening," "Mrs. Benson," "Night and Day" and "Sermon," "Bibliography."

1042 *Who's Who in America* (1995). 49th edition. New Providence, New Jersey: Marquis Who's Who, 1995.

The "standard of contemporary biography." James Purdy is listed as are many of his publications.

1043 *Who's Who in Writers, Editors and Poets: United States and Canada, 1992-1993*. Highland Park, Illinois: December Press, 1992.

A reference work containing very brief biographical information and lists of works for over 9,000 writers. Purdy is listed.

1044 Wilmeth, Don B. and Tice L. Miller, editors. *Cambridge Guide to American Theatre*. New York: Cambridge University Press, 1993.

A basic reference source for "concise, carefully selected and authoritative information on a broad spectrum of topics relating to the American theatre from its earliest history to the present." Purdy is listed along with the titles and dates of his plays. Listed are: *Cracks* (1963), *Wedding Finger* (1974), *Two Plays* (*A Day at the Fair* and *True*, 1979), *Scrap of Paper* and *The Berry-Picker* (1981), and *Proud Flesh* (four short plays, 1980).

# Index

*References are to item numbers.*

267